CHIEF OF STATION, CONGO

Praise for *Chief of Station, Congo*

"Remember the Cold War? Larry Devlin does, and his very inside, very honest, and very unapologetic account of clandestine operations, cynical bargaining, and an idealistic desire to stop the Commies—the basic stuff of CIA activity in the Congo during the early 1960s—is as good as it gets."　　　—SEYMOUR M. HERSH

"This memoir shows the author in best light as a station chief with personal courage and cultural astuteness, a quick thinker in sticky situations, many potentially lethal. The hair-raising incidents—often at roadblocks, once with burglars in his house—so common in Devlin's narrative will instill those interested in operational intelligence careers with the 24/7 risks of a posting in the field, while his involvement with political developments in chaotic, post-independence Congo contributes primary testimony to the history of the period. . . . Including his personal impressions of Mobutu, the eventual victor in Congo's early 1960s turmoil, Devlin's retrospective will rivet the espionage set."　　　—*Booklist*

"In this vivid, authoritative account of being CIA station chief in Congo during the height of the Cold War, Devlin brings to life a harrowing tale of postcolonial political intrigue, covert violence, and the day-to-day reality of being a key player in a global chess match between superpowers. . . . While the rest of the book is full of exciting cloak-and-dagger derring-do and scrapes with death, it is this incident that haunts Devlin. He devotes the last chapter of the book to a point-by-point refutation of his or the agency's involvement in Lumumba's death. That alleged assassination is often used to illustrate the hypocrisy in U.S. foreign policy. Devlin's straightforward, plainly written approach to the task lends credence to his assertion of innocence."　　　—*Publishers Weekly*

"A spy comes in from the dripping heat. . . . An unusually open look at CIA operations in the Eisenhower–Kennedy era, adding an interesting, perhaps controversial footnote to the still-much-debated death of Lumumba."   —*Kirkus Reviews*

"If one man personified the cold war in Africa—that ruinous contest between the greatest powers in the world's weakest states—it was Larry Devlin. Smart, ambitious, and hard as bullets, a second-world-war veteran who equated communists with Nazis, he was one of the CIA's first station chiefs in Congo, where he arrived just days after it was made independent by Belgium in 1960—at two weeks' notice. . . . His adventures, which he tells quite well, included dodging cannibal mutineers and murderous Western mercenaries; surviving numerous mock executions; and driving around Kinshasa with a rigid corpse sticking out of his trunk."
                                                      —*The Economist*

"Devlin clearly loved his job. He deals with individuals, power-brokers. . . . The book is part memoir, part documentary, part B-movie screenplay. . . . The book covers much more of interest, including the Cuban missile crisis. But the main thrust is Devlin's central role in countering Lumumba and those around him, while building up pro-U.S. figures and backing Mobutu."
                                                      —*Socialism Today*

"One of those agents, indeed the very chief of the Congo's CIA 'station,' has now come forward with a memoir of his years in the country. . . . In one striking tale, Devlin recounts how the U.S. ambassador, at a private dinner, made a casual criticism of one of Mobutu's mistresses. Word of the comment got back to Mobutu, who summoned Devlin and ordered him to arrange the ambassador's removal. Devlin explained that the ambassador was his boss and that Mobutu's request was impossible. Yet one month later, the offending diplomat was gone."
                                        —*San Francisco Chronicle Book Review*

"His memoir is filled with the sort of racy cloak-and-dagger details that you'd find in any good spy novel. . . . The Congo was clearly a fascinating, important, and lively place during the 1960s and Devlin's account offers a unique behind-the-scenes perspective of this harrowing episode of Cold War history."

—African Update, africanupdate.com

"Devlin's book is a gripping read." —The Hill

"Chief of Station, Congo: Fighting the Cold War in a Hot Zone, details the CIA's covert activities in undermining Mr. Lumumba, to the point that he should be poisoned, a task Mr. Devlin was asked to carry out. . . . But whatever flack he might take for his role, Mr. Devlin's book details for the first time the CIA's—let's say—unofficial account of how Mr. Lumumba died. . . . Apart from covert dealings, the book also details interesting Indiana Jones–like tales. In one incident, someone plays Russian roulette [with] Mr. Devlin, in another he is lined up to be shot by firing squad. In his quest to stem Soviet influence, Mr. Devlin was willing to work with the devil. Readers get treated to meetings with the notorious mercenary Bob Denard, who has been involved in overthrowing several governments in Africa." —Embassy

"In a twenty-six-year foreign service career, I have served with a number of outstanding station chiefs, but Larry Devlin is in a class by himself. Some will differ with the tactics used from time to time and many will differ with his assessment of Mobutu, but Larry presents an honest account and it is important to remember that we were at the height of the Cold War in a tumultuous country where everybody played rough. Danger was our constant companion as Devlin describes so graphically in this gripping true tale of power and intrigue."

—Frank Carlucci, former secretary of defense
and deputy director of the CIA

"In Chief of Station, Congo, Larry Devlin has done a superb job of capturing the Kafkaesque chaos of the Congo's early years of independence and reminding us of the Cold War mentality that shaped American goals. Devlin's account of the twists and turns in both Congolese politics and American policy sheds new light on some old controversies, notably the U.S. role in the death of Patrice Lumumba and the Mobutu *coup d'etat*.... Equally important, it's a lively and engaging page-turner...."

—ANDY STEIGMAN, associate dean at the School of Foreign
Service at Georgetown University and
former ambassador to Gabon

"It has been my privilege to have known Mr. Devlin for much of my own career in CIA. I served with him briefly in Brussels, for most of his second tour in Kinshasa, and as a fellow chief of station when he was in Laos and I in Cambodia. I was also chosen by Director William Colby to assist the Church Committee in its investigation of allegations concerning the death of Patrice Lumumba. I can attest that this vivid account of Mr. Devlin's experiences in Congo contains neither exaggeration nor falsehood in its account of the experiences of this remarkable man. Indeed, it sometimes downplays the impact he had on the events of those perilous times. It was an honor to have served with and for him, a view shared by virtually all of my former colleagues in CIA."

—JOHN H. STEIN, former deputy director
for operations, CIA (1981–84)

CHIEF OF STATION,

CONGO

FIGHTING THE COLD WAR IN A HOT ZONE

LARRY DEVLIN

PUBLICAFFAIRS
A Member of the Perseus Books Group
New York

Published in the United States by PublicAffairs™, a member of the Perseus Books Group.

PublicAffairs books are available at special discounts for bulk purchases in the U.S. by corporations, institutions, and other organizations. For more information, please contact the Special Markets Department at the Perseus Books Group, 2300 Chestnut Street, Suite 200, Philadelphia, PA 19103, or call (800) 255-1514, or e-mail special.markets@perseusbooks.com.

Library of Congress Cataloging-in-Publication Data
Devlin, Larry.
   Chief of station, Congo : fighting the cold war in a hot zone / Larry
   Devlin. -- 1st ed.
      p. cm.
   Includes bibliographical references and index.
   ISBN-13: 978-1-58648-405-7 (alk. paper)
   ISBN-10: 1-58648-405-2 (alk. paper)
   1. Devlin, Larry. 2. Congo (Democratic Republic)—History—Civil War,
1960-1965—Personal narratives, American. 3. Diplomats—United States—
Biography. 4. Intelligence officers—United States—Biography. 5. Espionage,
American—Congo (Democratic Republic)—History—20th century. 6. United
States—Foreign relations—Congo (Democratic Republic). 7. Congo
(Democratic Republic)—Foreign relations—United States. I. Title.
   DT658.22.D485 2007
   967.5103'1—dc22
   [B]
                                                              2006028475

   PB ISBN-13: 978-1-58648-564-1

10 9 8 7 6 5 4 3 2

To Mary

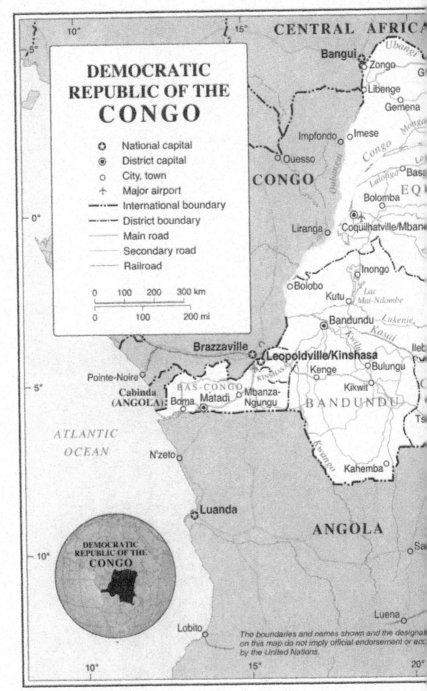

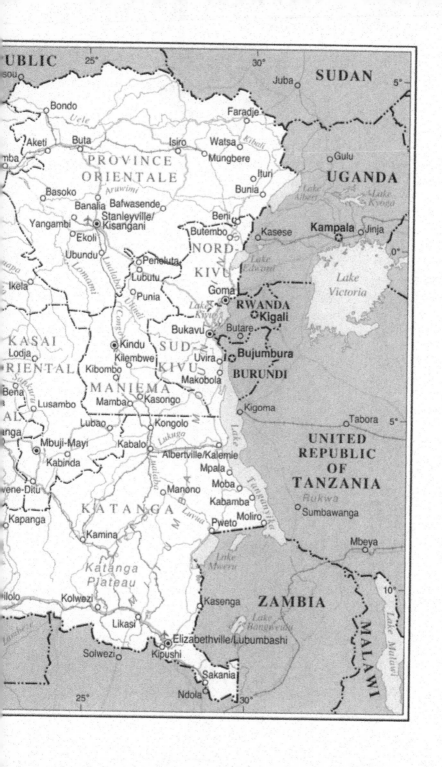

PROLOGUE:
CONGOLESE ROULETTE

I FIRST HEARD OF MY APPOINTMENT as Chief of Station in the Congo while I was in Washington, late August 1959, when the capital was dozing in the sultry summer heat. My initial impression was that though the Congo seemed to be a quiet, almost unknown diplomatic backwater, it would provide an excellent opportunity to meet and, hopefully, to recruit Soviets. A colleague of mine with personal experience in what was then the Belgian Congo—a vast African country still under colonial rule—advised me, "There are a lot of black-tie dinners. Take two tropical dinner jackets so you can have one at the cleaners at all times. And, by the way, you'll be on the golf course by two o'clock every afternoon."

Well, it didn't turn out quite like that.

I arrived on July 10, 1960, ten days after independence from Belgium and five days after the Congolese army had mutinied, throwing the country into chaos. My first taste—but by no means the last—of the lawlessness and arbitrariness of daily life in this newly born African giant came just a few days later.

I was picked up by a band of mutinous soldiers on the prowl in the center of Leopoldville (now Kinshasa). They took me to a dilapidated room at their base located between the European residential part of the city and the Congolese slums and began to question me in a rudimentary sort of way. My protests that I was a diplomat, and thus immune from arrest, were about as useless as tits on a boar.

It was hot and stuffy in the room. Five soldiers were slumped against the grimy walls smoking marijuana, laughing, and talking in Lingala, one of the four main native languages and the official language of the Congolese army. A tall, rangy fellow in filthy pants and shirt detached himself from the group and came over to me. He jerked a battered chair away from the wall and straddled it. The room grew very quiet. The tall soldier reached down and slowly took off his boot. The others were grinning, nudging each other.

"Come over here and kiss my foot, *flamand*," he said in broken French. *Flamand,* or Fleming, was the worst insult the Congolese felt they could use against a white man.

I had already seen this scenario played out to its own unique Congolese conclusion. The soldiers would stop a white person on the street and order him to get down on his knees and kiss a proffered foot. Once the man bent down, a boot would go into the back of his head, smashing his face into the pavement. If the victim didn't initially obey, he'd be clubbed over the head with a rifle butt or beaten in some other manner. If you ever wanted a definition of a no-win situation, that was it.

I made up my mind not to kiss that damned foot, and started trying to talk my way out of my predicament. I also started to sweat. The tall soldier and his scruffy comrades let me spar briefly with them before the mood became belligerent.

"Ever played Russian roulette?" the tall soldier asked.

He pulled a revolver from his holster, showed it to me, and ostentatiously turned his back so I couldn't see what he was doing. He appeared to remove some bullets, spun the chamber twice, and held out the gun to me. I shook my head. The other soldiers were watching me with grim satisfaction.

"Then I will do it for you," the tall soldier said. He got up from his chair and put the gun to my head.

I was damned scared, but I was also damned furious. *"Merde!"* I said.

He pulled the trigger. I heard the pistol's hammer click as it hit an empty chamber. Relief flooded through me. But I was anxious not to show it and give the soldiers the satisfaction of knowing that they had scared the hell out of me.

Then, to my horror, the tall soldier— without spinning the chamber—cocked the gun again.

"Now, you kiss my foot," he said grinning. The other soldiers watched with sour, sullen expressions.

My heart was racing ninety miles a minute. *"Merde!"* I shouted as he pulled the trigger.

The hammer clicked again on an empty chamber, but this time I was not euphoric. I now believed this sadist would kill me. I made a half-hearted effort to remind him of the Geneva Convention concerning the treatment of prisoners, and cited the fact that diplomats cannot be arrested, let alone shot to death by soldiers playing games.

"Just kiss my foot, *patron*, and you have nothing to fear," he said. "Two chances wasted."

I shook my head. There was a roaring sound in my ears and the blood pounded at the back of my head. I heard the hammer click three, four, five times on an empty chamber.

"Last chance, *patron*," he teased. "Kiss this foot."

I wanted to run. I wanted to fight. I certainly did not want to die. At that point, I was undoubtedly a little crazy. I remember yelling *"Merde!"* at the top of my lungs as he pulled the trigger for the sixth and last time.

It took me a while to realize that what I was hearing was a room full of Congolese soldiers roaring with laughter. The tall soldier had removed all the bullets from his revolver, and I was the only one not in on the joke. *Congolese* roulette.

Suddenly, they were my friends, laughing, and slapping me on the back. They offered me a drink from a bottle of wine they had scrounged from somewhere, and we were all big buddies. When we had finished the wine, they dropped me near the Memling Hotel in the center of the city and went off to look for more fun.

It was a far cry from black-tie dinner parties and leisurely golf. Same place, but a totally different world.

1

I GREW UP IN SAN DIEGO in southern California, my father an army colonel who fought in World Wars I and II and my mother a schoolteacher. Both were extremely patriotic. I enlisted in the army in World War II, rose through the enlisted ranks, attended officers' candidate school, and reached the grade of captain serving in the Mediterranean and European theaters. While in Corsica, waiting to land to southern France, I met my first wife, Colette Porteret, now deceased. She was a second lieutenant in de Gaulle's Free French army, having escaped from France to join the Free French forces, where she commanded a forward ambulance platoon. After the war, we were married in France and returned to the United States where I completed my undergraduate studies before going on to Harvard's graduate International Relations program, a precursor to the Kennedy School. I obtained my master's degree and had plans to continue with a doctorate.

Those plans changed dramatically and definitively when Professor William Y. Elliot invited me and three other students to his office in Cambridge one wintry Sunday afternoon in November 1948. There we met McGeorge Bundy, who was secretary of the Council on Foreign Relations in New York and later became national security adviser for Presidents Kennedy and Johnson. Bundy made a convincing argument that the newly formed Central Intelligence Agency in Washington could play a key role in thwarting Moscow's ambitions for world domination without having to resort to open warfare in the nuclear age. The Cold War, for better or worse, was under way and, to my mind, was better than a hot one, which I knew something about. Bundy's argument was in line with my own convictions and I joined the Agency shortly thereafter. After serving in Europe under non-official cover, several years in CIA headquarters in Washington, and a tour in Brussels, I was posted to Leopoldville, in the Congo, as Chief of Station.

The crisis exploded when I was taking a short vacation in France while on my way to the Congo. I was with Colette and our young daughter, Maureen, who liked to tell everyone that she was "almost nine." The Congolese army's mutiny set off a panic exodus by the country's white community and created a dangerous power vacuum in a nation that was literally only six days old. The French media was full of stories of atrocities committed by the mutineers. Plantation owners had been killed, nuns raped, and businessmen beaten up. I quickly halted my vacation after partially convincing my daughter, but not my wife or myself, that as a diplomat I would be safe. It was not easy to leave after hearing Maureen cry out, "Daddy, don't go. They are killing people down there."

I rushed to Paris, then on to Brussels, desperate to reach my new post. Brussels airport was a scene of utter confusion. All the flights to the Congo had been cancelled and SABENA's fleet, the former national airline of Belgium, was commandeered to fly in Belgian troops to restore the peace and to evacuate the refugees. The only way was to go to Brazzaville, capital of the French Congo, which lies on the north bank of the Congo River facing Leopoldville on the south bank, and then take a ferry across. Although not the most auspicious way to reach your first post as station chief, it was a route that many others were to follow in those hectic first weeks of independence.

In those days, Brazzaville was a small, sleepy town with a strong French flavor—low-lying stucco buildings with green tin roofs, sidewalk cafes, bars with zinc countertops, a few high-rise hotels, and walled gardens brimming with bougainvillea, cannas, and hibiscus. It could have been the tropical version of a rather run-down French provincial town.

I headed straight to the American Consulate. The ground floor offices were jammed with people, most of them Americans. Everyone was talking about the Congo, the mutiny, and his or her "escape." I found Alan Lukens, the U.S. consul, on an open porch at the rear of the building, chatting with American refugees. Most were missionaries who had arrived from their stations in the interior of the Congo, and Lukens was trying to find out if there were other Americans still there and what the Congolese thought of the mutiny.

I introduced myself to Lukens, a cheerful and competent man who was to lose his wife, his children, and his mother in a plane crash at his next post in the Central African Republic. Somehow, he managed to recover from this terrible tragedy and go on to become an ambassador and establish a new family. He said he had been alerted by cables from Washington and the embassy in Brussels about my projected arrival and was instructed to do his best to get me across the river to Leopoldville.

"I'm sorry we couldn't meet your plane," he said. "I've got only two vehicles, and they've been tied up with the refugees. Many of them have nothing but the clothes on their backs and we've also got all the wives and children from the Leo embassy. Somehow we've got to make room for them all here, God knows how."

The poor guy looked completely worn out. "It's too late to get to Leopoldville now," he said. "The ferries have stopped for the day." He looked around at the crowded porch. The late afternoon heat was stifling and the lushness of the vegetation was oppressive. "I can't even offer you a bed, only floor space," he went on. "Our apartment is filled with as many female refugees as my wife can pack in. But at least we can offer you something to eat this evening."

With the loan of a blanket, I spent a long, uncomfortable night alongside the other men, including the consul himself, on the cement floor of the consulate. Bullfrogs in the garden kept up a deafening din. Dread and foreboding appeared at every turn of my thoughts, fueled by the horror stories I had heard since my arrival. What was waiting for me across the Congo River?

The next morning brought more doom-laden stories from new arrivals. Several people urged me to stay in Brazzaville or do anything but go to Leopoldville. One kind lady told me I was signing my death warrant. But curiosity, not to mention duty, called, and I found myself impatient to see what was happening on the other side.

I decided to take only one bag with me. My most difficult decision was to leave my Colt .45—a weapon my father had carried in two world wars—but I was strongly advised to leave it at the consulate. The mutineers, I was told, would shoot anyone they found carrying weapons.

Fortified by a robust breakfast, I went down to "the beach," the Brazzaville dock where the cross-river ferries came in. There was a crowd of anxious Belgians waiting to see if the incoming boat would bring family members or friends from Leopoldville. When the overloaded ferry finally pulled in, the passengers fled from it as if escaping their wildest nightmares. The whole noisy, unruly scene was unsettling.

I stood back and took my first real look at the river and what lay beyond. The wide stretch of swirling, coppery-sheened water between Brazzaville and Leopoldville is known as the Stanley Pool, named for the famous British explorer Henry Morton Stanley, who made an epic journey across Africa from east to west in 1877. A good part of his route was down, or alongside, the Congo River, and he was the first white man to follow its winding course to the Atlantic Ocean.

Feted in Europe as a hero, Stanley became King Leopold II's point man in Africa and helped the Belgian monarch secure the river and its huge basin as Leopold's personal property. The deal was signed and sealed at the Berlin Conference in 1885 when the European colonial powers formalized the divvying up of the African continent between them. A single man—the Belgian government, parliament, and people had no say in the matter—now controlled a country as large as the United States east of the Mississippi and bigger than England, France, Germany, Spain, and Italy combined. The king named his new domain the Congo Free State, created his own flag—blue with a gold star in the middle—a new anthem ("Towards the Future,") and referred to the vast territory as "a slice of magnificent African cake."

Over the next twenty-three years, Leopold plundered the country with a cynical brutality rarely matched in colonial history. This great river was the conduit of discovery, punitive expeditions, proselytizing missionaries, conquest, and trade.

The river had also been the route the humanitarian whistle-blowers had traveled. The first was George Washington Williams, a remarkable black American Civil War veteran, lawyer, journalist, and minister who had spent six months in the Congo in 1890 and prepared the first scathing report on the administration of the country, written as an *Open Letter* to King Leopold. Williams was followed by Edmund Morel, the British shipping functionary-turned-activist; Joseph Conrad, whose time as a Congo riverboat captain inspired his book *Heart of Darkness*; William Sheppard, the black American missionary who discovered the orderly and well-governed Kuba Kingdom and befriended its artistic people; and Roger Casement, the British consul who was knighted for his well-documented revelations but later, having given his body and soul to Ireland's cause during the First World War, was captured, tried, and hanged for treason. But the one man of note who never sailed upon this great flood of water, nor ever put a foot on Congolese soil, was the country's owner, Leopold II, King of the Belgians.

The few passengers on the ferry, all men, were not in a talkative mood. We paced about the deck, nervously eyeing each other. Huge patches of water hyacinth torn loose from small streams upriver swept past on the rapid current of the river like little islands of green and purple. Between the two cities the river spread itself in a broad expanse of coppery brown, rushing toward the rapids. In the distance, the city of Leopoldville looked modern, with high-rise white buildings glassy and pale in the morning light. Here and there, columns of smoke rose in the distance. But everything seemed peaceful and quiet.

As the ferry approached the Leopoldville dock, mutineers in full battle-dress with leaves and brush tied to their helmets lounged about; some of them were carrying rifles, others machetes. I was soon to learn that this type of camouflage, known as *matiti*, was not a good sign: the troops were dressed for combat. The mutineers taunted us, motioning us forward. One soldier, swinging a machete, kept repeating in French, "Come, *Flamand*, we will kill you."

We stepped off the boat and walked single file, eyes straight ahead, moving not too fast and not too slow through the unruly mob. One of the soldiers, eyes wild and grinning maniacally, swung a machete close to my face. I kept going, avoiding eye contact. Fortunately, I knew how to find the American Embassy and, within a few minutes, was at my new post.

The embassy in Leopoldville was not then, and is not now, much to look at: a modest diplomatic mission in a tropical, ex-colonial country. The vegetation around it was prolific all year, though in the dry season the vibrant, green plants sagged under a thick layer of dust.

But the city itself was a modern metropolis. The Belgians had created a model state in the middle of Africa after the avaricious monarch willed it to Belgium in 1908. Leopold's legacy was appalling: a devastated landscape of burnt and deserted villages, a ruined agriculture, a declining birthrate, and an estimated ten million Congolese dead as the result of his misrule. In the half century since then the Belgians had built roads, railways, modern cities, hospitals, schools, even a university, and developed a sophisticated government infrastructure. They had also exploited the huge natural riches of the country. For Leopold, the lure had first been ivory then rubber; for his successors, it was copper, cobalt, and diamonds. Belgians, not Congolese, controlled all economic and commercial enterprises.

The real flaw in the Belgian government's strategy, however, was that political development lagged way behind the social and economic transformation. Up to the late 1950s, Belgium regarded the Congo as a docile and dependable cash cow, and it is clear that

Brussels expected to continue governing the mineral-rich region indefinitely. Many Belgians expressed the personal belief that the Congo would not be ready for independence for at least another hundred years.

The result was that the Congolese were well-educated and trained but only up to a limited level. At independence, the country had one of the most literate and healthy indigenous populations in Africa. But out of fourteen million people, there were fewer than twenty university graduates. There was no Congolese cadre of doctors, dentists, engineers, architects, lawyers, university professors, business executives, or accountants. The *Force Publique*, the country's army soon to be re-named the *Armée Nationale Congolaise* (ANC), was officered exclusively by Belgians; the highest ranking Congolese was an adjutant, a sort of senior sergeant, but only a few had recently gained that rank. What seemed clear was that Brussels planned to allow the Congolese their political freedom while keeping the military, economic, and commercial levers of power in their own hands.

Democracy came late to the Congo. The first political party was formed in 1956 and the first elections, of any kind, were local and held in 1957 with Brussels planning a long and gradual path towards independence. But Belgian complacency was shattered in January 1959 when a maelstrom of destruction and pillaging broke out in Leopoldville after the authorities banned a political rally. Shaken by the riots, the Belgian government dramatically reversed course. It was influenced by France's difficulties in maintaining control of Algeria and the fact that the British and the French had already begun the process of decolonization in their sub–Saharan African colonies. Ghana, for example, became independent in 1957 and Guinea followed in 1958. As British prime minister Harold Macmillan put it, Africans were well aware of the "winds of change" blowing through their continent.

Congo's first national elections were held in May 1960 with independence scheduled for June 30. Supervised by Belgian judges and other officials, they were the only free and fair elections held in

the Congo to date. The winners among the many parties and leaders were Joseph Kasavubu, a canny, inscrutable politician with a
strong tribal base in the area between the port city of Matadi and
Leopoldville, and the charismatic but temperamental Patrice Lumumba who had obtained some support in five out of the six
provinces. None of the parties received a majority. A parliamentary
deadlock between the two leaders and their parties resulted in
Kasavubu taking what was then believed to be the largely ceremo-
nial job of president while Lumumba assumed what was thought to
be the much more powerful post of prime minister.

Independence on June 30, 1960, brought pomp and ceremony
but also disharmony. King Baudouin, then king of Belgium, made
an ill-judged, patronizing speech, praising the "genius" and
"courage" of King Leopold and the subsequent development of the
country by "Belgian pioneers." Kasavubu's speech was conciliatory,
but Lumumba trashed the Belgians' colonial record, talked of the
need "to bring an end the humiliating slavery imposed on us by
force," and invoked the struggle for independence that had involved
"tears, fire, and blood." He ended, somewhat prophetically though
not the way he intended, by saying, "We shall make the Congo the
focal point of Africa."

A few days later, Lumumba promised all government employees
a pay raise—all, that is, except the army. General Emile Janssens,
the army's Belgian commander, made matters worse when he reportedly told his troops that "for the army, independence equals
zero." On the night of July 5–6, Congolese soldiers at the large
Thysville military base, which was downriver from Leopoldville,
mutinied. The revolt spread rapidly to other bases around the country as Congolese radio operators spread the word. Their grievances
were not difficult to divine. They were furious with Lumumba for
being excluded from the pay increases, and they had no love for
their Belgian officers who continued to treat them as if Belgium
still ruled the country.

That was when panic seized the European community as stories
of murder, rape, and pillage spread rapidly. The international media

began to take notice as grotesque reports appeared in major newspapers throughout the world.

The situation was, of course, not as bad as in Algeria where one million Frenchmen had settled, or in the colonies of Kenya and Rhodesia that had large British settler populations. The Belgian presence had always been limited to people required by the various Belgian enterprises and government services operating in the colony. Belgian citizens came out, served their time, and generally returned home. This policy, in effect, limited the number of Belgians with deep roots in the country. Nevertheless, the suddenness of the mutiny and the chaos that followed was bad enough—bad for the Europeans who still basically ran the country, and bad for the new, inexperienced government struggling to rule a vast country and a huge population bereft of the human material necessary for such a task. It was also pretty rough on us newly arrived diplomats.

My own office, which was also my place of residence in the coming months, was next to that of Ambassador Clare H. Timberlake—"Tim"—a man with whom I would share many moments of high drama and forge a close friendship. My first meeting with Tim occurred during a visit he had made to our embassy in Brussels from Bonn, Germany, where he was then serving as deputy chief of mission (DCM). He had come to Brussels to discuss matters related to the Congo and to meet me. Lean as a reed, Tim was a relatively short man with a Clark Gable mustache. After graduating from the University of Michigan, he joined the Foreign Service and served for twenty-nine years before being appointed to the Congo, his first ambassadorial post. He was a natural leader, prepared to make rapid, tough-minded decisions, the right man in the right spot at the right time. He will always remain in my mind as an outstanding ambassador and courageous public servant.

The embassy staff was small. With the evacuation of the wives, children, and non-essential personnel, only thirteen Americans remained. In addition to the ambassador, the key players were Rob McIlvaine, the deputy chief of mission, who had run a small newspaper before entering the Foreign Service; Jerry Lavallee, chief of the political section, had served as number two in the consulate, and Frank Carlucci, a young officer on his second overseas tour, had been there before independence. Lavallee and Carlucci had developed a useful range of Congolese contacts. Carlucci would have many close shaves in the months ahead and go on to greater things. Fitzhugh Green, the United States Information Agency officer, and Andy Steigman, a first tour officer, his wife Meryl, and I made up the rest of the group. My assistant was a young woman who handled the code work, kept the books, and typed and filed. Shortly after my arrival, a radio operator joined us.

Since I was assigned to the Congo before the country became independent, my cover was as a consul. Our mission was a consulate-general and not yet an embassy. And even though we had become a fully fledged embassy after independence, my title remained the same during the whole of my first tour in the country.

A number of Americans and a few Europeans had taken refuge with us. They were waiting to see if the political situation calmed down so they could return to their businesses or missionary stations. Most were men who had sent their wives and children out with the embassy evacuees, but a few wives remained. The sleeping accommodations within the embassy consisted of two one-bedroom apartments for junior personnel, so most of the refugees slept on the floor, although a few lucky ones found divans in some of the offices. At night, the men slept in one area and the women in another. There was no hanky-panky in the American Embassy.

During my first few days, I tried to get my bearings and to learn as much as possible from the refugees inside the embassy. Outside in the city, the mutinous troops, almost always armed and often drunk, roamed the streets. The sporadic sound of gunfire and explosions occasionally punctuated our days and nights, and the smell of smoke was often strong outside the embassy. But if I was to do my job gathering intelligence, it was imperative for me to get outside the embassy compound.

Shortly after my arrival, I drove in a borrowed car to a house in Binza—a suburb of Leopoldville on a hill overlooking the city— where I met an agent who had been on the books for some time. He was one of the few agents I inherited and I had to start building up a network from scratch. After he left, I was preparing to do the same when the telephone rang and a voice I did not recognize asked in French if "they" had reached my place yet. When I asked who "they" were, my mystery caller said that the Belgian military had killed several Congolese soldiers near the port city of Matadi. The Congolese were marching on Leopoldville, he said, and planned to pick up all the "Europeans" they could find (the Congolese called all white people "Europeans"). They would then hang twenty of them in the square in front of the Belgian Embassy.

I had no sooner ended that conversation than the phone rang again. Once more an unfamiliar voice asked me if "they" had reached my place. Again, I heard the story of the approaching Congolese soldiers and their plan to hang Europeans. I hung up and picked up my things to make a run for the embassy, but at the last minute I decided it would be advisable first to check with someone there. I reached Rob McIlvaine, who advised me to stay where I was.

"The Congolese may already be between Binza and Leopoldville, if our Belgian contacts have got it right," Rob said. "I personally don't think so, but no point in taking chances." So I waited.

There were more phone calls, all of which made me almost as nervous as the callers. I decided I'd better find a weapon. (Contrary to popular belief, CIA officers do not carry weapons. Exceptions are made, but only after approval from on high.) The only possible weapons I could find in the house were a claw hammer and a butcher knife. I looked for door keys and found none. So I propped chairs against the doors, even though that was pretty foolish because the doors were made of glass panels. Anyone standing on the other side could see the chairs and would have little difficulty breaking in.

The phone rang several more times, and the question was always the same. The callers were full of wild stories, but no hard facts. I listened for the noise of approaching trucks or jeeps, and my imagination soon began to play tricks, convincing me that I could hear vehicles approaching. I called the embassy again but still no hard news on what was really happening.

The sun went down about six o'clock with the sudden plunge into darkness that is so typical of the tropics, but I did not turn on the lights. After several hours of prowling around in the dark house, I stretched out on a bed, my "weapons" at the ready. I must have gone to sleep, for I was suddenly awakened by the sound of vehicles. I leapt out of bed and crept over to the window. Outside, a handful of Congolese soldiers were making camp. I had no idea how many of them had come into the neighborhood. The rest of the night was uneventful, except in my imagination. With first light, the soldiers began moving about preparing their breakfast. Fortunately, none tried to enter the house, and they seemed in no hurry to leave their post outside. My greatest fear was that, as time passed, they would get bored, begin looking for loot, and break into the house.

After several hours of creeping from window to window, I had had enough. I abandoned the hammer and hid the butcher knife in the sleeve of my suit coat. I knew that being caught with a weapon was dangerous, but at the time I thought it better to be armed. I opened the door and walked quickly to the car that was still in the yard where I had parked it the day before. I do not know what I expected, but whatever it was, it didn't happen. The soldiers in the yard looked up at me, but made no move to stop me. *"Bonjour, Flamand,"* one said, and that was it. The car started on the first try, and I was off. I drove as fast as I could, keeping a weather eye open for Congolese roadblocks, but there were none. The last hurdle was passing a small army camp at the bottom of the hill, a place where many whites had been arrested the night of the mutiny. I sailed past it and on to the embassy without a hitch.

The story of a Congolese column marching on Leopoldville turned out to be yet another false rumor, and I was never able to determine why a small group of mutinous Congolese soldiers decided to camp in that particular yard. It was the kind of thing that happened over and over again during that tumultuous time, periods of absolute terror that left you feeling like a fool afterwards for having had the living daylights scared out of you. A mutinous army is a dangerous and fearful thing. Without their officers, the soldiers no longer followed the chain of command and relied on their guns to make their own kind of law. The most frightening thing was the sense of anarchy throughout the city and, no doubt, throughout the country at large. Central authority had broken down; there was no one in control who could prevent random acts of barbarity.

2

SINCE WE HAD NOT YET RECEIVED our contingent of U.S. Marine guards to protect the embassy—which tells you what a sleepy, back-of-beyond post Leopoldville had been—I checked to see what weapons we had in case the mutineers attacked the building. All I found were six tear gas grenades. With the approval of the ambassador, I decided to rectify the situation.

Using my nose, literally, I started prowling the city at night, looking for mutineers high on marijuana or beer. The streets were largely deserted except for soldiers and lone women huddled in the dust roasting corn or frying suspicious-looking pieces of meat. The best technique was to find a soldier by himself, offer him a cigarette and, if he appeared friendly, tell him I was going on a hunting trip and would like to buy his rifle. It worked on a couple of occasions and, crazy though it may seem, it also worked with a soldier who had a Thompson submachine gun, which was a military version of the "Chicago piano" favored by Al Capone and other gangsters in the 1920s and '30s. A Belgian member of the Belgian Congo *Sûreté Nationale*, who was leaving the country, gave me two Browning semi-automatic pistols. Finally, a SABENA Airlines contact passed on a box of Czech fragmentation grenades that the Czechs or Soviets had inadvertently left at the airport.

None of us in the embassy was anxious to use these weapons. In any battle with the mutinous troops, we would certainly have been the losers. However, we took other precautions such as placing all of the embassy's and station's classified files in burn barrels on the second floor of the embassy. This was a source of daily irritation because each time we needed a file, we had to hunt through the barrels. But it was a thoroughly effective security measure because, if we seemed likely to be overrun, all we had to do was toss a match into each barrel.

Several times it looked as though the soldiers were about to attack the embassy, but on each occasion the crisis was defused. Happily, we never needed to burn the files. I was later told that, had we needed to burn them, the magnesium contained in the barrel was enough to have blown the roof off the building.

The threat of an attack never entirely disappeared, but it was only really serious during the first few weeks after my arrival. Our closest shave occurred on July 13, the day the Belgian paratroops landed and seized Ndjili, Leopoldville's international airport. The Congolese army was put on a war footing, somewhat haphazardly because each unit seemed to be acting on its own. The troops had been taught camouflage techniques by the Belgians, who presumed fighting would take place in the forest, not in the city. As a result, the troops appeared on the streets wearing their *matiti* foliage.

Only two of the embassy's Congolese employees, Sammy, the ambassador's driver, and Albert, who worked for the United States Information Agency office, turned up that day. When the soldiers arrived, these two courageously planted themselves in front of the embassy and tried to convince them that the embassy had nothing to do with the Belgian incursion and was a neutral diplomatic mission.

The situation was fraught and dangerous with racial overtones. The uneducated troops seemed to take the attitude, "black good, white bad." Any spark could have set off an attack.

Structurally, the embassy was indefensible. The architect had obviously never considered the possibility that the building—intended as a consulate—would ever come under military attack. The lobby had glass doors, and the brick latticework decorating the sides of the building made dandy ladders for anyone who wanted to pay a visit through the windows on the second and third floors.

Ambassador Timberlake called us together and outlined a plan of action. His assumption was that, if the troops smashed their way into the building, they would kill anyone in their way. Three of us—Tim himself, Rob McIlvaine, and I—were authorized by Tim to open fire if the soldiers attacked. I had a grenade in each pocket and a nine-millimeter Browning semi-automatic pistol in my belt under my coat. I had hidden the Thompson submachine gun in the hall ready for use to stem an assault on the front of the building.

Around mid-morning, an army jeep, mounting a fifty-caliber machine gun, pulled into the narrow driveway that separated the embassy from the sidewalk. The gunner slowly swung the weapon around, aiming it at the embassy's front door. When he pulled back the arming mechanism, I retreated into the hallway but kept the jeep in full view. Fortunately for us, the gunner forgot, if he ever knew, that the firing mechanism had to be turned three clicks before squeezing the trigger. The gun jammed. As he worked to clear it, I pulled out a grenade, ready to hurl it at the gunner if he opened fire. Fifty-caliber bullets have a terrifying, destructive power at close quarters and I knew they could blast a huge hole. I expected that the troops would then attack but I hoped that a grenade might set the jeep on fire and slow them down. We planned to retreat to the third floor and keep the attackers at bay by throwing grenades down the stairwell.

As I stood apprehensively watching the soldiers in the jeep, Ambassador Timberlake suddenly appeared at my side. "Come with me," he said curtly. He opened the front door. "Forget about that grenade in your pocket, just smile and translate everything I say." Tim spoke nearly fluent Spanish and German, but his French was rusty.

As we approached the jeep, two men aimed their rifles at us, but the ambassador appeared not to notice. "Thank God, you've come to protect us from the Belgians," he said, shaking his head angrily and pointing at his watch. "We've been waiting for hours for the Congolese army to defend us. The Belgians could be here any minute." Then he turned to me, as cool as could be, and said, "Why don't you offer our friends here some cigarettes?"

The soldiers put down their weapons, took the pack of cigarettes, and agreed they had indeed come to protect us. Tim, acting as though he had expected such a response, turned and pointed to the far end of Avenue des Aviateurs, where there was a statue honoring the aviators who first flew the African mail route, and suggested that it would be an excellent position from which to defend the embassy. To my astonishment, the soldiers nodded, quietly departed, and settled down near the statue.

This entire incident lasted little more than five minutes and was probably never reported to Washington. If it had been, people there would have had a hard time believing it. Diplomats, armed to the teeth and defending their embassy against unruly soldiers of the host country, contradicted all the principles and practices of normal diplomacy. But in our case it was a small victory for skilled diplomacy over violent confrontation and a personal triumph for our ambassador. Tim proved that day, as he was to prove many times in the days and weeks to come, that he was a man of excellent judgment and great courage.

The tension grew more acute with the news that the Belgian paratroopers were approaching the city. The Congolese army had occupied positions near the Royale, a new apartment building on Boulevard 30 Juin (formerly Boulevard Albert), Leopoldville's main street, where the UN mission to the Congo was later to establish its headquarters. The government, led by President Joseph Kasavubu and Prime Minister Patrice Lumumba, was still in place but invisible, unable to restore order. The day the Belgians entered Leopoldville, I was on one of my usual exploratory prowls and stumbled on an extraordinary meeting that may well have prevented a skirmish, not to say a battle, between the Belgians and the Congolese.

In the middle of Boulevard 30 Juin—a broad avenue with palm trees down the middle—I found the agitated commander of a Congolese unit talking to Justin Bomboko, the youthful Congolese foreign minister, and Archbishop Malula, the senior Catholic bishop in the Congo. As they talked, I could see them apprehensively eyeing a Belgian column that had halted a short distance away.

"My God, my God, someone tell me what to do," the Congolese commander said. "If they advance, we must open fire." Bomboko and the archbishop were remonstrating with him, trying to head off a clash. The archbishop mopped his forehead and looked disconsolately down the avenue.

"I've got it!," the archbishop said with a little squeal. "We'll have a parade!" He and Bomboko walked over to the Belgian troops and spoke to their commanding officer. In a few minutes, the Belgian unit's trucks were turned around, and each truck was filled with a mixture of Congolese and Belgian troops. The column then drove slowly down Boulevard Albert to the train station. The soldiers were clearly ill at ease and distrustful, but everything went off smoothly and a fight was avoided. As the column slowly passed the Regina Hotel, the proprietor made his contribution to the archbishop's novel peacekeeping effort. Waiters from the sidewalk cafe handed up free soft drinks and sandwiches to the soldiers in each truck.

During those early days, I ate my daily ration of beef stew and slept in the embassy every night. The embassy staff, confined to quarters for much of the time, formed a tight bond. All the city's restaurants were closed, and the mutinous soldiers did not encourage unnecessary exploration. However, since I had to go out to make useful contacts, I encountered the full range of unpredictable military behavior. I quickly learned to carry several packs of cigarettes and a supply of small bills ready for sticky situations.

During my first few weeks in the Congo, I had no car. All the embassy cars had diplomatic plates, which were of no use to me because I did not want to draw attention to myself, so I had to rely on cadging a vehicle. But the chaos worked in my favor in a curious way.

One evening, a Greek gentleman with his wife and teenaged daughter knocked on the embassy door and I let them in. The girl was in shock, and the man and his wife were almost hysterical.

"Soldiers stopped us at a roadblock," the man said. "They ordered us out of the car and when we got out, one of them began to fondle my daughter. She resisted and he tore her blouse. I knocked him down—I couldn't stop myself—and we jumped into the car and drove here."

They were convinced the soldiers must be in hot pursuit, and although there was no sign of them, they were understandably terrified. The man was also afraid that I would refuse to give his daughter sanctuary. He begged me to protect her, saying that he and his wife asked for nothing for themselves. They would risk the roadblocks if only we would protect their daughter. As he spoke, he wrote a check for a large sum, leaving the payee blank, and handed it to me. I tore it up and assured him that they could spend the night in the embassy.

The following day the Greek told me that he, his wife, and daughter were leaving for Brazzaville with some other refugees. He thanked me over and over again, and putting his hand in his pocket, fished out a set of keys to the Volkswagen Beetle that was parked outside.

"Here, Mr. Devlin," he said. "It's yours."

I laughed. "Thank you, but no," I said. "We can't accept gifts, but we were happy to help you and your family." He persisted. Finally, we struck a bargain. I told him I would be delighted to keep the car for him but that I would return it to him when he came back, or hand it over to anyone he might designate in his place. We decided on a code word that he would include in a letter carried by the person he sent to pick up the car. He went away happy, and I had a nice little car for my clandestine meetings. Some weeks later, a man carrying a letter with the code word from the owner of the Volkswagen visited the embassy to claim the car, and I handed it over. By then I had managed to buy the last remaining Peugeot 403 in Leopoldville, one of the great vehicular war-horses of Africa that served me well.

In late July, word reached the embassy that several Americans, presumably missionaries who were leaving the country, were being held prisoner at the beach where the Leopoldville-Brazzaville ferry docked and where I had landed. The ambassador asked me, in my function as consul or perhaps because I was near at hand, to see what I could do to obtain their release. Preparing for my first consular duty, I pocketed several packs of cigarettes as bargaining chips and set off.

The Americans were being held by a group of Congolese soldiers. There were three couples and a child who looked hopeful when I arrived. No one seemed to be in charge of the detail, and the soldiers were high as kites, although it was only eleven o'clock in the morning. The place was a mess: guns lying around, lots of beer bottles, all manner of trash and filth scattered across the bare, wooden floor. In my sorties around town, I had gradually developed a technique for dealing with the mutineers. I would try to determine the softest target in the group and begin a roundabout palaver that ended with the gift of a pack or two of cigarettes when I saw things were going my way.

That morning the business proceeded without a hitch, and the Americans were released. As I was about to leave, a big soldier jumped me and hit me with his fist, knocking me unconscious. I have no idea how long I lay there on the floor.

"Get up, you Flemish dog, you Flemish spy, get up!" I heard someone shout in broken French before I was dragged to my feet by a couple of soldiers.

"We're going to shoot you, Flemish bastard!"

There were about ten of them, and they seemed mad as hell. They yanked me outside and slammed me against a wall.

"I am *not* a Flemish spy! I'm an American diplomat," I protested. "I came here to obtain the release of those Americans, the people you've just let go to Brazzaville."

Nobody listened. They flung me up against the wall again while half a dozen formed a firing squad. It must have been around noon, and the sun was blazing down as if it had just discovered what hotter than hell meant. The soldiers went through a rudimentary firing squad routine, and my head was clear enough to realize that I was looking down six rifle barrels. I had always heard that people about to die see their entire lives flash before them. That didn't happen to me. I simply could not believe what was happening.

But then it hit me: they *were* going to fire. At that moment, the cavalry arrived in the form of Albert Delvaux, the Congolese ambassador to Belgium, who had not yet taken up his new post. He also had the rank of a government minister. Delvaux saw what was happening, jumped out of his car, and ran over to me.

"I can't do anything with them," he muttered in rapid French, "but I'll try to distract them. Just walk away. Don't run, don't run!"

The soldiers, one and all, adopted a respectful attitude as Delvaux walked toward them, and I tried my best to make a discreet exit from the scene. I could hear him arguing with them in Lingala as I walked away, all the time feeling an unpleasant itching sensation down my back. I kept walking and walking and finally got back to the embassy without further trouble.

A few hours later, there was another report of Americans being held at the beach. Once again I was sent to obtain their release, and I'll be damned if the same scenario wasn't played out just as it had been that morning. Cigarettes were offered, cigarettes were accepted, the Americans departed for Brazzaville, and, once again, I was accused of being a Flemish spy. They were the same troops who had been there earlier. When the time for the firing squad arrived, I looked around hopefully for Delvaux, or any influential figure, but none appeared. Not having a white knight at my disposal, I announced in desperation that I was the American consul and that no one had the right to shoot a consul. With that, I walked away. I heard them discussing the matter in Lingala, the word *consul* being the same as it is in French. While they talked, I walked, but I did not look back, fearing that it would provoke them to shoot.

I realized later that the word *consul* had done the trick. Before independence, consuls were important men in the Congo, men to whom the *Force Publique*, as the Congolese army was then called, had regularly presented arms. My mistake during previous incidents had been to use the word *diplomat* rather than *consul*. In retrospect, I doubt that the soldiers intended to shoot me. I suspect they were merely trying to humiliate and frighten me as they had done in the Congolese roulette episode. And, of course, they succeeded.

Later, I learned that Delvaux, along with Foreign Minister Bomboko, and Archbishop Malula, were on the streets every day trying to prevent incidents like the ones I had experienced before they got out of hand. They were extraordinary men facing extraordinary times.

It was a topsy-turvy world. A deadly game was going on but no one seemed to know the rules. The instant you did, the rules would suddenly change and you'd be in trouble again, as we were late one night when Ambassador Timberlake had asked me to drive to his residence with him to discuss our work. We were stopped at a roadblock commanded by an extremely short corporal who announced that we were under arrest for violating the curfew. Since curfews were regularly declared, but often not announced or enforced, it came as a surprise to be stopped for a curfew violation. I got out of the car to argue with the corporal, pointing out diplomats were exempt from such regulations, particularly ambassadors. That seemed to confuse him and he maintained that we were under arrest. As the argument continued, I banged my fist on the hood of Tim's car and told the corporal that I was the American consul and he had no right to arrest a consul or an ambassador. With that, he came to attention.

"*Monsieur le Consul*, you can go," he said. But then he turned in Tim's direction and glowered. "*Mais, ambassadeur, je m'en fous.* (I don't give a damn.) He's under arrest."

I tried to explain that the ambassador was a most senior, highly important diplomat, but I soon realized that I was not getting through. Wracking my brains for a solution, I finally said the ambassador was my deputy. The soldier looked doubtful then said: "*D'accord*, he can go, too."

Tim, who had heard the conversation, laughed as we drove up to his house. "Almost thirty years in the Foreign Service, and here I am back to being a vice-consul," he said wryly. He took the matter to heart, however, for I heard that when he was next stopped at a roadblock, he swallowed his ambassadorial pride and identified himself as the "American consul."

The Congo's internal turmoil was one thing, but a more sinister threat rapidly became apparent. Personnel from the Soviet Union, its Eastern European satellite allies, and communist China began to flood into the country. There seemed no doubt that those countries were making a special effort to establish a foothold in a continent where they had no history but where they sensed great opportunities for political and economic influence. These were made all the sweeter because any gains would be at the expense of the West. In the past, the European colonial powers had virtually shut the Soviet Union and other communist states out of Africa. But with the independence of Ghana in 1957 and Guinea in 1958, the Cold War struggle got rolling in earnest. These two newly independent countries declared themselves non-aligned but, sensing an opportunity, were more than willing to play the two superpowers against each other for their own purposes.

During July and August 1960, several hundred Soviet personnel entered the Congo. The count was based on a newly recruited and untried Congolese agent sitting at Ndjili airport and marking them off on a note pad as they came in. Any white person disembarking from a Russian plane was considered to be a citizen of the Soviet Union. There were also a number of twin-engine Russian Il–14 cargo/passenger planes based at Ndjili and at the airport in Stanleyville, the up-river capital of Orientale province. Each plane had two or three crews as well as mechanics, interpreters, and other personnel. The aircraft carried cargo that had come from larger Russian planes. Some of it was in boxes marked with a Red Cross symbol, but the boxes seemed remarkably similar to small arms and ammunition boxes. The planes were flying into the interior of the country but, since they seldom filed flight plans, it was difficult to find out where the cargo was going. Some years later, we found some of those boxes with Red Cross symbols still unopened in Orientale province, the center of the rebellion in 1964 and 1965. The boxes contained rifles, machine-guns, and ammunition. It thus appears the Soviets were planning support for a rebellion as early as July 1960.

We assumed that many, if not most, of the Soviets were intelligence officers, although it was impossible to confirm. Even when we had names, we could not be sure we had true identifications, since Soviet intelligence officers sometimes use different names when they change assignments.

In more settled places, identifying and attempting to recruit the opposition's intelligence officers usually occupies much of a station chief's time and energies. But, in the Congo, the first priority was to single out the key Congolese players and get a handle on the political situation that, like desert sand, was constantly shifting under our feet.

The political situation was worsening daily. On July 11, the day after I arrived, the southern province of Katanga—the producer of the Congo's rich copper and cobalt exports—seceded, taking with it the country's major source of revenue. Led by Moise Tshombe, the provincial president, and Godefroid Munongo, the influential minister of interior, Katanga's secession was supported by the powerful Belgian mining interests in the province. It followed the army mutiny by less than a week, and encouraged other potential secessionist movements, notably the diamond-rich South Kasai in the center of the country.

Patrice Lumumba, who as the head of the government was the central political figure of the moment, found himself having to deal with many unfortunate things: an army mutiny for which he was partly responsible; the secession of the country's wealthiest province; and a government paralyzed by personal and tribal rivalries, including his own with President Kasavubu. Compounding the political difficulties, the army mutiny had produced a mass flight of Belgian businessmen, technicians, and some senior military and police officers, bringing the economy to a virtual standstill.

Lumumba, three years younger than myself, was born in Kasai province and educated up to primary level at a Catholic missionary school. (He was later denied entry into Lovanium University in Leopoldville because only single students were admitted, and he was married.) He worked as a postal clerk in Stanleyville, edited a quarterly review, and wrote articles for local publications. In 1956, he was arrested on charges of embezzlement and imprisoned for a year. On his release, he moved to Leopoldville and became a sales director at a brewery. He was active in politics and helped to form the *Movement National Congolais* (MNC), which later split into two wings. However, his branch won a parliamentary plurality in the May 1960 general election and he became prime minister. He was a powerful, at times mesmerizing orator who could whip a crowd into a frenzy. A passionate nationalist, his emotions often swamped his political judgment, and as time went on he became increasingly unstable and unpredictable.

Most of us at the embassy regarded him as a disaster in the making. There was no reason to believe that he was a Soviet agent or even a communist, but he was all too close to the Soviet Union and its allies for comfort. The ambassador and I concluded that while Lumumba thought he could use the Soviets, they were, in fact, using him.

The Soviets' image of unwavering support for Africa's downtrodden people was occasionally undermined by unintentional self-parody. Shortly after the Congo became independent, Moscow announced that it was sending food for the "poor, hungry, oppressed workers and peasants" of the Congo. Sure enough, a Soviet ship arrived at Matadi, the Congo's primary seaport. It was full of wheat. Unfortunately, the Congo did not possess a flour mill, so it had to be loaded on a ship once more and sent elsewhere to be milled. This episode did not match Moscow's fraternal dispatch of snowplows to tropical Guinea two years earlier but it made clear that our Cold War adversaries were not ten feet tall.

The Soviets were also not immune to the daily hazards that we encountered on the streets of the capital. One day I was downtown, walking past the New Stanley Hotel, when a truckload of Congolese soldiers with fixed bayonets pulled up and dashed inside. I was wary but curious and waited across the street to see what would happen. A Congolese civilian who came out told us the troops were reacting to a rumor that there were communist spies in the hotel. In due course, the soldiers emerged with three "communist" prisoners: Ralph Bunche, the interim United Nations representative to the Congo; the Israeli ambassador; and the Soviet ambassador, a minister from one of the Soviet republics.

Bunche and the Israeli knew that discretion was the better part of valor and promptly obeyed the order to get into the back of the army truck. The Soviet ambassador who had yet to appreciate the value of that stratagem, remonstrated loudly in English. He proclaimed he was the ambassador of the USSR sent to help the poor, downtrodden, oppressed Congolese masses. Unfortunately, he did not speak French or any African language, and the Congolese soldiers did not understand English. He refused to climb into the truck. Without further ado, the soldiers stepped forward, grabbed him, and tossed him into the vehicle as casually as if he had been a sack of Soviet wheat.

He picked himself up and turned to the Israeli ambassador. "You speak French," he said. "Tell them that I am the Soviet ambassador and that I am here to help the poor Congolese workers and peasants." The Israeli gave him a quizzical look. "And what concession is the Soviet Union prepared to make to Israel?" he said.

Later Ralph Bunche, a light-skinned African-American, told Timberlake that he was greatly amused by the whole episode. "Can you imagine this chocolate boy being taken for a communist spy?"

he asked. The Congolese soldiers, most of whom were jet black, looked upon Bunche as just another "European."

We led a strange life in those early days in the Congo, which was a far cry from what people usually imagine diplomatic life to be. There were no cocktail parties or receptions, and certainly no golf and drinks in the clubhouse. Fitzhugh Green, the USIA officer, tried to get in a round of golf, but he played only one or two holes when he decided the game was not worth the risk. Some mutinous soldiers probably high on beer or hash, or both, were taking a little target practice with Fitzhugh as the bull's eye.

I thought someone was taking a pot shot at me in August 1960 when I received a cable instructing me to remove the rods from a small atomic reactor at Lovanium University. The cable said the request had come from the United States Atomic Energy Commission. The United States had given the reactor to the Congo as an expression of appreciation for having provided the uranium for the first American atomic bombs. I was to advise Monseigneur Gillon, the university's rector, who was described as an atomic physicist, of my plans (I had no plans) to remove the rods and bury them where they could not be found.

There were no other details, not even a hint of how to handle a hot atomic rod. Perhaps they thought I was expendable. As for burying the rods where they could not be found, I could not think of a way to do that in a country where a white man stood out like a cigar store Indian. As for taking the rods out into the countryside, I wondered how to get them past a dozen or more check points before I was clear of civilization. Even then, my experience in North Africa during World War II convinced me that no matter how hard one tried to act without being seen when nature called, someone would pop up and be looking at you at the crucial moment. However, I was expected to carry out orders.

I put my fears in neutral and drove to Lovanium, passing through three road blocks on the way. When I told Monseigneur Gillon of my instructions, he was horrified and said it was a crazy idea. He shared my view that it would be nearly impossible to carry out the mission in secrecy and said it would be much safer to leave the rods in the reactor. I reported his views to Headquarters and, happily, never heard another word about the matter.

Before independence, the Congo had been of limited interest to the United States. When we wanted to know something about the country, we asked the Belgians, our NATO ally. This changed when the Cold War reached the Congo. Neither the Soviet Union nor China was represented, although Czechoslovakia had managed to establish a consulate in Leopoldville headed by a member of its intelligence service. Our general practice was to establish a liaison link with the security services of the host country. However, we thought it would be unwise to do that with the Lumumba government because it was perceived to be hostile to the United States and friendly with the Soviet Union. This soon became more than a perception when we learned that Soviet "technical advisers" were working with the Congo's *Sûreté Nationale,* the country's internal security service. Any information we might have given the Congolese would almost certainly have reached the KGB.

In my early days in the Congo, I was sometimes followed when I left the embassy. Fortunately, the surveillance was obvious and amateurish. I'd leave the embassy on foot and the surveillance team would lock in on me. But, after a block or two, someone from the embassy would pick me up in my car, leaving the team jumping up and down in frustration like the Three Stooges.

The Cold War, like it or not, had come to a hot country and the battle lines were rapidly being drawn in the streets of Leopoldville and across this enormous, fragile country. It was my job to do something about it, and the first task was to create a network of agents and then mount clandestine operations against the Soviet Union and its allies, which were clearly setting their sights on influencing, if not controlling, Lumumba's fledgling government.

Our problem was that we were starting from almost zero. Before independence, our consul-general had worked almost entirely with the host country's officials, the normal practice in colonial territories. Jerry Lavallee and Frank Carlucci, the embassy's political staff, were the only people in the embassy who had made useful contacts among the Congolese prior to independence. They were primarily engaged in working with members of the Congolese government, if and when they could be located. This was not easy because the Congolese leaders were unused to running government departments, or indeed dealing with foreign diplomats and conducting conventional diplomacy. Also, they sometimes ran into difficulties of their own with the mutinous soldiers. My experience when Albert Delvaux had come to my rescue was fairly typical.

Recruiting agents is not, or should not be, a rapid process. The process begins with spotting someone who seems to have access to information of interest to the U.S. government. Alternatively, he (or she) may be in a position to support American policies or objectives. Next, you attempt to determine his motivation, his political views and opinions, whether he has problems—money or otherwise—details of his family life, any personal idiosyncrasies, and so forth.

If you decide the person is both useful and recruitable, you try to establish a close relationship. You do things that you believe would amuse or interest the person. If he likes jokes, you tell jokes. If he enjoys discussing literature or economics, you discuss literature and economics. If he is fond of food and drink, you wine and dine him. The first three steps—spotting, assessing, and developing—are all the preliminaries for the final and crucial step, recruitment. You then pop the question and hope for an affirmative answer. The process has a lot in common with seduction.

There is no single factor that motivates men or women to become spies. Money is often the key, but there are numerous other reasons. One agent with whom I worked in another country did so because of his own personal beliefs. He was convinced that the United States had saved his and his wife's lives during World War II, and his cooperation was his way of re-paying a debt of gratitude. He accomplished extraordinary things for us but would never accept a penny. When we lunched together, he insisted on taking turns in settling the bill. Others cooperated with us because they believed it was in their interest to do so. They wanted the United States to support them in achieving some objective, usually political. But, of course, every individual is different so motivation has to be extremely carefully assessed.

I spent hours in bars, hotel lobbies, newspaper offices, walking through the market, and sitting in the parliamentary visitors' gallery—you name it, I did it. While hard slog and dogged persistence are crucial to intelligence work, a little luck never hurt. And lady luck, as it turned out, smiled on me in the Congo.

At the embassy, all sorts of visitors dropped in to see me, not only because my door was open to all comers, but also because legitimate diplomats, such as Jerry Lavallee and Frank Carlucci, sent people to my office whom they thought might prove useful. Sometimes there is friction between Foreign Service officers and CIA personnel in an embassy. But not in the Congo. Ambassador Timberlake set the tone from the outset, making it clear that he would not tolerate any kind of turf wars or infighting. Further, I was truly blessed with strong and competent colleagues, and we worked with each other in a remarkably harmonious way.

My visitors included Congolese politicians, tribal leaders, and people who were political neophytes with ambitions. One of my regular visitors was Albert Kalonji, the leader of the Baluba tribe in the southern Kasai province whose title was Mulopwe, variously translated as "king," "emperor," or, sometimes, "god." He led the other wing of the MNC that had broken away from Lumumba's faction. He detested the prime minister and blamed him for the slaughter of many of his fellow tribesman. When Katanga seceded, Lumumba sent troops to crush the rebellion and en route they passed through Kasai, killing many of Kalonji's Baluba followers. Kalonji was seeking American support to overthrow Lumumba, and he wasn't the only one, for several other politicians visited me with the same idea in mind.

Another Congolese who came by regularly was Paul Bolya, a junior leader of the Mongos, one of the larger tribes in Equateur province. He headed a political party called the *Parti National Popu-laire* (PNP). During the recent national elections, he had reportedly received financial backing from the Belgian government and Belgian businessmen with interests in the Congo to the point where the PNP became known as the *Partie des Nègres Payés* (Party of Bribed Negroes). Although he had not done particularly well in the elections, he nevertheless had great ambitions and hoped to add American support to the Belgian largesse.

Some of these visitors led legitimate ethnic or political groups while others were merely looking for a handout. But I found them all useful because, knowingly or unknowingly, they helped me get a better grasp on the Congo's complex political and tribal structure. I listened to all of them, as intelligence officers must, but expressed no opinion as diplomats are obliged to do.

3

WHEN I WAS A SMALL BOY, my mother read me a story called *The Man Without a Country*. I remember thinking how terrible it would be never to be able to return to one's country. It was comforting to know that I was not in that situation at present, but it never occurred to me that I would spend much of my life abroad, and I certainly never thought I'd spend so much time in a place like the Congo. Yet I had always been interested in international affairs. Growing up during the Depression, I became a great admirer, along with my parents, of President Franklin Roosevelt's social and economic policies. Later, we supported the way he stood up against Nazi Germany. Two other public figures also fascinated me, as different as day from night: Edward R. Murrow, the radio journalist, and Adolph Hitler. I had read *Mein Kampf*, and here, plainly, was evil writ large. Murrow's calm but gripping broadcasts from Europe of Hitler's expanding power and conquests convinced me that only force would stem the Nazi tide.

It may seem old-fashioned now, but I was raised to believe that I owed a debt to my country and that I would serve it whenever the need arose. After the end of World War II, it was clear that the Soviet Union and its Eastern European allies represented a real and present threat to the United States. Winston Churchill, with President Truman at his side, had put it well in his famous speech in Fulton, Missouri, in 1946. He spoke of an "iron curtain" having descended across Europe, dividing east from west, and the desire of the Soviet Union for "the fruits of war and indefinite expansion of their power and doctrines."

The United States arrived late in Africa. While in favor of independence, the Eisenhower administration calculated that decolonization was safe in the capable hands of the European powers—its NATO allies—with their deep knowledge of Africa and their large economic stake in the continent. In the State Department, Africa was the poor relation, handled as a subsidiary of the Middle East Bureau. It was not until 1957 that a separate Bureau of African Affairs was established. In the CIA, our Africa Division was created in mid-1959, just a year before the Congo became independent.

In contrast, the Soviet Union under Nikita Khrushchev, who had been in power for six years and was bubbling with confidence, ideas, and energy, was beginning to take serious notice of Africa. Khrushchev believed in reaching out to the newly independent countries in order to expand the Soviet Union's influence in the world and outflank its superpower rival. He traveled to India, Burma, and Afghanistan offering economic aid and technical expertise, and he financed the Aswan Dam, the high prestige project of Gamal Abdul Nasser, Egypt's nationalist, anti-Western leader.

In 1958, President Charles de Gaulle suddenly offered France's African colonies independence with the stipulation of still being associated with France, or the colonies could opt for complete independence. Guinea was the only country that chose to go it alone, and the French pulled out, taking everything movable with them. Khrushchev quickly stepped into the breach with generous economic aid and Soviet technicians. By 1960, the Soviets had had nearly three years to develop an African strategy, one that fit into their world strategy. The United States, on the other hand, suddenly found itself in an area about which it knew very little, but which required it to act while it developed new policies.

Back in the Congo, events were moving so fast, I often slept on a divan in my office, not having had time to look around for a house. It was a bit like military service again: a group of men separated from their wives and families by the nature of their jobs amid difficult circumstances. Tim had a residence but spent long hours in the office. I would join other embassy officers meeting with Tim in the evenings to discuss the evolving political and security situation. He was not finicky about rank; he allowed each of us to hold forth before giving us his opinions. He maintained close contact with the British, French, Belgian, and Italian ambassadors and briefed us on their views. Our goal was to try to reach a consensus on what was happening and how it affected U.S. policy. Of course, the embassy could not establish policy, but given that Washington had only a limited grasp of the situation our views often *became* policy—a rather unusual dynamic dictated by the extraordinary situation in which we found ourselves.

It was hard to keep up with developments then, and it's still not easy to follow them almost half a century later. So much happened in a few intense days in July, and it began five days before I reached Leopoldville. The army mutiny, which had begun in Thysville on the night of July 5, spread to Leopoldville the next day, paralyzing the new government. Lumumba went to Thysville to try to pacify the soldiers by promoting all soldiers one rank and dismissing General Janssens, the unpopular Belgian commander. On July 7, a train full of Belgian refugees from Thysville arrived in Leopoldville and the passengers' stories of rapes, beatings, and shootings sent a wave of panic through the European community. The following day was anarchy as several thousand Europeans fled across the river to Brazzaville. Embassies sent their families and non-essential staff in the same direction while the U.S. Embassy became an informal refugee center. That evening, Lumumba gave way to the mutineers' demands and dismissed all their Belgian officers.

He and President Kasavubu flew around the country desperately trying to calm the situation but with little success. Sometimes their presence had the opposite effect. As a speaker Lumumba was a great stem-winder and he chose to attack the "Belgian colonialists" with such virulence that his speeches often led to riots and the beating of any available European. I noted in a message to headquarters that he was born to foment revolution but not to govern once it had succeeded, suggesting that he was a Thomas Paine rather than a Thomas Jefferson.

On July 9, the Belgian government announced that it was sending 1,200 paratroopers to reinforce the 2,500 soldiers already stationed at two bases: Kitona near Leopoldville and Kamina in the southern province of Katanga. Brussels promised that the troops would not intervene unless specifically requested to do so by the Congolese government. The next day, Moise Tshombe, the provincial president of Katanga, asked the Belgian forces to restore order in Elisabethville, the provincial capital, after mutinous soldiers had killed six Europeans. During the following week, Belgian troops went into action in many parts of the country.

In response, Lumumba and Kasavubu requested the United Nations, via Ralph Bunche, the UN representative in the Congo, to intervene and help restore order. This idea actually originated with Ambassador Timberlake who was acting on his own initiative because he was worried that the chaotic situation would be exploited by the Soviet Union. He thought that the Belgian forces should be put under a UN umbrella until they could be replaced by UN peacekeeping troops from other countries. He concluded his cable to the Department of State with, "this should keep the bears out of the Congo caviar."

On July 11, Lumumba and Kasavubu flew to Luluabourg, the capital of the diamond-rich province of Kasai. The situation was so bad that they authorized the use of Belgian troops to restore order. While they were there, Tshombe declared Katanga independent and Lumumba and Kasavubu, realizing that the country was beginning to fall apart, flew to Elisabethville to negotiate with him. But at the airport, the local authorities refused Lumumba and Kasavubu permission to land. They were forced to return to Leopoldville empty-handed.

On July 13, as the turmoil continued, Belgian troops killed several Congolese soldiers in clashes in the port city of Matadi. Justin Bomboko, the pro-Western, fun-loving foreign minister, and Antoine Gizenga, the deputy premier (a morose type believed to be a

Marxist and the leader of a key political party allied with Lumumba), asked Ambassador Timberlake for two thousand U.S. troops to restore order. Tim, who did not trust Gizenga, told the two men that it would be a serious error to invite any major power to send troops to the Congo. Instead, he again recommended that the Congolese seek the assistance of the United Nations. Knowing that a request for U.S. troops would have no appeal in Washington, Tim stressed in his cable that a large UN peacekeeping force would be required to put an end to the rioting.

Lumumba apparently had not been consulted about the appeal for U.S. troops and denounced it. Instead, he and Kasavubu sent another request for UN intervention, but this time they accused the Belgians of attacking the Congo and of masterminding Katanga's secession.

Khrushchev had not paid much attention to the Congo until fighting broke out between the Belgians and the Congolese on July 11. He had been preoccupied with the shooting down of the American high-altitude U–2 spy plane in May, deteriorating relations with communist China, and the Soviet downing of yet another American reconnaissance plane—this time a RB–47—on July 1 over international waters. Khrushchev, using what had become a standard Cold War communist tactic, accused the Belgians of trying to prevent Lumumba from adopting an independent policy and of being behind the Katanga breakaway. On July 12, Khrushchev publicly condemned Western policy on the Congo and expressed full support for the Kasavubu-Lumumba government.

The UN Security Council met on July 13 and 14 at the request of its respected secretary-general, Dag Hammarskjöld, to discuss the Congo crisis, which he declared "posed a threat to international peace and security." After some opposition by the Soviet Union, a Tunisian-sponsored resolution was passed calling for the withdrawal of Belgian troops from the Congo, and authorizing the dispatch of a UN military force "to provide military assistance" in consultation with the Congolese government.

In a remarkable *tour de force*, Hammarskjöld and the U.S. Air Force had an advance guard of the UN force, consisting of Tunisian soldiers, in Leopoldville on the evening of July 15. They landed within forty-eight hours of the resolution being passed, and a mere four days after Katanga's secession. By the end of July, UN soldiers had arrived from Tunisia, Morocco, Ghana, Ethiopia, Malaysia, Sweden, and Ireland and had spread throughout the country. Troops from other nations soon followed. General Carl von Horn, a Swedish officer with UN experience in the Middle East, was put in command. The massive airlift was mainly an American affair, although the Soviets flew in the Ghanaian contingent and some food supplies.

Ambassador Timberlake asked me to meet the first American planes to determine if the squadron commander needed assistance. The Congolese deputy defense minister was also at the airport, representing his government. (A Katangan, he abandoned his post and returned to Katanga the following day.) When the American C–130s landed, I contacted the squadron commander who said he needed a relatively small amount of additional fuel. I told him that someone had cut the fuel line between Matadi and Leopoldville and, as a result, the Belgian forces had taken control of all aviation fuel supplies. He was aware of the problem but insisted he needed to top off his tanks to enable him to reach Accra where he could refuel.

I immediately contacted the senior Belgian air operations officer. He categorically refused to supply any fuel, explaining that the Belgian military needed it to carry out its mission. He then closed his office, saying he needed to get some rest. I followed him at a distance to another hangar area and waited to make sure he was out of the way.

I returned to the Belgian military's offices and asked to speak to General Gheysen, the commander of the Belgian operation. I repeated my request for fuel but made no mention of seeing his air operations officer. The general, who appeared fatigued and to be drowning in paper, instructed his aide to locate the officer. When the aide was unable to find him, the general said he had given orders for a strict control of fuel supplies. I commiserated with him, saying that, as an ex-military man, I fully understood his reasoning. I added, however, that as a diplomat I had another perspective. If one of the C–130s should crash as a result of insufficient fuel, the United States, the United Nations, the Belgian government, and God knows how many other politicians would blame General Gheysen. In short, he would become a sacrificial lamb. After wrestling with himself and no doubt mentally cursing the air officer who could not be found, the general agreed to provide the necessary fuel on the understanding that this would be the last emergency request for American or United Nations planes.

Meanwhile, the Belgian troops had moved into action in Leopoldville for the first time and occupied Ndjili, Leopoldville's international airport, on July 13. Kasavubu and Lumumba, still trying to pacify the country, announced that the Congolese government was breaking diplomatic relations with Belgium. They followed this bombshell with another—an appeal to Khrushchev, suggesting they might be forced "to ask for the intervention of the Soviet Union" if the West "did not stop its aggression against the Congo." Khrushchev replied promptly and sympathetically but refrained from making any commitment.

Lumumba appeared to the Belgians, and to a somewhat lesser extent to us in the embassy, as the instigator of the declaration while Kasavubu was an almost passive observer. It was an alarming development, whichever way you looked at it and confirmed our suspicion that Lumumba was playing into Soviet hands. The Belgians, for their part, interpreted the move as positive proof that Lumumba was under the sway of the Soviets.

Breaking relations benefited neither the Congo nor Belgium. The country depended on Belgium economically and in many other ways, and Belgium, of course, had large commercial interests in the Congo. Further, Belgian citizens would be at a great disadvantage without the protection of an embassy.

On July 17, Major-General Henry Alexander, a British officer on loan to Ghana who had led the first Ghanaian troops to the Congo, returned to Leopoldville from Stanleyville, capital of the Orientale province, with some more disturbing news. Kasavubu and Lumumba had issued an ultimatum that if the United Nations did not expel the Belgians by midnight on July 19, they would ask the Soviet Union to intervene. Alexander sent a message asking Ralph Bunche, the UN representative, General Roger Gheysen, the commanding general of the Belgian forces, and Ambassador Timberlake to meet him at the airport to discuss this disturbing news. Tim asked me to accompany him.

When we arrived, we found Justin Bomboko, the Congolese foreign minister, and Thomas Kanza, the Congo's ambassador to the United Nations, waiting for us. (Coincidentally, Kanza was the country's first university graduate and Bomboko its second.) General Alexander told us that no one could expect the United Nations or anyone else to get the Belgians out in such a short time span, adding parenthetically that the Congolese leadership "had not yet come down from the trees." Luckily, neither Bomboko nor Kanza appeared to have heard this offensive remark.

Everyone present agreed that the ultimatum was unfortunate and that, even if the Belgians wished to depart, which they clearly did not, they could not get out in the two days left before the ultimatum expired. Bunche said that the United Nations had never been served with an ultimatum before and would not accept one now. Bomboko and Kanza appeared nearly as shocked as Bunche and said they would try to get the ultimatum reversed at the next cabinet meeting after Kasavubu and Lumumba returned from Stanleyville.

The ultimatum did, however, have the immediate effect of putting pressure on the Belgians to withdraw their forces. The United States, working with Hammarskjöld, helped to produce an agreement with the Belgians that their troops would leave Leopoldville by July 23. Lumumba's move backfired in several important ways. It antagonized Ralph Bunche and other UN officials by triggering violent incidents against UN personnel and showed a lack of appreciation for the organization's hard work. I believed it also increased Khrushchev's interest in the Congo and convinced him that Lumumba might be useful in furthering his African strategy. It certainly alarmed American policy-makers in Washington.

When the embassy stopped providing us with stew once a day, I started going to a restaurant that a hardy Belgian businessman had reopened at the New Stanley Hotel. The fare was simple, a *plat du jour*, take it or leave it. The clientele, almost entirely male, was loud and raucous, and the conversation centered on business and the problems posed by independence. But, for me, it was a good place to make contacts because it was really the only place to eat for people who did not have a cook at home.

On my first day there I ran into Pierre Sumialot, the prime minister's private secretary, and invited him to lunch. A relatively small man, he was a surly sort of guy, but I wanted to get to know him better. He no doubt found me of little interest, but since I was paying for his lunch, he answered a few innocuous questions while carefully chewing his food. I was already in the assessment stage but my recruitment efforts never went beyond that point.

During lunch the news that Lumumba and Kasavubu were on their way back from the interior spread through the restaurant. I decided to get out to the airport as soon as I could. I had an embassy car, and Sumialot agreed to join me. I was delighted to have him along to deal with the dicey Congolese roadblocks on the airport road. What made those checkpoints so nerve-wracking, no matter how many times I went through them, was the knowledge that the soldiers were also nervous, and you never knew what a nervous man with a finger on the trigger of a loaded rifle would do.

Ambassadors were normally the only diplomats who flew their country's flag on their limousines, but during those early days in the Congo we all flew the flag in the hope that it would provide some protection. On the way to the airport, Sumialot and I were stopped at three different roadblocks. The first time, Sumialot identified himself and we went through without any hassle. I had just begun congratulating myself for having had the foresight to invite him when we reached a second roadblock. Sumialot identified himself again but the soldiers told us, in less than polite terms, to get out of the car. After a great deal of poking around inside the vehicle, they let us go on.

At the third roadblock, it was the same drill. So much for the clout of a prime minister's secretary. While we waited for the soldiers to complete their inspection, I pointed to the flags on the embassy car. For lack of anything else to say, I explained the meaning of the stars and stripes: thirteen stripes represented the thirteen original colonies and the stars represented the states.

The word colonies caught Sumialot's attention. He aggressively demanded to know if the United States had thirteen colonies. Assuring him that was not the case, I provided him with a short version of the war of independence against Great Britain by the thirteen original colonies.

The story seemed to astonish him, for he immediately asked how we could be friends with the British if they had been our colonial masters. I explained that nearly two centuries had passed since that time, a fact that seemed to surprise him.

We arrived at Ndjili airport, which was under Belgian control, just in time to see Kasavubu and Lumumba descend from a DC–3. The Belgian general who commanded the Belgian troops at the airport met them and invited the two men to inspect an honor guard of Belgian paratroopers.

Lumumba was angry and made it abundantly clear that he and Kasavubu were not interested in inspecting foreign troops that had arrived uninvited in their country. A group of Ghanaians, including the Ghanaian ambassador to Moscow who was in Leopoldville for reasons unknown to us, clustered around the Congolese leaders. They listened as Lumumba expressed his anger. The Ghanaians completely ignored Kasavubu, who looked uncomfortable and out of place in the uniform of a lieutenant-general. As commander-in-chief of the Congolese army he was entitled to wear it, but his dumpy figure did not lend him the martial impression that was intended.

Sumialot had abandoned me for Lumumba's entourage, leaving me on my own and unable to get close to Kasavubu or Lumumba. I had, however, managed to hear enough to know that Lumumba and presumably Kasavubu both looked upon the Belgian troops as invaders and a threat to their new country's independence. I decided to return to Leopoldville and this time the twenty-minute journey took more than an hour. At each roadblock I was held up at gunpoint, and soldiers crawled into the car to search for God knows what. One held his rifle by the barrel and pulled it after him, risking shooting himself. I had visions of the gun going off and the other soldiers opening fire on the assumption that I had been responsible.

When I returned to the embassy, I reported to the ambassador and sent off a report to CIA headquarters. Tim met with several of his ambassadorial colleagues and called a staff meeting in his office. He told us that Lumumba and Kasavubu had broken diplomatic relations with Belgium and that he had decided to send Jerry Lavallee and me to the airport to talk to them. The two men reportedly had returned to the airport and planned to fly to the interior once more. Our mission was to try to convince them that the rupture in relations with Belgium was not in the best interest of the Congo and, hopefully, to persuade them to reverse the decision. Tim assured us that the Belgian ambassador and the Belgian government fully supported such an outcome.

With flags flying on the embassy sedan, Jerry and I set off for Ndjili airport. When we got there we found Kasavubu and Lumumba with their entourage on the same DC–3 in which they had arrived that afternoon. They had tried to leave for Stanleyville but the Belgian pilot had cancelled the flight pleading radio trouble, possibly at the request of the Belgian military or embassy. The Belgian honor guard had been replaced by a hundred or more Belgian civilians, waiting for a flight home. They were in an ugly mood, shouting and cursing the two men and Congo's independence. A bored-looking Belgian officer with a squad of soldiers sat smoking a cigarette, apparently unaware that the situation could get out of hand at any moment.

Jerry and I worked our way through the crowd and climbed up the steps to the plane's door where we were admitted by a frightened Congolese. Kasavubu and Lumumba were sitting near the rear of the plane. They greeted us politely and Jerry introduced himself and made the argument for maintaining diplomatic relations with Belgium.

"I cannot discuss such matters," Lumumba interrupted, "while I am being held prisoner."

"But you aren't a prisoner," I said.

Lumumba turned his head toward the window and looked down on the roiling mob of angry Belgians. He had made his point.

It was obvious that we were not going to be able to talk to them in that situation, which could deteriorate at any moment. I said I would look for transportation to take them back to Leopoldville while Jerry continued to argue the importance of retaining diplomatic relations with Belgium. As I left the plane, the crowd pressed in on me, cursing in French and Flemish. They had learned that we were Americans and immediately assumed we were conniving with the Congolese leadership to their detriment. Most of the Belgians in the Congo appeared convinced that the United States intended to take over the copper, cobalt, and diamond mines and other profitable Belgian businesses. This belief was never raised at an official level but it was a widely held misconception in the Belgian commercial community.

I managed to get through the crowd to the Belgian officer in charge and asked him to help me find transportation for the Congolese leaders.

"What do you mean?" he asked, indignant as a wet hen. "Why should I help you? Why should I find a car for someone like Lumumba?"

After trying unsuccessfully to explain the obvious, I set out to find vehicles. Outside the terminal, I found a Volkswagen van with a Congolese driver and a large Mercedes-Benz sedan that had been commandeered by the Belgian army. Since the keys were in the sedan, I performed a Huck Finn. I "borrowed" it for the night.

When Kasavubu and Lumumba hurried down the steps from the aircraft and got into the sedan, the mob set up a roar and began rocking the car in an effort to tip it over. I found myself fighting off a half-crazed man who was trying to pour a jerry can of gasoline over the car to set it on fire.

The Belgian officer belatedly realized that he had the makings of a serious incident on his hands and ordered his troops to push the people back. With one of Lumumba's aides driving, the sedan took off in a hurry, followed by the entourage in the Volkswagen van.

Jerry and I departed almost as rapidly as the Congolese, but when we reached Leopoldville, Lumumba refused to talk to us. Kasavubu, whom we concluded was playing a waiting game, simply went home to bed.

Shortly after the airport episode, a Congolese clerk from Lumumba's office came to the embassy one evening to ask for visas. It rapidly became clear he did not know what a visa was, other than that it had something to do with travel. When I asked if he had passports to put the visas in, he shook his head. Who wants the visas? I asked. Lumumba and his staff, he replied. They intended to go to the United States to see President Eisenhower and Dag Hammarskjöld, the United Nations Secretary-General. I was astonished. I knew that Eisenhower was not expecting a visit from Lumumba and that such visits are normally planned far in advance.

Tim told me to stall while he requested instructions from Washington. I told the clerk that we would need to have passports for Lumumba and those traveling with him. I explained that if they had not yet printed Congolese passports, they could make do with small notebooks containing the biographical data and official stamps required in most passports.

Tim alerted the State Department of Lumumba's plans. Eisenhower approved the visit, as did Hammarskjöld. The latter agreed to delay an already scheduled trip to the Congo in order to be in New York when Lumumba arrived. We were authorized to issue visas to Lumumba and his group, and Tim and I received instructions to return to Washington on temporary duty. Since there were no commercial flights operating to and from the Congo, we flew out on one of the U.S. Air Force C–130s supporting the United Nations operation.

The C–130 is a large cargo aircraft. Inside, it looks rather like a boxcar. Once the plane had reached its cruising altitude, we each borrowed blankets from the crew and stretched out on the deck. It was almost as cold as it was hard, but Tim and I had had little sleep over the past few days, and it did not take us long to nod off. The whole trip was uncomfortable, but I was delighted to be returning to Washington. I had never been recalled like this before and the entire episode felt like a historic adventure. I would later be recalled on similar trips from various parts of the world, but that first journey stands out in my mind as by far the most exciting.

We woke at first light and a crewmember offered us coffee and C-rations, the first that I had had since World War II. They were much better than those I remembered but that might have been because we were hungry. We landed at Wheelus, a United States Air Force base in Libya, which was a country still ruled by King Idris and friendly towards the United States. We were able to wash, shave, and answer questions about the Congo as we ate a proper breakfast.

The next stop was another American airbase outside Paris. The squadron commander met us and we received the full-blown four-star-general treatment due to Tim's ambassadorial rank, and the fact that Tim was the first senior American official to leave the Congo since the mutiny and the creation of the UN mission. Leading the group was General Lauris Norstad, the NATO commanding general, a gaggle of other generals, as well as two American ambassadors, Houghton of France and Burden of Belgium. Norstad looked around the aircraft and asked where we had slept. When Tim told him, the general turned to the squadron commander and suggested that better sleeping arrangements be made when we returned to Leopoldville. We adjourned to the base club where Tim thanked the Air Force for its magnificent support of the UN operation in the Congo and for the embassy. He also answered questions concerning developments in the Congo and predicted that the U.S. Air Force would remain involved in supporting the UN mission for some time to come.

We moved on to Ambassador Houghton's office where we were joined by Ambassador Burden for more detailed talks concerning the Congo and its problems. We were provided lodging at Ambassador Houghton's residence and dined there with the two ambassadors. During our discussions, Tim brought up a delicate matter: "*Time* magazine plans to do a cover story on Lumumba with his picture on the front of the magazine." He continued, "Celebrity coverage at home will make him even more difficult to deal with. He's a first-class headache as it is."

"Then why don't you get the story killed?" Burden asked. "Or at least modified?"

"I tried to persuade the *Time* man in Leopoldville until I was blue in the face," Tim replied. "But he said there was nothing he could do about it because the story had already been sent to New York."

"You can't expect much from a journalist at that level," Burden said pulling out his address book and flipping through the pages. He picked up the phone and put a call through to the personal assistant of Henry Luce, *Time*'s owner.

Luce soon returned the call. After a brief, friendly exchange that made clear his personal relationship with Luce, Burden bluntly told him that he would have to change the Lumumba cover story. Luce apparently said that the magazine was about to go to press. "Oh, come on, Henry," Burden said, "you must have other cover stories in the can." They chatted for a few more minutes before Burden hung up.

A few days later in the United States we picked up a copy of the magazine with a new and different cover story. Lumumba had been relegated to the international section. (Hammarskjöld and Tshombe would be the only major figures in the Congo drama at that time to make it onto a *Time* cover.) On arriving in Washington, I spent the night with my parents in their apartment in Arlington, Virginia. We talked late into the night for they were curious to know about life in the Congo. I left out my firing squad and Russian-Congolese roulette experiences: they were worried enough already about my safety. The next morning as I was preparing to leave, Bronson Tweedy, who as chief of the African Division was my direct boss, called to say that Allen Dulles, the director of the CIA, had already asked for me twice. This taught me a lesson: the key men in Washington get to work well ahead of the others and generally stay at their desks late into the evening.

Dulles could have been sitting in the law offices of Sullivan and Cromwell in New York making a fortune, but he chose to work for a relative pittance in Washington. I had first met the CIA director in Brussels in 1958 when he visited our offices. I was assigned to serve as his driver, bodyguard, and general man Friday, for in those times directors traveled without an entourage. While lunching with him in Brussels one day I asked if the press rumors that he planned to retire soon and be replaced by General Mark Clark were true. Dulles laughed. "When it is announced that I have submitted my resignation, you will know that the president has fired me," he said. I saw him on a number of occasions during my early years in the Congo, and got to know him socially after I returned to Washington. He loved the intelligence game. His core belief was that only a thin line separated the Cold War from a hot one and he was passionate about the CIA's role in preventing the world from slipping across that line into a nuclear conflict.

Dulles queried me at length about the main political players in the Congo, particularly Kasavubu and Lumumba. He seemed to have a detailed understanding of the country's political situation and believed the international stakes were high. His view was that the United States could not afford to lose the Congo to the Soviet Union. He impressed on me that I would be playing a key role in his plans.

While intelligence operations were, for him, "the great game," it was a game with incalculable consequences. Before my return to Washington, I had learned as much as possible about the influx of

Soviet "technicians" in the Congo, most of whom were almost certainly KGB or GRU (the Soviets' military intelligence organization) operatives. I outlined to the director my belief that, if the Soviets achieved their objective of influencing and eventually controlling Lumumba, they would use the Congo as a base to infiltrate and extend their influence over the nine countries or colonies surrounding the Congo—Congo-Brazzaville, the Central African Republic, Sudan, Uganda, Rwanda, Burundi, Tanganyika, Rhodesia, and Angola. Had the Soviets gained a position of control or influence in the nine countries and colonies, they would have had an extraordinary power base in Africa. In addition to gaining control or influence over the minerals, raw materials, and oil produced in Africa, it would also have greatly increased their influence in the third world, as well as extending their influence within the UN.

The Soviets' long-term objective would be to outflank NATO in Western Europe if they could extend their influence to include bases along or near the Mediterranean. Control of the Congo, moreover, would give the Soviet Union a near monopoly on the production of cobalt, a critical mineral used in missiles and many other weapons systems, since the Congo and the USSR were the world's main suppliers of the mineral. Such a scenario would put the United States' own weapons and space programs at a severe disadvantage.

Dulles expressed considerable interest in this assessment, but I suspect I was preaching to the choir because he had probably already reached the same conclusion.

While in Washington, I made my case for more personnel in the Leopoldville station. I had a first-tour station assistant who was responsible for administrative tasks and a temporary duty communications officer, but I needed operations officers. All African stations were small and most had yet to prove that they merited additional personnel. In retrospect, I should have insisted on having an additional four or five qualified officers. They would be required if the station expanded its network of agents as I hoped and expected it would in the next few months. The way it came out was that I was authorized to send a cable to a number of stations asking if they could spare an officer for a temporary duty assignment to the Congo.

I did obtain one extra officer, Jeff, who would be my deputy. But his file did not impress me. He had only one overseas tour under his belt and that had been as a psychological warfare officer. He seemed an enthusiastic sort, but enthusiasm does not always equate with ability and productivity. I agreed to take him on a temporary duty basis with the understanding that the Africa Division would try to find a more qualified officer for the job. It turned out that my doubts were groundless. Jeff was not only a hard worker but he was also brimming with original ideas. He was to become one of my closest and most trusted colleagues throughout my CIA career and remains a close friend to this day.

During my stay in the United States, I spent time with the Africa Division desk officer responsible for the Congo. He was one of the people who had predicted a quiet tour in Leopoldville. Before I had left for my new post, he had urged me to send at least one cable every week, just to remind headquarters that the station existed and that I was still around. From day one, I had deluged headquarters with cables so his advice seemed rather quaint. My evenings were spent with my parents and seeing them every day was one of the pleasures of this unexpected trip home.

The return trip was a marked contrast to our journey from Leopoldville. Tim and I went by commercial jet to Paris and then made our way to the airfield where we had been met some ten days earlier by the military and diplomatic brass. Another C–130 was waiting but the squadron commander had taken to heart General Norstad's suggestions. The plane was full of supplies for the United Nations troops but, strapped to the deck at the back, were two beds neatly made up with sheets and Air Force blankets. I have since flown most of the best airlines all over the world, but nothing matched that horizontal ride, with several tons of cargo, across the Mediterranean and the Sahara Desert back to the Congo.

Lumumba appeared to many Western nations to be on the same track as other leaders who believed they could use the Soviet

Union without falling under its sway. The Soviets had a reputation for providing aid, funds, and weapons until the leader in question became almost totally dependent on the USSR. Once they reached that point, the Soviets could be expected to remove their velvet gloves and demand payment in the form of control. In New York, Lumumba's visit went well. He adopted a more conciliatory attitude and impressed Hammarskjöld—the first time the two men had met—with a clear and eloquent presentation of his case. He accepted the terms of the UN peace-keeping force for the Congo and declared he wanted the organization to remain to help retrain the Congolese army after the Belgians had gone. At this stage, Hammarskjöld's impression of Lumumba appeared to be positive.

In contrast, Lumumba's time in Washington was a disaster for the young prime minister. He did not see President Eisenhower, who was vacationing in Newport, Rhode Island. Christian Herter, who became secretary of state after the resignation of John Foster Dulles, deflected his request for an airplane, financial aid, and technicians by pointing out that all American assistance to the Congo was being channeled through the United Nations. Lumumba had other disappointments. While staying in Blair House, the residence across from the White House where the government lodges official guests, he asked to be provided with female companionship. When told that Blair House did not provide women for its guests, he was offended and noted that France and some other European nations were more hospitable.

Fifteen years later, Douglas Dillon, the deputy secretary of state who was present at the meeting between Lumumba and Herter, appeared before the Senate Select Committee appointed to study alleged assassination plots. He testified Lumumba "would never look you in the eye and his words never had anything to do with the matters under discussion. You had a feeling that he was a person that was gripped by this fervor that I can only characterize as messianic. He was just not a rational being."

Lumumba seemed to have misinterpreted the mood in Washington, failing to realize what a negative impact his threat to turn to the Soviet Union for assistance had made on the administration. While not as extreme as the Belgians in their distaste for the man, the U. S. government's view of Lumumba was hardening.

Meanwhile, Hammarskjöld had arrived in Leopoldville and was shocked by the chaotic situation and the tension in the city. The burning issue was Katanga. The Congolese cabinet, under deputy prime minister Antoine Gizenga, demanded immediate action by the UN forces to remove the Belgian troops from the province and to reunite it with the rest of the country. Hammarskjöld urged patience, saying negotiations were necessary to facilitate the entry of UN troops. Neither Gizenga nor Lumumba, back in New York after an abortive trip to Canada, was prepared to be patient. Lumumba threatened to call another Security Council meeting and made a point of contacting Soviet diplomats.

Since its secession on July 11, Katanga province had been operating as an independent state. Tshombe's government had the support of the powerful *Union Minière du Haut Katanga* mining company, the Belgian Consulate, the Katangan Gendarmerie under the command of Belgian officers, and Belgian technicians who kept essential services running. With our help, Hammarskjöld persuaded the Belgian government to make a public commitment to withdrawing its troops from the province. On August 2, Hammarskjöld announced that UN troops would begin to move into Katanga on August 6. Bunche was dispatched to the Katangan capital, Elisabethville, to prepare the way. But on arrival, Tshombe made it clear that he would use force to prevent the plane from landing. Bunche, like Kasavubu and Lumumba earlier, had to return to Leopoldville, his mission a failure.

Hammarskjöld realized that he would need a new Security Council mandate to extend the UN's authority to the breakaway province. The Security Council met on August 8 and passed a resolution calling on the Belgians to withdraw their troops from Katanga immediately, and declaring that a UN military presence was necessary in the province. The organization, however, was not given a mandate to become involved in Katanga's internal affairs, whereas Lumumba wanted the UN to expel the Belgian military from Katanga *and* take action to end Tshombe's secession. Hammarskjöld took the position that Katanga's secession was an internal political matter that should be resolved by Lumumba and Tshombe working together.

Shortly after Katanga declared its independence, President Eisenhower asked Allen Dulles if he had a good man in Elisabethville. Dulles is said to have replied that one of his best men was there. After the meeting, he called Bronson Tweedy, chief of the Africa Division.

"Who have we got in Elisabethville?" he asked.

"Elisabethville?" said Tweedy. "We haven't got anybody in Elisabethville."

"Then find someone today and send him out there as fast as you can," Dulles said.

One of our station chiefs in North Africa was about to return to the United States after completing his tour. He had booked a leisurely trip home for himself and his family. You can imagine his reaction when he received a cable ordering him to proceed immediately to Elisabethville.

I was delighted to have an officer in Katanga, but when he arrived he showed little interest in the job. Since the United States did not recognize Katanga, it was difficult for me as an accredited diplomat to the Congo to visit the breakaway province. But we kept in close touch by cable and "back channel" notes. (A back channel note either goes by pouch or by cable but doesn't get any distribution beyond the addressee.)

Our man in Elisabethville began to complain about his raw deal, especially his aborted trip home, and grew more angry and bitter as time passed. One day, I received a cable from him and the message was short but not sweet. He announced that he was planning to leave Elisabethville that night and return to the United States. I realized that time was too short to send him an encoded cable so I took the risk of calling him on an open radio frequency. I tried to reason with him, reminding him of the embarrassment his departure would create, especially for the director who was relying on him. He didn't budge. Aware that Tshombe's Belgian intelligence officers were probably eavesdropping, I had been trying to use double talk to make my point, but exasperation finally got the better of me. "Listen to me, godammit!" I shouted. "This is a direct order. You are to stay at your post. If you don't, I'll have your ass, if it's the last thing I do."

He remained in Elisabethville until he was officially relieved. Some years later I served under his direction. Gentleman that he was, he never mentioned the matter and never seemed to hold a grudge against me.

When Lumumba returned home, things got worse. Whatever rapport he and Hammarskjöld had in New York faded away, and I think the two men never really understood each other. Lumumba seemed as angry with the United Nations as he was with the Belgians and with us. His hostility was reinforced by two members of his staff. Serge Michel, his private secretary, was a French leftist with strong anti-Western views. The French had condemned him to death *in absentia* for his support of the Algerian rebels, and a friendly foreign intelligence service had identified him as a Soviet agent. Madame Andrée Blouin, Lumumba's protocol chief who had arrived from Guinea immediately after the independence ceremonies, was a striking, light-skinned beauty. She was anti-white and reportedly had considerable influence with Lumumba. In addition, he was surrounded by a group of radical, anti-Western Ghanaians and Guineans. The Guineans were particularly vitriolic in their criticism of Westerners while speaking favorably of Soviet and other Eastern Bloc diplomats.

Lumumba was not the only problem. The feeling of insecurity in Leopoldville came from other elements as well, notably the unruly youth groups that held noisy street demonstrations against Lumumba. The Guinean police contingent, although officially part of the United Nations operation, took sides with Lumumba, and ruthlessly put down these demonstrations.

The Congolese army remained fragile, having never been brought fully under control after the mutiny. It still lacked trained

Congolese officers and relied on a few senior sergeants who had been named or elected officers after the departure of the Belgian officers. In fact, most units elected their own commanders with the result that those in charge were not necessarily the most competent, and the troops did pretty much as they wished. The soldiers drinking in bars or wandering the streets were generally armed and had a disconcerting habit of threatening or beating whites for no apparent reason. Seemingly powerless, Lumumba turned a blind eye to these incidents. This led to misunderstandings with Western embassies and a general feeling that, if he was unable to control his own army, he was not the right man to run the country.

In retrospect, I think that Lumumba's actions and statements may well have resulted from his limited education and his total lack of experience in dealing with sophisticated leaders and governments. While I never believed that Lumumba was a communist, I did believe he was politically naïve and inherently unstable. Our view in the embassy was that he did not have the leadership qualities to hold this vast, disintegrating country together and, sooner or later, the Russian bear would seize its chance and pounce. This may seem far-fetched years after those hectic days at the height of the Cold War, but the Soviets had long before demonstrated their ability to work from within to control trade unions, peace groups, political parties, and other groups in Europe and Asia. There was no doubt in our minds that the Congo was a strategic linchpin in that epic struggle.

4

WHEN I ASKED FOR EXTRA HELP during my Washington trip, I realized I was taking the risk of having stations dump marginal personnel on me. The first officer to arrive, "Dad," as I will call him, was about ten years my senior, had been chief of a large and important station, and had held senior posts in Headquarters. He was, however, no longer a career officer, for reasons that were never explained to me. He was on a contract and, having started off my own CIA career that way, I understood the difficulties of his position. His cover in the Congo was as a businessman.

Before picking him up, I drove randomly through Leopoldville for about thirty minutes to make sure I was not under surveillance. At the pick-up point, I stopped just long enough for him to jump into my car. After taking additional counter-surveillance measures, we drove to a safe house where we talked at length.

Dad's specialty was psychological warfare, for which the station had no immediate need but would find useful in the future. Given his long experience, however, I assumed he would have a well-rounded knowledge of all intelligence disciplines, an assumption that was to prove incorrect. He was never able to recruit or handle agents but he did participate in two key operations and provided me with some good advice.

After I had probed Dad's operational experience, I asked about his French. He had had the usual two or three years of French in school but, never having used it, could not put a sentence together in the language, thus limiting his value to us. I told him to study French, to circulate using his business cover, particularly among the Belgian community—many of whom spoke English—and to target potential agents. Dad did not appear to have great potential for the Congo, but I could not afford to send him back without making an effort to use him.

When I had finished speaking, Dad asked me about the political situation, what I hoped to achieve, and how I proposed to go about it. I told him about some of my problems involved in obtaining approval of operations that I had submitted to Headquarters, qualifying my comments with such phrases as "if Headquarters will approve," "if Headquarters can find the money," and so on.

After listening to my complaints, Dad gave me the best piece of advice I ever received as a new station chief. He looked at me and said, "Are you or are you not the chief of station?" Without waiting for a reply, he went on: "If you want to be successful, you have to tell Headquarters what to do. Don't wait for Headquarters to tell you. You know why? Headquarters may know more about American policy but it won't know as much about the local situation as the officers in daily contact with it. A truly competent station chief has a much better grasp of the realities in the field, and his job is to make sure that Headquarters gets the whole picture. So make your recommendations clearly and strongly. Don't just sit back and wait for instructions."

In other words, fight like hell for the operations you believe are required to insure that American policy is implemented, but be prepared to give way if policy changes occur. I took Dad's recommendations to heart and followed them throughout my career as a chief of station. His approach almost always worked, but I also learned the need to bend when United States policy changed.

We received a number of other officers over the next few weeks. All but one served under non-official cover and thus were not in the embassy. Some were of little use and had to be returned to their posts of origin, while others did outstanding work and were a credit to the Agency. Two, in particular, deserve mention. The first,

Morgan, was a young man who carried the passport of a small European nation. At first glance, he appeared to be of questionable use because he spoke no French and had limited operational experience. I suspect the station that sent him to us may not have realized his full potential as an operations officer. I told him that I had no immediate plans for him and gave him three months to learn French and Lingala, which was one of the four vernacular languages of the Congo and the official language of the army.

I made this decision because the station was about to launch a major operation that, if it failed, would have risked the CIA's continued presence in the Congo. I wanted to insure that there was at least one officer who was absolutely clean and could maintain contact with some of our better sources if Jeff and I were declared *persona non grata*. Much to my surprise, Morgan's French and Lingala were both quite fluent within three months, and he proved a most useful agent. He went on to reach senior rank in the agency, always serving under non-official cover.

The other non-official cover officer, Bobby, was probably the best recruiter I ever met in the Agency. He was truly a legendary operator. A classics graduate from Fordham University in New York, he had been a naval officer in World War II. He had a brilliant mind, was highly imaginative, and was devoted to his profession. He was a pleasure to work with, not least because he had an infinite supply of fascinating stories that ran the gamut of the CIA operations in which he had participated as well as his experiences as the captain of a naval seagoing tug during World War II.

I picked up Bobby on a street corner shortly after dark less than fifteen hours after his arrival in the Congo. I had known him for some time and was well aware of his reputation as a recruiter. Even so, I was taken aback when, after a few brief words of greeting, he told me that he had already spotted two potential agents. He stressed that he had not yet recruited them but assured me they would work for us, and work they did. One, a Congolese, became a useful agent for renting safe houses, post boxes, and carrying out other support activities. The other, a refugee from one of the Soviet

Bloc countries, also proved to be a reliable agent and eventually became a career employee working under non-official cover.

One of our best agents was a "walk in," that is to say, he contacted the station and offered his services. Jacques was a Belgian citizen of mixed European blood who said that he had previously
assisted one of the Agency's European stations. When he decided to
move to the Congo before independence, the station suggested that
he contact the CIA representative in Leopoldville. He did so, but
my predecessor had no need for his services at that time. After the
army mutiny, Jacques again contacted the station. As with any
"walk in," we ran traces on him, queried the station for which he
had previously worked, and verified that he had a wide circle of
contacts in the Congolese community. He had come to the Congo
under his own steam—unlike most of the Europeans who were
working for large companies—obtained a piece of land, and began
his own plantation. As he worked side-by-side with his Congolese
labor force, this set him apart from most Europeans in the colony,
many of whom looked down on him. But he impressed the Congolese, and he quickly made many Congolese friends.

In fact, he appeared to be an intelligence gold mine. He told us
that he was friendly with, among others, a member of the government, the leader of Kasavubu's ABAKO youth group, the editor of
the leading Leopoldville newspaper, the president of the Congolese
senate, and several other less important figures. But we proceeded
carefully and as slowly as the Congo situation permitted. To check
his reliability we had him question his sources, particularly the government minister, the senator, and the editor, on subjects about
which we already had verified answers. In each case, he reported
factually and came up with the right answers. Jeff, my new deputy,
was his case officer and soon had him suggesting anti-Lumumba
story lines to his friend the newspaper editor, and getting steady
feedback from all his sources. Jacques was a prolific source of intelligence, providing insight into areas in which we previously had little or no access.

Since I had begun my career in the CIA under non-official cover, I was more aware of the problems that people like Dad, Bobby, and Jacques faced than many of my colleagues who had always served under official cover. These agents have special needs because they are both more exposed and less in the picture than operatives working under official cover. They hunger for information, for reassurance, for human company, and it is vital to try to satisfy those needs and maintain their morale.

We had one temporary duty officer who worked under official cover in the embassy. Mike was experienced and extremely competent, fluent in French, Italian, Arabic, and German. He had the kind of personality that allowed him to get along with almost anyone, a great attribute for an operations case officer. He had been sent to the Congo by his home station with instructions to develop contacts among that nation's troops assigned to the United Nations military force. Though I appreciated the other station's needs, I quickly drafted Mike to serve as a station case officer because we needed all the help we could get against our local and Soviet targets. Mike remained in the Congo for several months and provided invaluable service.

On my return from Washington, I found that Jeff had arrived to take up his duties, automatically increasing the station's operational personnel by one hundred percent. During the next few days I was busy catching up on events that had transpired during my absence, and Jeff was fully occupied reading the files of ongoing or potential operations.

I also spent considerable time reviewing with him what I expected of a deputy. Each chief of station has his own views on this subject, but mine were fairly simple. Harking back to my days in the military, I said that in my absence he would be in charge and should make decisions based on his judgment, the general directives we had received from Headquarters—vague though they might be—and on his knowledge of my views and objectives. While some chiefs of station were reluctant to give their deputies a free hand, I have always been convinced that a deputy must have full authority to act on any problem that may develop in the absence of the chief.

At that time we were still concerned by the possibility of the embassy coming under attack, so when we received a message reporting that the Belgian security service had left two Browning semi-automatic pistols in a safe house, getting hold of them was appealing. The pistols were apparently hidden under a bidet in the bathroom of the apartment for which we had a key. The only problem was that the Congolese might have discovered what the apartment had been used for. With that cautionary note in mind, I set off to recover the pistols. I took the usual counter-surveillance measures and entered the apartment building through the back door. I walked up seven flights of steps to avoid using the elevator. Had I been followed, the elevator lights would have indicated my location in the building.

Once on the seventh floor I listened at the door of the apartment to determine if anyone was there. Not hearing anything, I opened the door. The first thing I sensed was the smell of cigar smoke. I looked around and saw a fat cigar smoking in an ashtray on a table in the center of the living room. I did not know who had put the cigar there but I assumed the smoker was in the apartment and was either a Congolese *Sûrêté* member or a KGB technician. Whatever the case, I did not want to meet him. My desire to obtain the pistols suddenly evaporated. I closed the door as quickly and as quietly as possible and ran down the stairs three at a time until I reached the ground floor. I caught my breath before going out onto the street and tried to look like a normal person out for a stroll.

A week later, Jeff and I tried again. We followed the same procedures as I had on my previous visit. After walking up the seven flights of stairs, we listened carefully. When we heard nothing, we entered quietly, checked the rooms to insure that no one was there, and then removed the bidet. Underneath we found two rusty Brownings. We took them back to the embassy where Jeff disassembled them and put them in a bath of light oil in order to remove the rust. Sure enough, the embassy soon came under threat by some wild Congolese troops. Jeff hurriedly started to assemble the two semi-automatics, something he had never done before, while I stood at his side, urging him on. Happily an officer from the army headquarters managed to get the soldiers in hand and away from the embassy, so we did not have to use the pistols.

Shortly after Jeff's arrival, we had a chance to bug the telephones of an office belonging to the Czechs. We needed a house nearby to use as a listening post (LP), and Jeff found a house that was ideal for his family and suitable as an LP. Using his home for this purpose, however, was a personal sacrifice. It meant dedicating one room to the operation, a real complication for a man with a wife and six children. His wife could be cleared to monitor the recorder and change tapes as necessary, but it posed a security problem because he had to keep what went on in the room a secret from his children. As our families had not yet joined us, I stayed with Jeff until I could find time to look for my own place.

A technician had been sent out to help us complete the installation, and he and Jeff worked at night to dig a trench to bring the wires into the house. All went well but at one point, Jeff, who was inside the house, heard a wake-up-the-dead scream from the garden. He rushed outside and found that the technician, groping for the wires in the darkness, had wrapped his hand around a snake. Luckily, the snake was as startled as the technician.

5

LIFE IN LEOPOLDVILLE continued to be chaotic throughout the month of August with the troops still not fully under control. Lumumba, who was preparing to invade Katanga to crush Tshombe's rebellion, intensified his search for spies, saboteurs, and other enemies. His paranoia infected the troops who saw spies everywhere. They arrested United Nations personnel, Belgian businessmen, diplomats, and almost anyone who crossed their path, roughing up or seriously beating some of them. There were demonstrations in the streets led by pro- or anti-Lumumba union members, youth associations, tribal groups, and political parties. Meanwhile, Albert Kalonji, the Baluba leader in south Kasai, had followed Tshombe's example and declared his region independent. Rich in diamonds, south Kasai's secession further threatened the political and economic viability of the country.

Shortly after my return from Washington, I received several messages from Director Dulles advising us that policy-makers shared our view that we should try to remove Lumumba from power. In one of them, on August 26, he wrote:

> In high quarters here it is the clear-cut conclusion that if Lumumba continues to hold high office, the inevitable result will at best be chaos and at worst pave the way to a Communist takeover of the Congo with disastrous consequences for the prestige of the UN and for the interests of the free world generally. Consequently, we

concluded that his removal must be an urgent and prime objective and that under existing conditions this should be a high priority of our covert action.

I was authorized to spend up to $100,000 on my own authority on any operation that appeared feasible if time did not permit me to refer it first to Headquarters for approval. That was a huge vote of confidence. To the best of my knowledge, no other station chief had ever been given such latitude. At that time, station chiefs were required to ask for authorization for any operational expenditure of more than fifty dollars. I never spent anything close to the $100,000 on an operation, but it was nice to have the authority to do so if the need arose.

If further evidence was required that Washington supported our own conclusion about replacing Lumumba, that was it. What I did not know was that our government was prepared to go much further in removing him than I had ever considered in my wildest dreams.

Under the Congo's constitution, the president had the legal authority to dismiss the prime minister and replace him with another person. However, the replacement needed to obtain a vote of confidence from parliament in order to take over, and it was not clear if there was a candidate who could obtain sufficient support. Fortunately, a prime minister could be forced to resign if a vote of no-confidence was passed in only one of the two legislative houses. The senate was more conservative and appeared more hostile to Lumumba than the national assembly, so we focused our efforts on that body.

We were already monitoring parliament and encouraging and guiding the actions of various parliamentary opposition groups that we had penetrated. We were seeking political leaders who might marshal their supporters against Lumumba when a vote of confidence was called. We were also using Jacques to insert anti-Lumumba articles in the country's leading newspaper.

Ambassador Timberlake met President Kasavubu during this period and suggested that Lumumba was a dangerous man and implied that he should not continue as prime minister. Kasavubu ignored the advice. Around this time one of our agents told us that a group of anti-Lumumba leaders had prepared a plan to assassinate him, but when they broached the matter to Kasavubu, he said he was reluctant to resort to violence.

Lumumba spent the first part of August attacking Hammarskjöld as relations between his government and the UN deteriorated. Guinea regularly supported Lumumba's ranting, and the Soviet Union also issued an official statement backing Lumumba. The Soviets blamed Hammarskjöld for an airport incident in which eleven Canadian airmen, flying in support of the UN operation, were brutally beaten by Congolese troops. The Soviet Union noted that the use of technicians from a NATO country was setting a precedent that might be used to justify Soviet intervention in the Congo. The Soviet statement added that such actions could lead to the sending of volunteers from other African countries, and even from other continents, to help Lumumba's government. The United States interpreted this as a Soviet ruse to intervene more actively in the Congo.

I learned of the airport incident in which the eleven Canadian airmen had been beaten almost to death at Ndjili airport only minutes after Jeff had left the office to accompany a reports officer, who had been on temporary duty with us, to catch her plane home. Afraid that the same result could await Jeff and the visiting reports officer, I dashed out of the embassy toward my car in the hope that I could head them off before they reached Ndjili. In my rush, I did not see Carlucci coming up the steps and I collided with him, almost throwing him off balance. I apologized and explained briefly where I was going. Frank followed me saying, "If it is as bad as that, I had better come with you."

Despite our best efforts, we did not catch Jeff before he had reached Ndjili. When we reached the airport, it seemed empty. However, finding Jeff and the reports officer at the airport was easy; they were the only people in the rotunda. They told us that something must be wrong for there was no one at the SABENA desk. In fact, they had not seen any airline employees at all. After a few minutes, people started appearing out of back rooms where they had been hiding. The aggressive soldiers apparently had decided to find more fun elsewhere.

Lumumba demanded that the United Nations turn over control of Ndjili airport to his troops, threatening to take it by force if necessary. The UN had been trying to maintain order there since the incident involving the Canadian aircrew. Ralph Bunche asked to meet Lumumba to discuss the matter but the latter refused to see him. Lumumba, who often changed his mind and his tactics, did not follow through on his threat and the airport remained in UN hands.

The prime minister turned his attentions to Kasai and Katanga. He requisitioned five Air Congo planes to airlift two hundred troops, along with their gear, to Luluabourg in the Kasai. The excuse for the operation was that the troops were being sent to try to restore peace between the Lulua and Baluba tribes who were engaged in a fierce tribal conflict. The actual reason for sending the troops was that Lumumba wanted to defeat Albert Kalonji, a former political ally turned bitter enemy. Lumumba also expected that, once his troops had been successful against Kalonji, they would go on to crush Tshombe and reunite Katanga with the rest of the country.

While these preparations were under way, the Soviet Union told Lumumba that it was sending the Congolese ten Ilyushin–14 planes with crews, technicians, and interpreters to Stanleyville, Lumumba's political fief and later the center of the rebellion. The Soviets also advised the prime minister that they were shipping one hundred trucks for the army to the port of Matadi. Meanwhile, our embassy in Brussels reported another disturbing development: Albert de Coninck and Jean Terfve, two leaders of the Belgian Communist Party, planned to visit the Congo. The conclusion was clear. The Soviet Union intended to intervene directly in the Congo rather than channeling its assistance through the United Nations.

Other factors supported our analysis. Lumumba did not act like any other government leader with whom American officials were familiar. He came across as an unpredictable loose cannon, and his grasp on power was tenuous, made worse by the divided loyalties and indiscipline of the army. Some of his closest supporters, notably Anicet Kashamura, the fiery minister of information, and Pierre Mulele, the minister of education, acted and spoke like communists. In fact, the station had good reason to believe that Mulele was a KGB agent based on information received from our agent who worked as the minister's adviser. He had been recommended to Mulele by a communist lawyer of his acquaintance who had suddenly given up his law practice to become a baker in Guinea. Further, there was the influential presence of the tantalizing Madame Blouin, Lumumba's chief of protocol, and Serge Michel, the left-wing Frenchman who was his private secretary and confidant. In those days, when everything was measured in Cold War terms, we were convinced that we were observing the beginning of a major Soviet effort to gain control of a key country in central Africa for use as a springboard to control much of the continent.

With the full backing of Headquarters, the station began work on a plan to remove Lumumba from power. One of our early operations, organized by Jacques who provided minor financial support, was an anti-Lumumba demonstration when the latter spoke at a meeting of African foreign ministers held in Leopoldville on August 25. On his arrival, hostile demonstrators shouted "à bas Lumumba" ("down with Lumumba"), and when he began to speak to the delegates, the mob drowned him out shouting anti-Lumumba slogans. When a pro-Lumumba group turned up, the two groups threw stones at each other until the police arrived and broke it up by firing shots into the air. This undermined Lumumba's image of a man loved by his people and in full control of the nation. He had counted on the conference to strengthen his position within the pan-African movement, but instead the delegates were caught up in the reality of the Congo situation.

In early September, Jacques reported that Kasavubu was consider-ing dismissing Lumumba. We had any agent or cooperator who might see Kasavubu ready to urge him to dismiss Lumumba. Once we heard that Kasavubu might take this action, we drafted a "how-to" paper for the president outlining, step-by-step, the actions he should take before dismissing Lumumba and what he should do in the aftermath. Jacques passed on our brief to Kasavubu via an inter-mediary and reported that the president had glanced at it but made no commitment to use it. Jacques, however, assured us that Kasavubu would soon act against Lumumba, but he could not say when.

Thus we were not surprised when we heard on the evening of September 5 that Kasavubu had gone to the radio station and an-nounced that he was dismissing Lumumba for having "betrayed his trust" by depriving Congolese citizens of their fundamental liber-ties. Kasavubu also criticized Lumumba for having led the country into a civil war. He concluded his short speech by announcing that he was naming Joseph Ileo, the president of the senate, to form a new government. He instructed the army to lay down its arms and called on the United Nations to maintain peace and order.

Having concluded his announcement, Kasavubu returned to the presidential palace and went to bed. Our carefully prepared brief showed we had a great deal to learn about Congolese politics. It made sense to Americans, but we were not in America. Kasavubu, who knew his people far better than we did, had ignored much of our advice. He failed, however, to control the radio station, a key place in such a volatile situation and one we had emphasized in our paper. Also, Ileo, his prime minister-designate, was nowhere to be found.

Lumumba leapt into action and the first place he went was to the radio station. In fact, he was there on three separate occasions that night. Each time he appeared to be angrier than the last. He denied that Kasavubu had the constitutional authority to dismiss him, he accused the president of acting on behalf of the "Belgian and French imperialists," he denounced Kasavubu as a traitor, and he ended by announcing that he was dismissing Kasavubu from the presidency for betraying the nation.

The embassy and the station were humming with activity. We cabled Washington about Lumumba's dismissal and reported the prime minister's response, as well as the fact that Ileo had not surfaced. Fortunately, we had a good idea where he was. After a quick French lesson, we sent Dad to the home of Cyrille Adoula, a labor leader and senator opposed to Lumumba. Dad drove out to Adoula's modest house in the suburbs and knocked loudly on the door. Adoula finally opened it, rolling his eyes as he was wont to do when excited. Ileo stood defensively beside him.

"You've got to form a new government," Dad said as Ileo watched mosquitoes blacken the front porch light. "You're the prime minister now."

"Tonight? Now?" Ileo asked, beginning to shake his head slowly. "It's too dangerous to be out at this time of night. Tomorrow morning I'll get to work. Soon enough. And goodnight, sir."

Ileo closed the door and shuffled off to bed.

By this point, we were prepared to go to almost any length to get Lumumba off the air. We knew his power as a rabble-rouser, and we were afraid that his strident speeches would soon have his supporters thronging in the streets. We considered cutting off power to the radio station but neither Jeff nor I knew how. Finally, Lumumba himself made our rather wild plans redundant when he decided he had done enough for one night.

The next morning we learned that Soviet and Eastern European journalists were in the radio station filing their stories while American and other Western journalists had been excluded. We decided to have Jacques rectify that situation by organizing an anti-Lumumba demonstration using his contacts with youth and labor leaders. It was to target the radio station and expel any white journalists found there. Jacques, who had excellent contacts with the leadership of the ABAKO youth group, ardent supporters of Kasavubu, was to lead the demonstration. When everything was ready, Jacques called us and Jeff gave him the green light to go ahead.

We were congratulating ourselves that the station would soon be open to the Western press and that the demonstration would provide them with a story of how the youth of Leopoldville supported the president. At that moment an embassy officer, who naturally was not aware of our plans, stuck his head round our office door: "Have you guys heard? The Soviets have finally left the radio station," he said.

"When?"

"Just a few minutes ago. The Western press is now in there filing their stories. I think there was a tussle of some kind."

Jeff and I grabbed our car keys and rushed out the door to stop the demonstration, or at least redirect it. We agreed that we would try to intercept the demonstrators and tell Jacques to divert them to another target such as the prime minister's office.

We took off separately in the hope that one of us would reach Jacques and the demonstrators in time to change the plan. All white journalists looked alike to them and we didn't want them to attack the Western press.

Jeff reached them first. I pulled up my car and jumped behind a house on the line of march. The demonstrators were pouring down the street, shouting and waving their placards: "*A bas Lumumba! Liberté! Liberté!*" ("Down with Lumumba! Freedom! Freedom!")

I could see Jacques at their head, a blurred figure in a white shirt, gesticulating and shouting. Jeff ran out in front of the demonstrators, frantically trying to get Jacques's attention. Just as he reached Jacques, a unit of Guinean police, who were officially part of the UN forces but often acted on their own, pulled up in a flat-bed truck and opened fire on the demonstrators.

Bullets were pinging and singing all over the place. One demonstrator fell, wounded. Jeff was caught in the line of fire between the police and the demonstrators. He took off like a flash and jumped into a drainage ditch parallel with the street and started crawling in my direction as rapidly as I have ever seen a man crawl on his elbows and knees. Every so often, his rear end would appear and the Guineans would open fire on him. It was like the pop-up rabbits in a shooting gallery. When he was opposite me, he braced himself and hurled himself out of the ditch as the police again opened fire. He hit the ground and rolled behind the house where I was standing, stopping against my legs. He looked up, surprised to see me there, and said, "Jesus, you have an active station!" That's my guy, I said to myself.

Our next operation was less hair-raising and in more the classic mold. Eager to organize a vote of no-confidence in Lumumba in the senate, we focused on Ileo and Adoula, both of whom were senators and had long distrusted and opposed the prime minister. The operation to influence the vote of the Congolese Senate lasted several weeks. Frank Carlucci, who covered parliament for the embassy, gave us his advice about how a senate vote might turn out. The night before the no-confidence debate we huddled at the embassy in an optimistic mood. But Lumumba surprised us. He spoke to the senators for two hours and the censure motion was defeated by forty-seven votes to two, with seven senators abstaining, including Ileo and Adoula.

We had underestimated the potential for intimidation. Lumumba surrounded the parliament building with troops, and I heard stories of armed soldiers in the senate visitors' gallery. Also some senators believed that he and some of his close associates were prepared to resort to assassination, beatings, or other physical abuse to achieve their objectives.

Our failure on the senate no-confidence vote convinced us that we had to find a better solution. It was around this time that one of our agents reported that Lumumba was planning to assassinate the foreign minister, Justin Bomboko. Bomboko, along with Albert Delvaux, the minister and ambassador-designate to Belgium who had rescued me from the firing squad, had countersigned Kasavubu's order dismissing the prime minister. Lumumba was, apparently, about to take his revenge.

I had met Bomboko at Ndjili airport in mid-July, but I did not know him well enough to tell him that his prime minister wanted him killed. While the ambassador knew Bomboko, it was a delicate matter that, if badly handled, could result in Timberlake and some or all of his officers being declared *persona non grata* for interfering in the Congo's internal affairs. Such a matter could conceivably go further and trigger a break in diplomatic relations.

Eventually, Jeff and I came up with a solution. Dad, like Bomboko, resided in the Regina Hotel and had met him in the hotel bar on several occasions. The Regina was one of the oldest and most rundown hotels in town with little to recommend it, but at least it had a bar, live music, and dancing.

Although his French was limited, to say the least, we felt Dad was our best bet because he was in no way publicly connected with the embassy. I met Dad at a bar across town from his hotel and spent a couple of hours coaching him to say in French that he had something of the greatest importance and urgency to tell the minister.

"If Bomboko shows any interest," I said finally, "tell him that someone from the consular staff will interpret for him."

"Bomboko has a reputation as a swordsman. A ladies' man," Dad said. "He'll be in the Metropole bar. There is plenty of company every night. I could drop in and meet him there."

Late the next night Dad called to say that Bomboko was in his room and ready to listen. Within a few minutes, I was at the Regina. Bomboko was a short, chunky man with a handsome, jolly face and alert, intelligent eyes. In later years his dark hair developed a thick silver streak that enhanced the general elegance of his appearance.

I explained that I was there merely in the role of interpreter and was not speaking for the American embassy.

"Dad (I used his name) and a friend who refused to report the matter overheard two men discussing plans to assassinate you," I said in French. "One of the men said that the whole thing was too dangerous. The other one assured him that there was no danger because the prime minister had ordered it."

Bomboko's jovial face clouded over. "I'm a chief of the Mongo tribe," he said slowly. "Lumumba is no fool. He would not dare to have me killed."

We chatted for a few minutes, and I got up to leave.

"So, sir, what would you advise me to do?" Bomboko asked as I shook his hand.

"Well, I think you should surround yourself with as many Mongo brothers as you can. And I wouldn't sleep twice running in the same place."

Bomboko smiled as if he had a big secret. "Thank you, both. I do thank you. But I assure you, I am in no danger whatsoever."

The following morning as I was walking past the Regina I saw soldiers in the lobby of the hotel and others moving from room to room. I realized that they must be looking for Bomboko. I hurried back to the embassy where, to my surprise, I found him sitting in my office chatting genially with Jeff. Grinning, he explained that he had followed my advice and had not slept in his room the previous night.

"This morning I got back to the hotel very early," he said, "and I ran into Colonel Mobutu, the chief of staff of the army, who was watching as his troops went through the hotel. He told me to get out of there. The soldiers had orders to kill me, he said."

Bomboko asked where he might hide. Mobutu said go to the American embassy and ask for Larry Devlin.

I was surprised that he thought of me. I had met Mobutu only twice before, once in Brussels when Ambassador Burden gave a reception for the Congolese who had attended the Round Table Constitutional Conference in early 1960, and once on the street in Leopoldville when he was trying to sort out an incident with the soldiers.

I left Bomboko with Jeff and hurried to the ambassador's office.

"Smelly situation," Tim said, "I don't like it."

"You think it's a set-up?"

"It could be . . . Lumumba could have ordered Mobutu to send him to us."

"That would make sense if he wants to send his soldiers over here and close us down."

"I had Mobutu pegged for a moderate, a really competent guy," said Tim. "But he could be going along with Lumumba for his own reasons." Tim got up and started pacing. "After all, he was Lumumba's private secretary during the Round Table Conference. They're buddies and Lumumba appointed him secretary of state in the prime minister's office and then named him chief of staff of the army after the mutiny. I'm going to call the UN and ask them to take Bomboko off our hands."

The response was not helpful. The UN said it would provide protection only for the president and prime minister. They suggested we take Bomboko to the prime minister's residence or the presidential palace. Lumumba's residence, we knew, was not an option. We would be sending Bomboko to his death.

Before deciding what to do next, I went out and drove around town to check on the situation. There were many more roadblocks than usual, even in the *cité,* as the native quarter was called. It seemed clear that the army was still looking for Bomboko.

I returned to the embassy and reported to Tim.

He looked at me, obviously ill at ease. "Larry, I hate to have to ask you to do this, but I don't see any other way. We need to get Bomboko out of here because if we don't our staff could be in great danger. So, I want you to take him over to the president's palace as soon as you can."

I nodded.

"You shouldn't drive him yourself because of your diplomatic passport," Tim continued. "One of your agents should be at the wheel."

Unfortunately, that was out of the question. It would take too long to contact anyone and, besides, I did not want to expose my undercover people to the Congolese. Luckily, Jeff was still using his tourist passport since he had not had the time to obtain a diplomatic document. I did not like the idea of asking him—or anyone else for that matter—to do the job. There were army roadblocks all over the city. If caught, the driver would almost certainly be killed along with the foreign minister. On the other hand, I could understand Tim's concern about his staff and the diplomatic dilemma Bomboko's unexpected presence posed for all of us.

Returning to my office, I found Jeff working with Bomboko on speeches that we could arrange to have broadcast from Brazzaville.

"Jeff, I need you to drive the minister to the president's palace."

He looked at me for a moment. I knew he was thinking of what lay ahead. "Okay," he said with a wry laugh. "I guess that's what they pay me for."

If there had ever been a question about Jeff's qualifications for the Leopoldville job, it vanished with that response. He had come under fire in a fetid ditch only a few days before; yet he was prepared to accept this dangerous assignment without a murmur. Many officers would have asked why I was not prepared to do it myself. Jeff, who had not been in the Congo long enough to know the city well, only had one question. "Tell me how to get to the palace."

"I'll lead the way in my car," I said, drawing him a map. "If we run into a roadblock, I will crash my car into any Congolese army jeep or truck that gives chase. But in that case, afterwards you'll be on your own." "Okay," he said. "Let's go."

As we went down the back stairs, the acting assistant air attaché appeared and asked what we were doing. I told him, while Bomboko, as cool as a cucumber, and Jeff climbed into the van I had borrowed. Just as I was driving out into the street, the attaché and his sergeant came running up armed with pistols and a rifle.

"We'll follow the van and lay down covering fire if you get in trouble," he said. It gave Jeff and me a good feeling to know we were not alone on the mission.*

---

*Unfortunately, I no longer recall the assistant attaché's name, but if I could find it, I would ask the Air Force to commend him and his sergeant for conduct above and beyond the call of duty. We were all so busy in those days that I failed to write up the incident as I should have done, an omission that I deeply regret.

The drive to the presidential palace went smoothly. The road-blocks were so poorly placed that we were able to find a way around each one. But, when we arrived at the palace, the situation became more dicey.

A wall with high, metal gates in the front and the rear sur-rounded the building. Inside the wall, UN Tunisian troops were in defensive positions, but Congolese soldiers surrounded the palace outside the wall. As I pulled up to the front gate, Jeff stopped a hundred yards or so behind me. I leaned out the window and greeted the soldiers as though they were long-lost friends.

"Message for the President," I said, grinning cheerfully. "I fig-ured you guys wouldn't mind a few cigarettes for night duty." I held up several packs. The sergeant, who appeared to be in charge, smiled back, saluted, took the cigarettes, and opened the gate.

Watching Jeff in my rear view mirror start moving up the hill be-hind me, I paused for a moment so that we both went through the gate at almost the same time and drove up to the palace's entrance.

Kasavubu, who must have been watching, hurried out in his shirtsleeves to greet us. Bomboko thanked us and we bade them a hurried farewell, leaving the compound by the back gate. The Con-golese soldiers merely glanced into our vehicles and let us pass with-out incident. We returned to the embassy as limp as two dishrags.

Bomboko repaid the good turn in several ways over many years, but one just a few weeks later was especially memorable. He invited me to a celebration at the popular Zoo Restaurant. It was a favorite spot with the Congolese because the French woman who owned the restaurant had been the first restaurant owner to break the color bar that had banned Congolese from certain restaurants. Bomboko was being honored by his fellow Mongo tribesmen, and there was a lot of food, drink, speeches, music, and dancing and a good time was had by all. At the end of the evening, he initiated me into the tribe, making me an honorary Mongo.

6

IT HAD BEEN A ROUGH DAY, but there was more to come. That evening, Tim called me into his office along with McIlvaine, Lavallee, and Carlucci. We endlessly discussed the odds on Kasavubu or Lumumba prevailing in the power structure but came to no conclusion. Finally, Tim turned to me.

"You've been with Bomboko most of the afternoon and you saw Kasavubu, what do you think?"

"Well," I said, "I could run the blockade again and sit down with Kasavubu and Bomboko and try to obtain their views. Meanwhile, you could try to see Lumumba." As no one had a better idea than this, the meeting broke up, and I set out for the presidency.

This time there were surprisingly few roadblocks and a handful of cigarettes got me through the gate once more. I was shown into a small, windowless waiting room where I sat for a while going over in my mind what I was going to say to Kasavubu and Bomboko. The door opened. I looked up expecting to see a member of the president's staff.

Instead, Colonel Mobutu stood in the doorway flanked by two soldiers with submachine guns at the ready. I jumped to my feet. My first thought was that the army had captured the palace and that I might be Mobutu's prisoner. The guns were trained on me, fingers on the trigger. Mobutu looked very solemn.

"Wait for me outside," he said softly to the soldiers. He closed the door and shook hands with me.

"I'm anxious to talk to you," he said with a tight, little smile. He was in full military dress, tall, rail thin, and very, very young. He almost looked like a high school kid all decked out in an ROTC uniform. He was only twenty-nine and his voice, which would become gravelly with age, was a smooth baritone. He cleared his throat and put one hand in his coat pocket.

"The president and prime minister have dismissed each other. Political games!" He made a long, disdainful hissing noise. "This is no way to create a strong, independent, democratic Congo! So, where do we go from here?"

I assumed it was a rhetorical question and kept my mouth shut. He stared at me intensely. I had no idea where he was heading.

"The Soviets are pouring into the country. You must know that, Mr. Devlin?"

I nodded.

"I know we don't have enough educated Congolese to fill the shoes of all the Belgian civil servants who've left the country. But that doesn't mean I want Soviet technicians to take their place. We didn't fight for independence to have another country re-colonize us." He paused. "Did you know that during the past two weeks the Soviets have been in Camp Leopold II [later renamed Camp Kokolo, the main army camp in Leopoldville] telling our soldiers that the Soviet Union is the only truly democratic state and Marxism is the only road to freedom and democracy? They say that the Western countries are only interested in stealing the Congo's wealth while the Soviet Union is our real friend."

He stepped outside and muttered something to a soldier. He returned with some of the books and pamphlets he said the Soviets were handing out to the troops. I glanced at them and saw that they contained typical Soviet propaganda. I also noticed that most of them were printed in English with British spelling. (We later determined that they had been printed in Ghana.) The fact that the books were in English, of course, defeated the Soviets' objective of using them to influence the thinking of the Congolese soldiers since they hardly spoke broken French, let alone English.

"I met with Lumumba and asked him to tell the Soviets to stay away from the army," Mobutu said. "Lumumba said he would, but nothing's happened. He hasn't kept his word. Not to me. Nor to the army. When I asked him again about Soviet interference, Lumumba told me to mind my own business. He said that this was a political matter and none of my business. I tried to argue, but Lumumba said the Soviets would be allowed to enter the camp and talk to the troops as long as they wished, and that I was not to interfere.

"So . . . what it comes down to is this: I've called all of my area commanders to Leopoldville to discuss the Soviet problem. They are scheduled to go back to their posts tomorrow. They are all as unhappy about Soviet efforts to penetrate the army as I am."

Now I could see where he was heading, and a whirlwind of strategies started up in my brain.

Finally, he said, "Here is the situation: the army is prepared to overthrow Lumumba. But only on the condition that the United States will recognize the government that would replace Lumumba's. The government we would establish would be temporary and would stay in power only so long as necessary to get the Soviets out of the Congo and to create a democratic regime."

"And Lumumba and Kasavubu, what happens to them?"

"They'll both have to be neutralized," he answered without missing a beat. "We'll replace them with educated men, a government of technocrats, and I'll remain in the army."

Allen Dulles had made it absolutely clear to me that the United States wanted Lumumba removed from power, but I had always thought in terms of a legal or parliamentary change, not an army coup. The question was whether Washington was prepared to recognize a government installed by means of a coup to achieve its goal. Yet the more I considered Mobutu's plan, the better it sounded. After all, I had not been able to come up with a solution to the Lumumba problem. Nonetheless, I knew I did not have the authority to guarantee the United States' support for a *coup d'état* nor its recognition of the government that Mobutu was prepared to install afterwards. Furthermore, our government did not, to the best of my knowledge, have anything against President Kasavubu who, as chief of state, was a key figure.

As I dodged a reply to Mobutu's question, Bomboko appeared, shook my hand and slipped me a note. He turned to Mobutu and told him how Jeff and I had helped him get to the palace. I read Bomboko's note, which was succinct and to the point. "*Aidez-lui,*" it said. "Help him."

Mobutu and Bomboko recounted at length the ineptitude of the Lumumba government, about how he ran it as a one-man show, seldom listening to his ministers' advice, and about the threat posed to the Congo by the Soviet Union.

I was already well aware that Lumumba was toying with the Soviets' support. Although I did not believe that he was either a communist or a Soviet agent, I was convinced that he was being manipulated by the Soviets and that he would, sooner rather than later, fall under their control. I knew, however, that I did not have the authority to do what Mobutu and Bomboko wanted.

"I've got to get back to my commanders," Mobutu said, turning to leave. "I have to give them a 'go' or a 'no go' order. Lumumba doesn't know they're here, so they must get back to their bases before he finds out."

Both men were looking at me.

It was time to fish or cut bait. I was a young and relatively inexperienced station chief with one hell of a decision to make. I did not want to embarrass my country or the CIA. But I could no longer dodge the question of whether the United States was prepared to recognize a government installed by a military coup. If I refused to cooperate with Mobutu, he might decide that he had no alternative but to support Lumumba. That, in turn, would mean that Lumumba would appoint one of his men to replace Kasavubu, a person who would almost certainly follow Lumumba's orders. That would lead to a strong possibility of the Congo falling under the control of the Soviet Union.

So I held out my hand to Mobutu and said with as much conviction as I could muster: "I can assure you the United States government will recognize a temporary government composed of civilian technocrats."

Mobutu's face was totally impassive. His gaze was steady, unreadable. "The coup will take place within a week," he said. "But I will need five thousand dollars to provide for my senior officers. If the coup fails, we will all be in prison or dead. The money will be for our families. My area commanders were all noncommissioned officers and poorly paid so their families will not expect a large sum. But I have to assure them that they will not be destitute."

Having already vastly exceeded my authority, I made another promise on behalf of the U.S. government in a style that wasn't exactly consultative or democratic. I assured Mobutu that the money would be available and arranged to meet him in his office early that morning.

"You can trust him," Bomboko said, noting that I was in need of reassurance. "If he pulls it off"—at this *if,* I must have looked like a hooked fish gasping for air—"and he will, it will be a great thing for this country. Mobutu is nothing if not a patriot, a nationalist. You'll see, you'll see."

"I need to talk to the president," I said, suddenly remembering why I had come to the palace.

"Oh, him!" Bomboko said, his face breaking into an impish grin, "he's been asleep for hours!"

I left the presidential residence without further incident. A sleepy UN guard opened the gate from inside, and I did not see any Congolese soldiers outside. They appeared to be following Kasavubu's example. At high speed, I drove to the embassy, where Jeff was loyally waiting for me.

When I told him of the guarantee I had given Mobutu, I could see from his expression that he knew I had just put my future on the line. The first priority was to inform Headquarters. If they did not approve, I would still have time to tell Mobutu that my guarantee was no longer valid. Unfortunately, our communicator had lost radio contact with Washington and had been unable to reach Headquarters for several hours. The next step was to tell Tim. It was about 2:00 a.m. when I drove into the circular driveway of his residence, parked, and tried to ring the bell, which didn't work. So I had to resort to a little breaking and entering. Not a sound. I checked the windows and managed to force one open.

Once in the residence, I turned on some lights and found my way up to the ambassador's bedroom. I had to pound on the door to make him hear me over the racket made by a noisy window air-conditioner.

"It must be important if you are here at this hour," Tim mumbled sleepily. "I'll be right down. Fix yourself a drink and, while you're at it, make one for me."

I told him the full story. Tim mulled it over for a moment, sipping his drink. "Larry, tell me something," he said slowly. "Do you have a personal fortune or enough service time to qualify for retirement?"

I laughed. I had neither, and he must have known it. "Well, as it happens, I have both," he said. "If the coup fails, the two of us will be out of a job."

"Do you think I should contact Mobutu and withdraw my guarantee?"

"No, you did the right thing," he said quickly. "Lumumba is a wild man, a dangerous man. But I want to be sure that you realize the gravity of your action and the risk it poses for your future as a CIA officer."

I assured him that I was fully aware of that problem.

Back at the embassy, our communications were still down. I contacted Bobby, my ace recruiter and an experienced political action officer, because I wanted to take him with me when I met Mobutu later that morning with the money he had requested. As an American official, it would not be a good idea for me to be seen with Mobutu too often, especially after he had led a coup, and Bobby was the ideal man to maintain the connection.

Bobby and I arrived at army headquarters at the early hour agreed upon with Mobutu. An aide asked us to wait in the hall and assured us Colonel Mobutu would not be long. Suddenly, a squad

of soldiers armed with submachine guns filed in and took up positions directly opposite us.

"We have been set up," Bobby said softly. It did not look good.
We were working up a sweat when a soldier at the end of the line
put down his gun and went out, probably responding to a call of
nature. Bobby and I instinctively moved slowly toward the gun. It
was not a good solution but, if what we feared came to pass, we
wanted to be able to put up a fight. At that time, I was sick and
tired of the games it appeared the Congolese were playing, games
that could end my career as an intelligence officer, games that could
result in my death.

We were within reach of the submachine gun, should the need
arise, when Mobutu's secretary appeared to say he would see us. We
went in and I introduced Bobby as "Dr. Roberti," a representative
of major international business interests eager to prevent the spread
of communism in Africa. Should the need arise, we wanted a story
that Mobutu could plausibly use to explain Bobby's connection
with him.

Mobutu appeared relaxed and confident. He said he had met his
area commanders and told them that the coup was on. "I'll be setting a date and time shortly but it will be within the next week," he
said. "I'll take control of the radio station, announce the formation
of a new government, and declare the Soviet and Czech embassies
and the Chinese communist delegation *persona non grata*."

At the embassy, our communications were up and running again
and I finally sent off a full report of Mobutu's plan and what I had
promised the U.S. Government would do to support him. The full
seriousness of what I was doing hit me once again as I initialed the
cable. There was still time to warn Mobutu to call the coup off if
Headquarters disapproved of my actions. But that would fatally undermine my credibility with the young colonel, severely limit my
usefulness in the Congo, and almost certainly end my career.

Fortunately, I had other things on my mind, notably preparing
Bobby for his intermediary's role with Mobutu. I had warned him
that whenever he visited the military camp where Mobutu had his

headquarters, he could expect to be roughed up or given a difficult time by the soldiers. He had listened attentively and nodded.

Meetings with Bobby were always a bit of a walk on the wild side because I never knew what he would do next, but they were invariably instructive as I found out when I later visited him in his apartment. He was busy preparing for his first solo visit to Mobutu the next day. He showed me a briefcase that looked rather like the type of bag doctors used to carry when they made house calls. He also had a blood pressure gauge, a small rubber hammer for measuring reflexes, several other medical instruments, and about twenty bottles of aspirin and malaria suppressants. Removing the labels from the bottles, he explained that he had become a physician, to match his new title, and here was the proof.

"I don't intend to have those camp guards lay a finger on me," he said. "After all, I *am* a doctor." He tucked the aspirins and malaria suppressants into the pockets of the bag and winked. "I'm sure they can use some of these."

7

FOR THE NEXT FEW DAYS, we were on tenterhooks. Kasavubu came out of his slumber and ordered Lumumba's arrest. Jacques reported that the president had chosen loyal soldiers from his tribal region to carry out the order, and confirmed that Lumumba was under arrest and on his way to the military camp. I passed on the news to Headquarters as a done deal. But I had underestimated Lumumba's persuasive powers. He convinced the young arresting officer that it was illegal to arrest a sitting parliamentarian and then used the officer's jeep to drive through the native quarters of Leopoldville proclaiming his "victory" over Kasavubu. After whipping up the crowd, he went on to Camp Leopold II to harangue the troops in the base.

I hit the ceiling. Only an hour before, I had reported Lumumba's arrest and the debacle made me look foolish. I was frustrated, and I told Mr. Dulles in my cable that trying to accomplish anything in the Congo was like trying to hammer nails with ripe bananas. In less than an hour, however, I received a reply from Dulles expressing his confidence in me. He urged me to continue working hard, implying that it was my job to play the hand I had been dealt. To the best of my recollection and that of Jeff, we never received a reply to my report on Mobutu's coup plans and my promise to recognize a new government. If this was the case, and I believe it was, it made sense. If the coup failed, it could be blamed on me and the Agency would be at least partially off the hook.

On the evening of September 14, the Soviets were still prepared to bet the collective farm on Lumumba. Jeff and I were at a party, the first that we had had time to attend since arriving in Leopoldville, at the home of Alison "Tally" Palmer, the American vice-consul. Shortly after her arrival, Andrée Blouin, the prime minister's glamorous and beautiful chief of protocol, received a phone call and departed in a great rush. A few moments later, Jeff and I also had a call with the news that Mobutu was on the radio announcing that the army was installing a government of technocrats. We left as hurriedly as Madame Blouin. Jeff returned to the office while I went to the Regina Hotel and arrived just in time for Mobutu's press conference. I joined the crowd and managed to obtain a seat in the second row next to the chief of the Chinese communist delegation that was hoping to establish diplomatic relations with the Congo.

Mobutu began by saying that the army would hold power until the end of the year. The new government, known as the "College of Commissars," would be composed of university graduates, and Justin Bomboko would remain as foreign minister and would lead the new administration. Kasavubu, Lumumba, and Ileo, he said, were "neutralized," and the parliament would be closed until 1961. Holding up the books and pamphlets he had shown me earlier, he condemned the Soviet Union and its allies for trying to indoctrinate the military with communist propaganda and ordered the expulsion of all Soviet, Czech, and Chinese communist diplomatic and technical personnel within forty-eight hours.

When Mobutu finished, pandemonium broke out. Most of the journalists rushed for the door to file their stories, but some with limited or non-existent French hung around desperately trying to find out what Mobutu had said. Anti-Lumumba activists were cheering, and I saw some of the former prime minister's supporters slip out of the room. A number of people clustered around the young colonel congratulating him and wishing him well.

I felt a tug on my arm.

"What did he say? What did he say?" It was the leader of the Chinese communist delegation.

"You have just been expelled," I replied amiably.

It was an exciting moment. Our efforts to remove Lumumba and prevent the Soviet Union from gaining control of the Congo were at last bearing fruit. I believed then, and I continue to believe, that the coup was vital if we were to prevent the Soviet Union from obtaining a foothold on the African continent, one that could eventually threaten our NATO defenses. We were anxious that Mobutu and the young technocrats would create a viable government because it would ensure the success of our policy.

A major bonus was Bomboko, whose life we had helped to save, leading the new government. He was well respected by Ambassador Timberlake as an intelligent, competent, and pro-Western official, and the personal contact we had established with him would certainly prove helpful. Little did I know then how valuable he would become. Not long after that fateful night, Bomboko's wife gave birth to a son and they named him Larry Bomboko.

I dashed back to the embassy to send the news of the coup to Headquarters. The Agency had special code words for reporting coups, war, and other major crises but, for the life of me, I couldn't recall the right word for a *coup d'état*. Jeff and I frantically searched our files but without success. In the end, I hazarded a guess, put the word on top of my message, and sent it off with a *flash* priority. Unfortunately, I picked the wrong code. The word I used signified a declaration of war, with missiles on the way, and resulted in President Eisenhower being rolled out of bed.

The next day, we found the correct word and Headquarters chided me with a long explanation of the proper procedure. But they were not too rough. After all, the operation was a success. I later learned that Eisenhower had called Dulles to discuss the coup and had asked if the CIA had a good chief in the Congo. Dulles is reported to have responded that I was one of his best. What else could he say? He was not likely to tell the president that he had made the mistake of sending an inexperienced station chief to the Congo. We had contributed to the objective of removing Lumumba from power and blocking the efforts of the Soviet Union to gain a major foothold in Africa. Mr. Dulles would have wanted to gain credit for the CIA for having achieved these objectives.

The United States did not immediately recognize the new government. The State Department reminded Tim that the Congo's constitution stipulated that the president was the *only* person who could legally nominate the prime minister and appoint a new government. Washington insisted that a way be found to legalize the illegal. In effect, this meant convincing Mobutu to recognize Kasavubu as president and have the latter name Bomboko and the technocrats as the new administration. It was also pointed out that the College of Commissars was an unfortunate name; it sounded too Russian, too communist. My job was to persuade Mobutu to make these changes.

Two days after the coup, I received a phone call from Mobutu asking me to come to his home in the military camp. I was not thrilled with the idea. For my own security, as well as Mobutu's, I didn't want to be seen with him so soon after the coup. But Mobutu insisted he needed to see me, and I could not ignore such a request. At that moment, he was the government and the success of our African policy depended upon him. I drove out to the military camp and after some relatively minor harassment, was allowed to enter.

The front door to Mobutu's house was unguarded, and I walked straight into his living room and into the middle of a press conference. There must have been well over forty foreign journalists present but no diplomats. Mobutu stopped speaking and heads swiveled to look at me. Furious with his lack of concern about security, I kept walking. Luckily, one of the American journalists came to my aid. "I'm glad you got my message," he said. "I was sure the embassy would want someone to cover this."

I hardly knew him but was grateful for his ingenuity and felt he had helped me out. I have often wondered if he had identified me as the CIA station chief. I took notes as Mobutu began speaking to give the impression that I was indeed covering the event for the American embassy. After it was over, I lingered talking to two

American newsmen until everyone else had gone. I excused myself and joined Mobutu in another room.

It was a small, scruffy room with battered furniture. Mobutu, looking none too happy, stood behind a scarred desk that had seen better days.

"Why should I deneutralize Kasavubu?" He started pacing back and forth behind the desk. He was like an angry, stubborn boy, and seemed thinner than ever. "Reversing myself would make me look like an idiot. And why? Just to please some American *fonctionnaire?*" he asked scornfully.

I could tell that he needed a good rant, so I let him go.

"This is a Congolese matter, a Congolese decision. It must be decided by us, not by the United States State Department." He stopped pacing and glared at me.

"You've got a legitimacy problem," I said. "Only Kasavubu can solve that."

"Legitimacy!" He threw up his hands in disgust. "*Hypocrisy,* you mean! Lumumba had to go, and you know it. He was leading us back into that colonial cage only this time the Soviets would have had the key."

"Okay. Hypocrisy, I'll buy that," I said. "But, at this stage, I think it would be wiser to follow the constitution than try to make new rules."

Little by little, the steam went out of his arguments and he finally agreed to consider the matter and let us have a quick response. That promise was all I could get out of him and we left it there. He did, however, come up with a less loaded name for the College of Commissars. He simply changed "Commissars" to "Commissioners."

Some former colleagues have criticized me for not treating Mobutu as a recruited agent, giving him orders, and insisting that he carry them out. The problem is that Mobutu was never an American agent so there was no question about handling him in that way. Instead, he was a cooperator, not a pussycat. However, we shared the same objectives in removing Lumumba from power and stopping the spread of Soviet influence in the country. Mobutu's concerns, of course, were limited to the Congo; our concerns had a much broader, global reach.

When the coup occurred, Khrushchev was on the *Baltika,* a Soviet ship, crossing the Atlantic Ocean to attend the UN's General Assembly annual meeting in New York. Soviet understanding of the events seemed equally at sea. The day after the coup, *Pravda* reported the coup had failed, Mobutu had been arrested, and that he was nothing but a "soap bubble." When the soap bubble refused to pop, the Soviet press announced that Moscow had decided to recall its diplomats temporarily.

The word *temporarily* was worrying because it indicated that the Soviet Union believed Lumumba would soon return to power. There was a risk that by sheer demagoguery he might still sway the crowds in his support. It was clear to me that Headquarters was determined to prevent Lumumba's return, so we could not rest on our laurels. As long as Mobutu stalled on my request to reinstate Kasavubu and have him officially appoint the new government, it was vital to maintain regular contact with Mobutu, either through our faithful and resourceful "Dr. Roberti," or directly myself.

In an effort to convince Mobutu to reinstate Kasavubu, I visited the military camp in late September. I parked my car some distance from Mobutu's house and proceeded on foot. As I turned a corner, I saw a Congolese in civilian clothes standing with his back toward me, watching a thin man in uniform who was walking away. The civilian pulled out a pistol and took aim at the uniformed man.

I do not remember thinking what I should do or of the possible consequences; I simply reacted. I jumped on the gunman, jerking his pistol arm down and then we were on the ground, fighting for control of the weapon. He tried to turn the gun on me but, remembering a trick from my army days, I managed to twist the gun barrel back and broke his trigger finger. Later, I recalled that our instructor told us this seldom worked but, that day, I was lucky, and so was the thin man. When I stood up, the thin man turned round: it was Mobutu himself.

Two soldiers rushed up. The would-be assassin was not moving as I had hit him on the head with the butt of the revolver, which I had managed to wrench away from him. The soldiers apparently assumed that I was the assailant since I had a gun in my hands, and they started to attack me. But Mobutu recognized me and called them off. He thanked me but was not effusive; it was just not his nature to be so.

I never told Mobutu that I had not recognized him as the target, but I did ask him not to mention me in connection with the incident. He kept his word, and I later heard that he told people he had jumped the gunman himself, which covered my tracks perfectly. Later, I asked Mobutu what happened to the gunman. He said he had released him because he had been a soldier and they had known each other when they were training to become noncommissioned officers. He also knew the man's wife and children and could not bring himself to hurt him or his family. The would-be assassin, it transpired, was a member of Pierre Mulele's tribe and had acted on Mulele's orders. Mulele was minister of education in Lumumba's government, a close associate of Antoine Gizenga, and later led a rebellion against the central government. We also had reason to believe that he was a Soviet agent.

This attempt on Mobutu's life was the first of several that week, all generated by Mulele. Later that day, one of our best agents, a European who worked as an adviser to Mulele, contacted me to report that another assassination attempt was planned for the following day. I warned Mobutu, and the plot was foiled. Yet another attempt was foiled two days later, thanks to our agent. Around midnight the next evening, I went to the safe house to meet the agent. He was not there, but I was not surprised because I knew he could only get away when Mulele called it a day.

At about two in the morning I was dozing in my chair when I heard a light tap on the door. I unlocked the door and the agent slipped in. He looked like death warmed over.

"There's a new plot to kill Mobutu and his family," he said. "But I can't tell you about it." We just sat there and looked at each other for what seemed two or three light years. "Mulele is suspicious," he said finally. "He's asking why have all the attempts to kill Mobutu failed? He's convinced his group has been penetrated."

"So he's going to try again," I said, trying to keep him talking.

"That's right," he said. "But this time it's my assignment. I've planned tomorrow's attack. Nobody knows about it except me, Mulele, and the four guys who are going to slip into the camp dressed as Congolese soldiers. They have orders to kill Mobutu and his family."

I took a deep drag on my cigarette. His logic was impeccable. The assassins themselves were most unlikely to give away the plan since doing so would mean their arrest and possible execution. That would leave my agent dangerously exposed. I assured him that I would never act in such a way as to put him at risk. He was frightened, but he had confidence in me and finally gave me the details of the operation.

Since the attack was to take place at six that morning, I had just more than three hours to warn Mobutu. Entering the camp at night was out of the question. No white person, particularly an American who did not speak Lingala, would be able to get past the guards. Reaching Mobutu by phone at such a time of night was impossible because he took the instrument off the hook in order to get some sleep. After the agent left, I returned home and began dialing Mobutu. The line was busy.

Happily, he was an early riser and just after five in the morning, he answered the phone. I told him I had to warn him of another assassination plot. He was businesslike as usual and asked all the right questions: when, where, how many men were involved, and so on.

I took a deep breath. "Now, listen carefully. Before I tell you the details, you have to promise me something."

"What's that?"

"You have to shake hands publicly with a couple of the attackers and let them go."

"And why in God's name would I do that?" he bellowed. "Men sent to kill me?"

"Simply because any future warnings will depend on you doing exactly as I say." He grunted his assent and hung up.

Four men were picked up as they entered the camp. Mobutu thanked two of them in front of numerous witnesses, handed them envelopes containing money, and let them go. The other two were locked up. I do not know what happened to the two that were released but our agent said that he never saw them again. The two prisoners were later released as the result of the UN's intervention and they returned to the Mulele fold.

Mobutu was one of the most courageous men that I have ever met. I have been with him a number of times when his life was in great danger, but he never flinched. The threat to his family, however, upset him greatly. Bobby and I noticed over a period of a week, or somewhat more, that the threat to his family and the pressure of being solely responsible for all governmental decisions sometimes seemed too much for him. At times, he seemed distracted and unable to concentrate on serious matters that required his attention. Also, he began to drink heavily.

The last thing we needed was a Mobutu who had had one too many drinks when dealing with the affairs of state. He was still, in effect, a one-man government since the College of Commissioners had not yet been sworn in. With this in mind, I went back to see him and suggested that he send his wife, Marie-Antoinette, and their children to Europe until the political climate improved. Mobutu jumped at the suggestion. His wife was reluctant to leave him but agreed to fly to Belgium where the children could be placed in the care of the Catholic priest who had officiated at their nuptial mass. Much to his relief, she left the next morning.

I called on Mobutu a few days later and was astonished to see Marie-Antoinette with him. She assured me that the children were safe and in good hands in Belgium. "If they are going to kill my husband," she said simply, "they will have to kill me." Married when I believe she was fourteen and he was sixteen, Marie-Antoinette was a strong woman, and she was not afraid to stand up to her husband. On several occasions in later years, she would sweep into the room where we were talking and tear into him about something that displeased her. He would switch into Ngbandi, their tribal language, which not many Congolese, let alone an American, could understand.

Mobutu was at his fearless best when the police mutinied. It was reported to me that Mobutu was on his way to their camp. I jumped into my car and set off, arriving just as Mobutu was entering the camp gate. There were several hundred policemen, all armed, shouting and waving their weapons. Mobutu stopped inside the compound and held up his hand for silence. As the turmoil gradually subsided, he began to speak while walking slowly towards the mutineers. Some shouted at him to stop, threatening to shoot if he continued to advance. Many pointed their rifles at him but Mobutu continued talking in a calm voice.

I could not make out much of what he was saying, but the thrust of it was that mutiny was no solution, that they must put down their guns and discuss their problems. Finally, they calmed down while Mobutu continued to advance slowly with no abrupt movements until he reached the first rank. He took the rifle out of the hands of a young policeman and continued down the line relieving the men of their rifles and telling them to put their weapons on the ground. At first hesitant, a few complied and, little by little, all of them put down their rifles. It was a great example of courage and of how a determined man who projects self-confidence and faith in his cause can pacify an angry, disorganized mob.

8

I WAS USED TO SURPRISES IN THE CONGO, but nothing prepared me for a cable from Headquarters that landed on my desk on September 19, 1960. It carried the code word PROP, was marked for my eyes only, stressed that I was not to discuss its contents with anyone, and was from Richard Bissell, the deputy director, plans, the officer in charge of the CIA's clandestine operations. The cable informed me that a senior officer, whom I would recognize, was arriving in Leopoldville around September 27 and would identify himself as "Joe from Paris." I was instructed to see him as soon as possible after he contacted me.

The mysterious Joe would explain his assignment, and I was to carry out his verbal instructions. This was most unusual because Headquarters normally sent orders to the field in written form. The intense secrecy was also strange. I later learned that PROP was a code word for a specific, highly sensitive operation that I would be directed to plan and implement. Knowledge concerning the operation was originally limited to Allen Dulles, Richard Bissell, Bronson Tweedy (chief of the Africa Division), Glenn Fields (Tweedy's deputy), and me. But the whole thing was highly intriguing because there was no clue as to the nature of the operation or my role in it. Although I didn't know it at the time, that cable was the beginning of an episode that was to plague me for the rest of my life.

About a week later, I watched a man I recognized get up from a table at a cafe across the street as I left the embassy. He was a senior officer, a highly respected chemist, whom I had known for some time. He walked over, and we got into my car. As we drove away, he turned to me.

"I'm Joe from Paris," he said. "I've come to give you instructions about a highly sensitive operation."

It was no surprise, but I said nothing until we reached a safe house. We sat down and he told me the story. He had come to the Congo carrying deadly poisons to assassinate Lumumba, and I was to do the job.

I'll never forget my reaction of total, fall-to-the-floor shock.

"Jesus H. Christ!" I exploded. "Isn't this unusual?"

I knew several Congolese who wanted to kill Lumumba, but that was not a method I had ever considered. Perhaps, naively, my tactics had been to try to unseat him in parliament, and when that failed I had supported Mobutu's takeover.

"Who authorized this operation?" I asked.

"President Eisenhower," Joe said. "I wasn't there when he approved it, but Dick Bissell said that Eisenhower wanted Lumumba removed."

I lit another cigarette and stared down at my shoes.

"It's your responsibility to carry out the operation, you alone," he said. "The details are up to you, but it's got to be clean—nothing that can be traced back to the U.S. government."

Neither of us spoke for a while. Then he leaned back and pulled out a small package. "Take this," he said, handing it over. "With the stuff that's in there, no one will ever be able to know that Lumumba was assassinated."

He handed over several poisons. One was concealed in a tube of toothpaste. If Lumumba used it, he would appear to die from polio. Joe made it clear that I could use other methods, anything that accomplished the objective, providing it was not traceable to the U.S. government.

The conversation was a nightmare. I did not approve of the operation, but I had to think quickly, and I did not tell Joe of my reservations. With more than a decade of service in the CIA, I had never heard of an operation to assassinate someone. I assumed that a decision to implement such an unorthodox operation could come only from on high, and I believed Joe when he said it had actually come from the president. I also knew that, if I refused the assignment, it would mean my immediate recall and replacement by a more compliant officer, in effect, the end of my career.

My mind was racing. I realized that I could never assassinate Lumumba. It would have been murder. While I could have justified the assassination of Hitler to myself, Lumumba's case was not the same. It would have been morally wrong. Also, even though I have been engaged in two major wars, I find it difficult to kill any living thing, even the smallest insect. But I kept that to myself. I had seen enough of local politics to know, deep down, that there were less drastic ways of assuring that Lumumba would not return to power. Further, even if I tried to assassinate Lumumba, which I had no intention of doing, and bungled the operation, it would be a disaster for the embassy, the Agency, and the U.S. government. It would seriously complicate our relations with the Third World, where it would be exploited by the Soviet Union, and it would almost certainly provoke a violent backlash against Americans and Europeans in the Congo.

In short, I believed that it was morally wrong for me or anyone under my orders to kill Lumumba, an act that I could not justify by any argument or rationalization. As for the pursuit of our policy in the Congo, I was convinced that the Congolese would solve the Lumumba problem themselves. It was really their problem, and I saw no reason to relieve them of their burden.

I followed orders, however, over the next few months keeping the operation to myself and reporting on its progress—or rather, lack of it—via the ultra-secret PROP channel. Fortunately, I had only one non-American agent with potential access to Lumumba's kitchen and living quarters. He was the man who had warned us of the assassination attempts on Mobutu and was by far our best source on Lumumba and his immediate entourage. When I asked if he could gain access to Lumumba's living quarters, he doubted that would be possible. Considering other options, at one point I requested a rifle with a telescopic site, but I don't recall it ever arriving. My plan was to stall, to delay as long as possible in the hope that Lumumba would either fade away politically as a potential danger, or that the Congolese would succeed in taking him prisoner.

While I dragged my feet on the assassination operation, I suspect that Bronson Tweedy, my immediate superior in Headquarters, did the same. Long after we had both retired from the Agency, I discussed PROP with Tweedy. He apologized for having signed off on Bissell's PROP cable to me, and I came away with the strong impression that he had carried on like a good soldier without believing in the assignment.

Back at the station, the operation had an unpleasant side effect in that it strained my relationship with Jeff, my loyal and trusted deputy. He would sometimes come to me to discuss potential operations or recently received intelligence just as I was leaving to attend to some aspect of the PROP operation. This produced a change in our relationship. He resented the fact that I must have appeared to be holding something back, but I could not explain why I seemed to be paying less attention than formerly to matters that were important to him.

In reality, I spent little time on the assassination plan because I was fully engaged in what I considered more important operations. The new government, led by Bomboko, was in place; Kasavubu had been "deneutralized" by Mobutu and was fully functioning once more as president; and the Soviets, Czechs, and Chinese communists had left the country. I was working closely with Mobutu and many of the new ministers, providing them with advice and guidance while obtaining intelligence on their plans and objectives. Only one of them, Justin Bomboko, had had any ministerial experience in government.

Mobutu, Bomboko, and Victor Nendaka, the new director of the *Sûreté Nationale,* formed an informal troika that remained at the center of power in the Congo during the next six years. I had met Nendaka in Brussels where he attended the Round Table Conference in early 1960. He had previously been vice president of Lumumba's wing of the *Movement National Congolais* but had broken with Lumumba before I met him. (The other branch of the MNC was controlled by Albert Kalonji of the South Kasai.) Nendaka visited the American embassy in Brussels and warned a political officer that Lumumba was already working closely with the Soviets. The officer, aware of my future assignment in the Congo, introduced me to Nendaka.

Nendaka was a tribal leader with roots in Orientale province. He ran for parliament but was defeated by Christophe Gbenye, possibly because of his break with Lumumba. He was largely self-taught and had a brilliant mind. His wife once told me that he had astonished her in the early days of their marriage by preferring to stay home and read books rather than go out to dance and drink beer as most of the other young men did. When Mobutu overthrew Lumumba, he failed to name a new head of the *Sûreté*. Nendaka, never one to miss an opportunity, appointed himself as director and thus became a key player in the new regime.

Although he had no experience in intelligence, he proved to be a quick learner. He recognized that American support was essential to the success of the new government and started to cultivate the most important officials in our embassy as I began to focus on him. The result was that we eventually became close friends, and our friendship continued until his death in Brussels in 2002.

Nendaka and I had only one serious disagreement. Early in our relationship, he told me that he expected me to hand over a list of my agents. I replied that I would do no such thing and offered him two options: either working closely together, as we had been, or each of us going our separate way. Nendaka reflected briefly, chose the former, and never raised the issue again.

The new Congolese government was guided by what became known as the Binza Group, named for the hilly district in the suburbs of Leopoldville where most of its members lived. The troika of

Mobutu, Bomboko, and Nendaka were its core, but there were other influential individuals also involved. They included Cyrille Adoula, the labor leader, senator, and later prime minister; Damien Kondolo, deputy commissioner for the interior and one of the few Congolese who had reached a relatively senior level in the colonial civil service; Mario Cardoso, deputy minister of education in Lumumba's government who resigned after only a few weeks in office; and Albert Ndele, the finance commissioner and later governor of the National Bank.

The group operated in many ways, sometimes as a pressure group and sometimes individually. It is difficult to know what was done on an individual basis and what had been cleared with other members of the group, but no major political decisions were taken without its approval. The Binza Group advised Kasavubu, but unofficially it was the power behind the presidency.

One day I saw how it worked. I was in Mobutu's office when Kasavubu called asking Mobutu for his support in a political initiative that he planned to take but was rumored to be opposed by the Binza Group. Mobutu assured the president that he could count on his support. Mobutu casually noted that the president's initiative might run into opposition in the army but insisted he would do his best to prevent another mutiny. Apparently that was enough to put the fear of God into Kasavubu, and he quickly abandoned the project.

Meanwhile, things were not going well for Khrushchev. When he left Moscow to go to the UN General Assembly meeting, his Congo policy appeared to me to be all too successful, but by the time he arrived in New York it was in shreds. No amount of shoe-pounding on his desk could change that. Lumumba had been sidelined and the new Congolese government was firmly in place. As for us, we had won a battle, but the war continued and we began to prepare for the next Soviet offensive.

9

COMMUNICATING WITH OUR FAMILIES was a problem during these early days. The post office had reopened, but mail took an eternity. The problem was partially solved by a group of American ham radio operators who established a regular watch over the single sideband frequency used by the embassy. The radio, an early acquisition from the American military, was often our only means of speedy and reliable contact with Washington. The station did not use it because it was insecure, but it was fine for speaking to family and friends. The operators were truly a great bunch, patching us through by telephone when we gave them the number, and I talked regularly with my parents.

Although I often sent reassuring letters through the Congolese post to my wife and daughter in France, it was a little like placing a letter in a bottle and throwing it into the ocean. Some arrived but many disappeared into a void. When I could find someone going to Brazzaville where the post office functioned in a reliable fashion, I would ask him to mail a letter to my wife and daughter. Unfortunately, I knew my family was watching French television and listening to the radio, both of which played up the more frightening aspects of the Congo story.

In September, I began receiving letters from Colette asking if she and my daughter could join me. I tried to discourage them because the political and security situation remained so unstable. Also, I explained that I was still living in Jeff's house and had not had time to find my own house or apartment. Nevertheless, my wife insisted on coming. As a World War II veteran and *Croix de Guerre* winner, she was not worried about the security situation. I finally went across to Brazzaville and telephoned her because we were not permitted to use embassy phones for private, long-distance calls (French personnel managed the phone and postal systems in Brazzaville, both of which functioned fairly well). I firmly told my wife that it was out of the question for her to come until the political situation was calmer. She listened patiently and then told me to meet the SABENA flight from Brussels on September 28.

Back in Leopoldville, I rented an apartment on Boulevard 30 Juin with a wonderful view of the city. I went on to the *Sacré Coeur* School for Girls where the good sisters assured me that there would be no trouble enrolling Maureen. Needless to say, I dutifully met the SABENA plane in late September and escorted Colette and Maureen to our apartment.

It is generally a mistake for a man to select a house or an apartment without consulting his wife, and I made that mistake. The apartment was not to Colette's liking, and I started looking around for something else. I had a stroke of luck when one of my contacts suggested the house that had previously been the residence of the senior SABENA representative in the Congo. Located on the road that ran parallel to the Congo River, the villa sat in an enormous garden with sweeping lawns, palm trees, and tropical plants. With an entry from two different streets the house was ideal for my work. Agents or contacts could come to the house and enter the study without being seen by others in the house. There were three bedrooms with bathrooms, a large and comfortable salon, a dining room that could easily seat ten, and a veranda running the length of the salon and the dining room. Best of all, there was a large study or office to the right as one entered the foyer. Guests who were already in the salon or dining room could not see anyone entering my study. It was perfect for entertaining, which was also important for my work. The house had another advantage: servants' quarters or *boyerie*, as they were called in the Congo. Thus, we had a place for a live-in servant, a rarity in Leopoldville after the banning of Congolese in the European areas of the city at night following the riots of January 1959.

The house had magnificent views of the river and was in the heart of the most desirable district of Leopoldville. Important for me was the fact that it was only a few minutes' drive from the embassy. I often received cables at night that required immediate action, and in the event of a coup, an army mutiny, or some other unexpected crisis, I was not likely to be cut off from the embassy.

Tim's wife, Julie, accompanied by three daughters, arrived in the Congo shortly after Colette and Maureen. Happily, one daughter was only a few months older than Maureen and the second was about a year younger. They attended the same school as Maureen and were soon the closest of friends. A delightful, outgoing person, Julie visited my office, introduced herself, and said she had a little something for me from Headquarters. Laughing, she fished in her purse and handed me a snub-nosed .38 pistol. It was a small, air weight Smith and Wesson that carried five rounds, a defensive weapon that was easily carried in a belt holster or even a pocket. Normally, CIA officers do not carry weapons, but I gladly accepted it.

My duties seldom brought me into contact with United Nations personnel. I did my best to avoid them, for I realized that the CIA could not afford to be suspected of running operations against an international organization. I had met Ralph Bunche when he visited the American Embassy and at the airport meeting with General Alexander. I was later to meet various UN officials once parties and diplomatic receptions returned to embassy life, but I was fully aware of the need to avoid establishing an operational role with the organization's personnel.

Ambassador Timberlake believed that Bunche, Andrew Cordier, who served briefly as Bunche's replacement, General von Horn, the military commander, and many other UN officials with whom he dealt were competent and fair. However, the character of the UN operation changed dramatically on September 8, 1960, when Rajeshwar Dayal, an Indian diplomat, assumed control of the

United Nations Congo operation as the Secretary-General's personal representative.

Dayal was a thorn in the embassy's side from the moment he arrived until his departure in the spring of 1961. He demonstrated a strong anti-American bias throughout his six-month "reign." I use the word reign intentionally because he seemed to think of himself as a ruling monarch. He had a way of needling Americans, particularly at one-on-one meetings where there were no witnesses. I recall one such incident that sent me through the roof. "Ah, Mr. Devlin," he said. "I so admire America and Americans. You make the very best air-conditioners, the best refrigerators, so many fine machines. If only you would concentrate on making your machines, and let us *ponder* for you."

Dayal carried this anti-American attitude into his work. Though Bunche and Cordier had sometimes adopted positions that the embassy found unacceptable, we always knew that these officials were sincere and that their decisions were not based on personal prejudice. Unfortunately, Dayal appeared to be respected and admired by Hammarskjöld and we wondered if the Secretary-General really knew the man. Perhaps Dayal's influence derived from his reportedly close association with Jawaharlal Nehru, Indian's influential prime minister, and Hammarskjöld believed that he needed to retain India's support for his UN diplomacy. Whatever the reason, Dayal's views often seemed to be based on his prejudices and yet they carried considerable weight with Hammarskjöld, who seemed to rely almost exclusively on his advice insofar as the Congo was concerned. This situation posed serious problems for the embassy, as well as for the new College of Commissioners government.

Dayal did not treat the Congolese any better than he treated the Americans. He was a Brahmin and we believed that his condescension came from his exalted place in the Indian caste system. He seemed to regard the Congolese as untouchables, although some appeared to be less untouchable than others.

Dayal and his wife acted as though they were royalty. During the first year after independence, food was in very short supply. The wives of the embassy officers, including the ambassador's wife, spent long hours every day scouring the markets. Meat, cheese, butter, milk, and many other products were seldom, if ever, available in Leopoldville. The UN established a commissary for its employees, but non-UN employees were not allowed to shop there. When the commissary did not have just what the Dayals wanted for their table, a UN helicopter would fly Mrs. Dayal across the river to Brazzaville where food was much more plentiful. If American wives wished to shop in Brazzaville, they had to wait in long lines to obtain a place in an overcrowded African Queen–like ferry to cross the river. On the rare occasions when Mrs. Dayal visited the local markets, she was guarded by at least two jeeps full of armed UN soldiers. The Dayals' regal airs, not surprisingly, did not endear the couple, or the UN in general, to the Congolese or the diplomatic community.

There was a fair amount of friction between the two groups that, on one occasion, struck close to home. One Sunday afternoon when my wife and I were visiting Jeff and his family, Jeff's eight-year-old daughter, Emily, was hit by a truck while out riding her bicycle. Her hip was shattered and she was in a bad way. Jeff tried without success to locate one of the few medical doctors remaining in Leopoldville before calling the United Nations hospital for help. An ambulance was dispatched and Emily was taken to the hospital.

She waited in pain on the ambulance litter for half an hour before a sleepy Indian doctor appeared. "What's the matter with her?" he asked, breaking into a wide yawn.

"I think her hip is smashed. Maybe her leg is broken, too," Jeff said. "We haven't been able to find a doctor. So we came here to the hospital."

The doctor suddenly woke up. "She's the child of a United Nations employee?" he asked. "You're with the United Nations?"

"No," Jeff said. "American Embassy."

The doctor shrugged. "Only United Nations employees and their dependents are allowed here."

He was either impatient to get back to sleep or he had decided to be as nasty as he possibly could. When we asked for an ambulance to take the child to the Reine Elizabeth Hospital (now Ngaliema Hospital), he refused. Emphatically. When Jeff and I picked up the litter and started to carry her to the hospital, he ordered us to put it down and to return the litter to the ambulance. With that, Jeff and I lost our tempers and Jeff told him to get out of our way before we physically removed him. When the doctor accused us of threatening him, Jeff replied that it was only a statement of fact. With that, the Indian scuttled away and we departed on foot carrying Emily's litter.

Although there was no doctor on duty at the Reine Elizabeth Hospital, we eventually located Doctor William T. Close, a New York surgeon who happened to be in the Congo at the time of the mutiny. Bill Close remained in the Congo for sixteen years, making financial sacrifices and facing extraordinary dangers. One day while operating on a drunken soldier who had accidentally shot himself, the soldier's drunken friends stood in the operating room pointing their guns at Bill and threatening that, if the soldier died, they would kill him. Bill and his wife, Tine, did many wonderful things, saving lives and providing medical help for many Congolese who would otherwise not have received medical care. Many of us in the diplomatic community owe the Close family a great deal for their help and friendship. Emily, Jeff's daughter, was one of his triumphs, for despite Bill's protests that he was not an orthopedic surgeon, he repaired her shattered hip, and she walks today without a limp.

From the moment that Dayal arrived, six days before Mobutu's coup, it was clear that the new UN representative was going to play an active role in Congolese politics. At that time, Lumumba was working hard to woo the leftist African governments. Guinea supported him without reservation; the Moroccan government waffled and sent a delegation to the Congo to assess the situation before reporting to the king; and Egypt made plans to recall its troops. Nkrumah, Ghana's president and perhaps the most influential African leader at that time, warned Hammarskjöld that Ghana would be forced to withdraw its troops if Lumumba were not allowed to use the radio station, which the UN had closed to all political parties. The UN, taking note of these developments, withdrew its troops from the airport and the radio station, thus temporarily appeasing Lumumba.

Although Hammarskjöld had, for all intents and purposes, caved in, the Soviet Union continued to accuse him of acting in the interests of the "imperialists." Meanwhile, Khrushchev was pushing to abolish the position of Secretary-General and replace it with a troika composed of a representative of the Western powers, a representative of the socialist (communist) states, and a representative of the so-called non-aligned nations.

After the coup, the United States remained concerned that Lumumba might find a way to return to power. Although the Soviets were gone, the radical African embassies continued to work actively to restore him to power. Dayal was also making every effort to call parliament into session, hoping for reconciliation between Kasavubu and Lumumba. Reconciliation was impossible, but by supporting that line Dayal placed himself in direct opposition to American policy. We were never sure how long Mobutu could keep the lid on the political pot.

Lumumba remained in the prime minister's residence and offices; however, it was easy for his political supporters to slip in to see him. He was not under house arrest at the time. He was under the protection of the UN. The Congolese wanted to arrest him but could not get past the UN to do so. Similarly, it was easy for Lumumba to leave, for the troops assigned to guard him were generally from countries that supported him and refused to recognize the College of Commissioners' government. Visitors had only to drive into the compound using a UN vehicle.

Lumumba not only could but did leave his residence. On several occasions he appeared in the *cité* , the native quarter that surrounded the residential areas occupied by Belgians and other foreign nationals. Escorted by UN troops, he gave speeches in the cafes and bars, claiming that he would soon return as prime minister.

While Mobutu seemed to be in control, we found it difficult to assess Lumumba's support among the political and tribal leaders. Mobutu had countered Lumumba's popularity in several ways. He had gained considerable popularity himself. Not surprisingly the man in power, particularly if he has the knack of appealing to the crowds, gains a great deal of support. He is also in a position to manipulate the political leadership.

Mobutu also had another trump card. The young university students and graduates he had called to manage the government represented many tribes and regions. That, in turn, had won many supporters for the new government as tribal and regional loyalty played, and continues to play, a major role in African politics. The university graduates, although young, were leaders within their tribal communities because the Congolese generally have a high regard for educated persons. University graduates were members of an extremely small elite group in 1960.

Lumumba was more politically adept than Kasavubu. If parliament were called into session, Lumumba could use bribes, threats, extravagant promises, or blackmail to obtain a majority, especially since the conservative Katanga legislators, who favored Kasavubu, had returned home. Tim and I urged Mobutu and the commissioners to arrest Lumumba. With a legally valid arrest warrant, we believed the UN would allow the Congolese arresting officers to carry out their duties.

The arrest might have worked had Dayal not replaced Cordier at that moment. Dayal refused to accept the commissioners as the legal government of the Congo, and he refused to take many, if any, of the Congolese players seriously. Despite his extremely limited experience in the Congo—less than one month—Dayal argued that the political impasse could not be solved without Lumumba. Our view was the direct opposite: the crisis could not be resolved *with* Lumumba actively involved because he was the main obstacle to a solution.

Hammarskjöld and Dayal did not claim that Lumumba remained the legal prime minister, but they rejected the American view that he had lost his position when Kasavubu dismissed him. The UN, moreover, guaranteed Lumumba's security while at the same time refusing to protect the commissioners, some of whom were attacked and severely beaten by Lumumba's supporters while UN troops looked on. Dayal seemed to be trying to keep Lumumba in the wings, ready to return to the political scene at the appropriate moment. I was truly concerned that, with Dayal's assistance, the pendulum might swing Lumumba's way with the fickle Congolese politicians. In such a case, the Western nations would be out and the Soviets and radical Africans would be in. The Soviets would then be in an even better position to move ahead in trying to gain control of the Congo as a first move to spreading their tentacles across the continent.

With Dayal's rejection of the arrest warrant, the commissioners' government decided to take Lumumba by force. This step, of course, would have resulted in war between the United Nations, which was still protecting Lumumba, and the Congolese government. Tim and I recognized that this would never do, because it would cost the Congolese government the support of the United States and a number of European states.

I spent hours with Mobutu trying to insure that he recognized the seriousness of the situation and that he would not permit his troops to be used in such a way. Tim worked to convince Bomboko not to attack the troops guarding Lumumba, and I also did my best to get this across to Bomboko and as many of the other commissioners as possible. We managed to keep the lid on, but it was a close-run thing.

Dayal went on to add insult to injury in his dealings with the commissioners, many of whom had called upon Belgian technicians they knew from the past to assist them. Just as the African leaders of the former French colonies turned to French technicians and the British were asked to return to their former territories, the Congolese naturally turned to Belgians who were familiar with the country, its people, and the indigenous languages. In many cases they were called back to fill jobs that they had held for years. The

UN tried to provide technicians from other countries but many were totally unsuitable for their designated jobs, professionally inept, unable to speak French, or simply patronizing.

An example was a World Health Organization (WHO) chief for the Congo, a Haitian exile, who believed that there was no need to try to prevent malaria. The Belgians had begun a system in Leopoldville of spraying stagnant ponds with oil and fining people who allowed water to build up in their gardens. The Haitian put an end to this effort, and told me that the only solution was to permit people to catch malaria and then build up a resistance to the disease. This policy resulted in an enormous number of deaths from malaria, particularly among young children.

The UN demanded that the Belgians withdraw all their teachers. Then the UN brought in a number of teachers, though not nearly enough, to replace all the Belgians. In short order, most of these teachers left the Congo. One, a Haitian, remained in the Kasai, and the UN representative of that area, in an effort to put a good face on the problem, gave a welcoming dinner for the man. All senior Kasai ministers were present. The Kasai minister of education gave a welcoming speech, saying that he appreciated the fact that the Haitian had accepted a position so far from home. The Haitian, in responding, said that he felt that he was at home because he had traced his ancestry and was a pure Luba. With that the Kasai minister, who was a Lulua, a tribe in deadly conflict with the Luba, yelled, "*Salaud!*" and tried to choke the Haitian. The UN was forced to hide the man for the night and to smuggle him out of Luluabourg the next morning.

The United Nations, at Dayal's urging, asked Belgium to withdraw its advisers and technicians from Katanga and those serving the new Congolese government. The United States did not recognize the so-called independent state of Katanga and thus did not object to a request that Tshombe be deprived of his Belgian advisers. Such a move could contribute to the unity of the Congo. But the same did not apply to Leopoldville, the seat of the only Congolese government that we recognized. We realized that, if the

Belgians withdrew their technicians from the capital, it would very likely lead to chaos and undermine the economy. The Belgians rejected the UN's request and their advisers and technicians remained in both places.

The friction between the Congolese and Dayal intensified. At the celebrations to commemorate the founding of the UN, Congolese soldiers prevented all but a handful of Congolese officials from attending. Kasavubu, Mobutu, and Bomboko boycotted the ceremonies. A furious Dayal told a group of journalists that Mobutu was an incompetent officer, adding that the army should have been disarmed and retrained after the mutiny. (This was the only policy advocated by Dayal with which I concurred.) He went on to say that the UN would never recognize a military leadership and that he hoped parliament would soon meet. He capped this by asserting that Lumumba remained the head of the legal government of the Congo.

Dayal finally said in anger all the things he had denied or avoided saying in his meetings with Tim and the other Western ambassadors. He confirmed our fears that the UN wanted to restore Lumumba to power. There were rumors that Dayal intended to have the army disarmed. We knew if that happened it would mean civil strife, the end of Mobutu, and the collapse of the commissioners' government. It would also mean the return of the Soviets.

Dayal's outburst was soon followed by a written report to Hammarskjöld in which he reputedly referred to Mobutu's arbitrary assumption of power, claimed that the ANC was the source of lawlessness (partially true in that it was *one* of the sources), and blasted the Belgians for their involvement in Katanga and Leopoldville. Dayal claimed that he had always followed a policy of "strict neutrality," and asserted that the Congo had only two legitimate institutions of government: the chief of state and the parliament.

Tim and I had our hands full trying to prevent the situation from getting even worse with an open break between Dayal and the Congolese government. It may not be clear why the station was engaged in what was essentially a diplomatic initiative that was the responsibility of the embassy. However, there were a number of reasons. First, some of the senior Congolese officials and political authorities had become agents. Second, I had developed a close, personal relationship with other political leaders and was well-placed to talk turkey with them. Third, Tim expected everyone in the embassy to pitch in and do his part as needed.

We faced a difficult problem because many of the Congolese were not much more helpful than Dayal. Prevented from arresting Lumumba, Mobutu ordered his troops into the *cité* to round up Lumumba supporters and to stop the former prime minister and his followers from holding meetings and handing out propaganda. The soldiers, if indeed one may call a bunch of ex-mutineers *soldiers*, did what they did best. They drank, smoked pot, beat and shook down civilians, and stole whatever they could lay their hands on.

Automobiles were a special prize. Stories of car theft became common gossip, and I began to wonder how I would react if they tried to steal mine. The answer was not long in coming.

I was returning home late one night when I was stopped at a roadblock in front of the *Sûreté* building. I had taken the precaution of removing the ignition key from my key ring. As I got out of the car, I slipped the key into the cuff of my pants. The roadblock was manned by only two soldiers, a Mutt and Jeff pair, with the big one well over six feet and the little one hardly taller than his rifle. They jumped into my automobile, clearly with the intention of stealing it, but found no key. I tried to move away, but the big one jumped out of the car and grabbed me. Holding me, he demanded the key. I insisted that I did not have it, that it must be in the car. I even helped them look on the floor but no key. The little soldier went on looking. Still no key. They made me empty my pockets. That brought them a few dollars worth of Congolese francs and half a pack of cigarettes, but no key. The big one held me by the front of my coat and my shirt with one hand and shook me. When that did not produce a key, he pointed his submachine gun at my chest and threatened to shoot me. The little one threatened to take me to Monsieur Nendaka, the head of the *Sûreté*, if I did not give them the key.

Tickled pink, I took the little one by the arm and said in French, "Let's go see Monsieur Nendaka." I started walking rapidly toward Victor Nendaka's house located almost directly across from the *Surêté*, holding the little soldier by the arm all the while.

The other soldier caught up with us near Nendaka's house. He swung at me twice with the butt of his weapon, but I managed to duck both times. At that moment, a man I recognized as someone I had seen around the *Surêté* came out of the house. He realized that there was a problem and asked me if I needed help. I gave him my card and said I wanted to see Nendaka. The big soldier tried to make me shut up, but after a few more questions, the *Surêté* officer, followed by the two soldiers, took me to the house where I was greeted by the houseboy who recognized me as someone who visited his *patron* regularly. The houseboy explained that Nendaka was in conference but offered me a drink while I waited. Once again the tall soldier tried to intervene, but since I was in Nendaka's home I felt surer of myself. I told both soldiers to wait outside and, surprisingly, they obeyed me.

After my problem with the soldiers had been cleared up, Victor offered me a double whiskey. A few minutes later, I heard cries and yells from the two soldiers. Victor smiled. My captors, he explained, were getting a taste of the *chicotte*, a rawhide whip.

*At the Leopoldville Beach, late 1960 or early 1961,
the Chief of Station, Congo.*

Larry Devlin, Captain of the Hoover High School ROTC, Age 17, January 1940.

Sergeant Joseph Walters, Martine Porteret (Colette's sister), Larry Devlin, Colette Porteret, and Captain Albert Lepore in front of the church on our wedding day.

Left to right: Me, "George," visitors from DC, and on the right Jeff, my deputy, 1961.

A Congolese paratroop camp, 1960.

Some Watutsi dancers at a party on my front lawn.

*Ambassador Claire H. "Tim" Timberlake and Mrs. Timberlake,
First Anniversary of Independence Celebration.*

*Me, Frank, Victor Nendaka, and Justin Bomboko,
who were two key allies.*

Left to Right: Foreign Minister Justin Bomboko, Betty Godley,
President Mobutu, Ambassador Mac Godley, Larry Devlin,
Frank, and Surete Chief Victor Nendaka at ambassador's residence.
The lunch was held to restore relations between Mobutu and Godley.

Mobutu. This photograph was presented to me on my last day as Chief of Station. The president had written on it in French: "To my old and excellent friend, L. Devlin, to whom the Congo and its chief owe so much."

The certificate naming me an Officer of the Order of the Leopard. (Members of the order cannot be arrested in Zaire without the approval of the president. Some of the boys in DC wish that Bush had created such an order.)

Larry and Mary at home in front of Larry's Great (4 greats) Grandmother's portrait. Family legend has it that the portrait was done in New York City by Gilbert Stuart in 1810.

At home in Virginia.

With a friend who had just been decorated standing in the entry hall of CIA in front of the monument to those whose sacrifice was much greater than our own.

My daughter Maureen.

Photo of Maureen's Intelligence Star, the CIA medal awarded for valor. It is similar to the military Silver Star. (We were, and perhaps still are, the only father and child team to have received this decoration.)

10

WHILE RELATIONS BETWEEN the United Nations and the Congolese government were degenerating further, I received a message from Bronson Tweedy asking me to agree to the temporary assignment of a senior officer to concentrate on the ultra-secret PROP operation under my direction. The message was couched in the friendliest of terms. Tweedy suggested that my other responsibilities were too heavy to permit the necessary focus on this operation and that I needed somebody who would get the job done.

It was clear, however, that Dick Bissell was dissatisfied with my failure to assassinate Lumumba. I sent in regular progress reports, but Headquarters wanted action. Either I had to get the job done myself or agree to put it into the hands of someone else. I knew that I really did not have the heart for the operation and had no intention of carrying it out. I also knew that I could not do justice to all of my other work and give the PROP operation the time and effort that it required.

I agreed to Headquarters' plan and learned that the person assigned to handle the operation was Justin, an officer several grades senior to me whom I had known casually several years before. When he arrived, we had a frank talk about many important matters. He made it quite clear that he recognized my position as chief of station and agreed that he would work under my direction. He also said he was opposed to assassinating Lumumba. He thought the best solution was to capture him and turn him over to the Congolese government for trial. A third country national agent was about to join him and assist him. I had no need or reason to meet this agent whose brief was to work solely for Justin on the operation.

Justin got down to work immediately, but with concentric rings of troops around Lumumba's residence—UN peacekeepers inside the fence and Congolese soldiers around the entire block—there was little chance of getting close to him.

The night of November 27, 1960, changed the entire political situation in the Congo. During a tremendous thunderstorm, Lumumba slipped through the Congolese lines and set out for Stanleyville. Numerous stories circulated concerning how he managed to escape, but I have never believed it worthwhile to determine which, if any, was correct. One was that he took advantage of the storm and, accompanied by a few followers, drove away in a darkened car while the Congolese and the United Nations troops were seeking cover. Another had it that he escaped dressed in the uniform of a Ghanaian UN soldier with the help of the Ghanaian ambassador.

Just how he managed his escape is of little importance. The fact is that he did get away and, in all likelihood, he received some assistance from the UN peacekeepers assigned to protect him. On the morning of November 28, a Moroccan soldier informed his superiors that a black car had left the compound during the night. It was not until that afternoon that UN troops searched the residence only to find it empty.

I learned from Bomboko of Lumumba's escape, and Bomboko, along with the other commissioners, was greatly concerned. Confusion reigned and no one seemed to be organizing a chase. Of course, no one knew where Lumumba was actually headed but Stanleyville, his political fief, seemed a good bet. He had left a letter in his residence saying that he was going to Stanleyville to attend the funeral of his baby daughter who had been born dead in Switzerland, but we did not know whether that was true or merely intended to throw his pursuers off track.

I met with the commissioner of the interior, Mobutu, and Nendaka to discuss the escape and suggested that they trace the various routes that Lumumba might have taken. If he was trying to reach Stanleyville, he would have to use several river crossings along the way. Since ferries were used for most river crossings in the Congo, setting up checkpoints at those crossings offered the best way to try to catch him.

On November 29, I met with Colonel Louis Marlière, the Belgian army *Force Publique* officer who had done so much during the mutiny to restore order. He was also one of a limited number of Belgian officers who had been popular with the Congolese soldiers. I had heard that he had been the godfather of Mobutu's first son, an action unfavorably viewed by his colleagues. Mobutu had kept him in Leopoldville as an adviser and, not surprisingly, Marlière had matters well in hand. I found him with a book of maps planning where soldiers should be sent to head off Lumumba before he reached Stanleyville.

I had been scheduled, in Rome, to attend a meeting of the chiefs of station working in Africa. In view of Lumumba's escape, however, I sent a cable recommending that I miss the meeting. An immediate reply asked me to come, if only for twenty-four hours, because Dick Bissell wanted to discuss the Congo situation with me. I arrived about six in the evening in Rome where John, a senior administrative officer and an old and esteemed friend, met me. John drove me to the home of Tom Karramessines, a senior CIA officer, where we were joined for dinner by Dick Bissell and Bronson Tweedy. We talked Congo until nearly one in the morning when I left for my hotel, happy to find that they very much appreciated the success of the station's operations and fully supported our efforts. All of my operations were discussed at length with one exception, the PROP operation. Much to my surprise, Bissell did not mention it.

The next day when the chiefs of station meeting broke for lunch, Bissell and Tweedy took me to lunch for two more hours of Congo talk. I made it to the airport just in time to catch my plane. I was settling into my seat when my eye caught the headlines of a news-paper someone in front of me was reading: "LUMUMBA CAP-TURED." We had been so busy talking about the Congo that we had not checked with the embassy or the station for the latest information on Lumumba.

Captain Gilbert Pongo, an army captain, captured Lumumba in Kasai province on his way to Stanleyville. Some Lumumba support-ers claimed that Ghanaian troops refused to assist their leader. The Ghanaian commander, however, requested permission from UN headquarters to rescue Lumumba but General von Horn, the UN military commander, reported that the request was refused, pre-sumably after Dayal had consulted Hammarskjöld in New York. (One can imagine what Dayal's personal recommendation would have been.) The irony is that Lumumba might not have been cap-tured at all had he not spent so much time speaking at public meet-ings along the way. Anicet Kashamura, Lumumba's minister of information, reported that Lumumba spent five hours addressing one public meeting during which he denounced the clergy, the "Western imperialists," Mobutu, and Kasavubu.

Lumumba was returned to Leopoldville by air on December 2, 1960. The Congolese soldiers, as was their unfortunate custom with prisoners, beat him while television and still cameramen cap-tured the scene at the airport. The beating, immortalized on film, aroused the African-Asian group at the UN as well as other nations that had not played a major role in the Congo crisis, and it neatly served the purposes of the Soviets.

My job, however, was not to keep up with debates and diplo-matic maneuvering at the UN; it was to prevent the Soviets from implementing their African policy. Had Lumumba succeeded in reaching Stanleyville, chaos would have returned. He would have declared himself the prime minister of the Congo, and the Soviets, Soviet Bloc countries, Chinese communists, and a number of African and the so-called non-aligned nations would have estab-lished embassies in Stanleyville. The civil war that was to break out and persist in the mid-sixties would have begun in 1960 while Khrushchev was still actively pursuing his African policy.

With the capture of Lumumba, his deputy prime minister, Antoine Gizenga, announced in Stanleyville that he was acting prime minister and head of the only lawful Congo government. While he did not pack Lumumba's political wallop in the international community, this put the cat among the pigeons once again in Washington.

Gizenga managed to gain control of Orientale province, which had long been a Lumumba stronghold. That was bad enough, but worse yet, many of the Congolese soldiers rallied to his side. These units began taking over other areas to such an extent that they gave the Stanleyville Lumumbists a Christmas present. On December 25, some sixty soldiers from the Stanleyville garrison moved south into Kivu, the eastern province, and into its capital, Bukavu, where they captured the provincial president, several of his ministers, and the commander of the Bukavu garrison whose troops preferred to join the attackers rather than fight.

From Bukavu, they moved south along the shores of Lake Tanganyika, gathering additional Congolese troops to their cause until they eventually joined forces with the Balubakats, the political party of the Baluba tribesmen who were Tshombe's main opponents in Katanga. Together, the Baluba and Gizenga's forces occupied Manono, the largest town in northern Katanga and proclaimed it the capital of "North Katanga," which they declared to be a new province. Other Lumumbist troops moved west into the northern reaches of Equateur province. All this happened rather rapidly and, once again, it appeared that Mobutu and his government were likely to fall.

I spent hours pouring over maps and meeting Mobutu, Bomboko, and Nendaka to discuss ways of stopping this new threat to their regime. I submitted several plans to them, but nothing happened. I was not, however, the only one concerned by the rapid expansion of the areas controlled by the Stanleyville forces and the fact that the government troops seldom, if ever, were willing to fight. Colonel Marlière, ever resourceful, developed a plan to recapture Bukavu. The problem was that the Bukavu airport was in Burundi, then held by Belgium as a trust territory.* That problem was effectively skirted when the necessary arrangements were made with the Belgian government, and one hundred loyal Congolese soldiers were flown into Burundi, where the Belgian authorities "expelled" them by truck into the Congo at a point near Bukavu.

However, when the Congolese soldiers arrived, they discovered that the Bukavu garrison had gone over to the Stanleyville forces. So, without further ado, the "valiant" Congolese troops surrendered rather than fight. As 1960 drew to an end, the situation remained unchanged with the Lumumbist forces, led by Gizenga, in control of Orientale province, a small piece of northern Equateur province, and a strip of varying width along the east side of the country running from Orientale down to north Katanga.

The Soviet Union failed to take advantage of the situation, waiting to see what action, if any, the more radical African nations (Ghana, Egypt, Guinea, Morocco, and Mali) would take. The leaders of those countries met in Casablanca to discuss the possibility of aiding Lumumba and Gizenga, but as so often happens when a group of egocentric political leaders gets together, they were unable to agree on a plan of action. As a result, Khrushchev hesitated and the Soviet Union missed an excellent opportunity to obtain a foothold in Africa. The conditions could not have been more favorable. A pro-Soviet rebel government was firmly installed in the east of the country and the anti-Western Dayal was running the United Nations operation in Leopoldville. Although Dayal regarded Gizenga with the same disdain he reserved for almost all

---

*Belgium's legal role in Burundi was that of a trustee. It was supposed to oversee the development of Burundi, but, in reality, Belgium ruled Burundi as it would a colony. Burundi and Rwanda had been German colonies prior to World War I.

Congolese, it is most unlikely that he would have acted to prevent the Soviet Union from supplying technicians, money, and weapons to strengthen the Stanleyville regime.

While we were worrying about that possibility, we had a brief break in our normal schedule. Louis Armstrong, the bandleader and great jazz trumpeter, was touring Africa on behalf of the United States Information Agency (USIA). For reasons that escaped us in the embassy, the USIA decided to have him play in Elisabethville, capital of the so-called Independent State of Katanga, a political entity that our own government did not recognize.

Ambassador Timberlake decided to make the best of a bad situation by attending the concert. The object was to talk to Tshombe, the elected president of the Congolese province of Katanga, without recognizing him as the president of an independent state. Tim assumed Tshombe would welcome an opportunity to meet a senior American official. Tim and Julie asked several of us to accompany them in order to contribute to the charade that we were indeed flying to Elisabethville merely to attend the concert.

While most of our party was assembled at the airport waiting for Lieutenant Colonel Edward Dannemiller, the army attaché, and his wife to arrive along with Frank Carlucci, Tally Palmer, the vice consul, drove into the hangar blowing her horn and screaming, "They are killing Carlucci and the Dannemillers." Stretched across the back seat of her convertible was the warrant officer from Dannemiller's office. He was covered with blood with a knife sticking out of his chest.

On hearing that Carlucci and the Dannemillers were in serious trouble, I threw the classified pouch that I was carrying to my wife for safe keeping. Mike, the temporary duty officer from our station, and I immediately set off in my car to try to help them. Tim, Julie, and my wife remained in the airport hangar at Ndjili to look after the warrant officer who had been stabbed. When Mike and I were stopped at the airport gate by a UN guard who presented arms with his submachine gun, I reached out and snatched it. Mike took off at full speed heading back toward Leopoldville.

In 1960, there was only one village between Limité, a suburb of
Leopoldville, and Ndjili airport. In short order, we found a crowd
throwing rocks at a burning embassy sedan near the village. Assum-
ing that Carlucci or the Dannemillers were still in the car, I fired a
short burst into the air, and when the crowd broke, I ran over to
the burning car, pulled open the doors, and found it empty. Mike
checked the trunk. Also empty. I grabbed a Congolese and asked
where the *mondeles* (white people) had gone. He pointed toward
the village and made a gesture as though he were cutting his throat.

Mike began looking for Carlucci and the Dannemillers on one
side of the highway, and I ran from hut to hut on the other. At the
end of the village I came upon two freshly dug plots, each about six
by three feet. A shovel was resting beside one of them. I thought
for sure Frank Carlucci and Dannemiller or his wife were in those
plots. I asked the man standing near them to dig. Just as he got going, someone from the embassy arrived and told us that the Dannemillers and Carlucci had arrived at the airport. (I never did learn
what those grave-like plots were for.)

When Mike and I got back to the airport, we found a visiting
State Department doctor working on the warrant officer. Carlucci
was bloody from knife wounds, but in less serious condition than
the warrant officer from Dannemiller's office. Finally, we had to
leave for Elisabethville without Carlucci or the Dannemillers.

I later learned that a cyclist had turned directly in front of the
embassy vehicle carrying the Dannemillers and Carlucci. The warrant officer, who was driving, swerved to avoid him, failed, and
skidded to a stop. The law in the Congo, at that time, called for
anyone involved in such an accident to turn himself or herself in at
the nearest police station as rapidly as possible because the Congolese customarily lynched the person driving a car involved in a
fatal accident. Instead, the warrant officer jumped out of the car
and ran to help the cyclist who had been killed instantly.

The first man out of the village happened to be the brother of the
cyclist, and, taking the law into his own hands, he stabbed the warrant officer. Frank Carlucci ran to help the officer while Danne-

miller rushed to get his wife on a bus that had stopped nearby. Carlucci, who had been on the wrestling team at Princeton, succeeded in fighting the man with the knife, getting rather badly cut up in the process, until Bob Heavey, the embassy administrative officer, came by on his way to Ndjili. Heavey leapt out of his car and fought back-to-back with Carlucci until Tally Palmer drove up.

Heavey and Carlucci managed to lift the badly wounded warrant officer into her vehicle, but as the crowd moved in, they were unable to get into her car. They were saved when a Nigerian UN police patrol pulled them out of harm's way. Prior to that awful incident, Heavey had not impressed me, but from then on I held him in high esteem. As for Carlucci, I had always seen him as an extremely competent Foreign Service officer; but he now stood out in my mind as an extremely courageous man. He was a good friend to me in the Congo and now, some forty-six years later, he remains a respected friend. The warrant officer survived after being rushed to a hospital in Leopoldville.

Finally, we climbed aboard the plane and headed for Elisabethville, arriving in time for a late lunch. Tshombe and a delegation of Katangan officials met us at the airport where a band played and cameras were in evidence on all sides. Tshombe clearly wanted to use the ambassador's visit for his own propaganda purposes. From the airport we drove to Tshombe's palace, formerly the residence of the Belgian governor of Katanga province, for lunch. It was a grand affair by African standards. There were a number of Katangan ministers and their wives, several of Tshombe's Belgian military and civilian advisers, and, of course, Louis Armstrong and his wife.

While we were having an aperitif, someone noticed that Louis Armstrong had disappeared. It turned out that he was in front of the residence where a band was playing. Mrs. Armstrong laughed and said that Louis always loved bands, adding that he got his start as a young man playing with street bands in New Orleans.

There were speeches after lunch in which Tim was careful not to say anything that would imply recognition of the Katanga. Tshombe could be addressed as *Monsieur le President* since the United States recognized him as president of Katanga province. After the formalities, Tim, Tshombe, and Godefroid Munongo, the Katangan minister of the interior, withdrew for private discussions.

Unfortunately, nothing worthwhile came out of these talks apart from providing Tim with an understanding of what it was like to deal with the Katangans. While Tim was meeting with Tshombe, I circulated and talked with Colonel Crevecoeur, the Belgian officer who commanded Tshombe's army; Major Weber, a Belgian officer who served as an adviser to Tshombe; and to several Katangan ministers. I did not gather any new intelligence and we already knew that the Belgian officers and senior civilians were either extensions of the Belgian government, *Union Minière*, or both. We also knew that they were completely committed to the cause of an independent Katanga.

After the long lunch and Tim's meeting with Tshombe, we adjourned to our quarters for a siesta before the Louis Armstrong concert. Driving to and from the concert was a show in itself. Tshombe's people had arranged the transportation, and we were paraded through a succession of Elisabethville neighborhoods. The drive was arranged with the intention of giving the impression to the people of Elisabethville that the United States respected Tshombe and that, eventually, we would see the light and recognize an independent Katanga.

Tim admitted afterwards that Tshombe had gained more from our presence than we had from meeting him and his ministers. The concert was sheer joy to those of us who love jazz. Louis was at his best, although judging by the polite but unenthusiastic applause I had the impression that the Africans did not appreciate jazz as much as do Americans and Europeans.

After the show, Tim called us aside with news that there had been a firefight near our homes in Leopoldville. Colonel Kokolo, commander of the Leopoldville garrison, and several members of his staff had been killed at the Ghanaian embassy when the Congolese government tried to force the Ghanaian ambassador to leave the country.

Mobutu, Bomboko, and Nendaka had consulted me several days previously over the problems with the Ghanaian ambassador who was spreading pro-Lumumba propaganda in the *cité* and among the Congolese soldiers. Bomboko, exercising his functions as foreign minister, had asked the ambassador to cease and desist, but the warning went unheeded. When Bomboko sought my advice, I naively suggested that all they had to do was declare the ambassador *persona non grata*, and he would leave the country.

"I've already done that," Bomboko replied.

"And what happened?" I asked.

Bomboko shrugged. "The Ghanaian government just ignored it."

I then suggested they send a special envoy to deliver a letter from President Kasavubu to President Kwame Nkrumah asking the latter to recall his ambassador. They followed my advice but Nkrumah refused to see the Congolese envoy or to accept the letter.

Since Ghana refused to play by the rules of international diplomacy, I recommended that the Congolese have a plane standing by and that they send a group of unarmed officers to the Ghanaian embassy along with a bus or a limousine. If the ambassador continued to refuse to leave, the officers should carry him to the vehicle, drive him to the airport, and put him on a plane to Ghana.

The Congolese followed this scenario to the letter. Colonel Kokolo and his men removed their pistol belts in plain view of the embassy, and, unarmed, went up the steps to the porch and knocked on the embassy door. When it was opened, they were met by a burst of submachine gunfire and were all killed. In response, Mobutu ordered his troops to surround the embassy. But the UN immediately sent in Tunisian troops, the contingent that was closest to Mobutu and the College of Commissioners' government, to defend the embassy. The result was a firefight that went on for most of the night and into the next morning when a cease-fire was finally arranged.

In Elisabethville we knew only the limited amount of information that Rob McIlvaine had been able to cable the ambassador. Tim, Julie, Colette, and I were greatly upset because the Ghana embassy was located less than one hundred yards from our home and it was close to the American residence where our daughter was being cared for by the Timberlakes' nurse. We wanted to leave immediately to return to our children, but it was impossible to fly at night in the Congo. There were no navigational aids and no lights. The pilots told us that we would have to wait until first light. It was a long, anxious night for all of us.

Rob McIlvaine met us at Ndjili airport the next day and assured us that our children were safe. His sixteen-year-old son, Steve, had crawled down the drainage ditches to reach the younger children and serve as their protector. Far from being traumatized by the events of the previous night, Maureen and the Timberlake children were full of stories about the adventure. Maureen later commented that she had felt better once a man—sixteen-year-old Steve—had arrived to protect them. When we returned to our home, we found that a few stray rounds had hit our house and that the back steps were covered with blood where someone had been shot.

THE AMERICAN presidential election in November 1960 captured the interest of the Congolese political intelligentsia, though not the masses. Members of the commissioners' government were particularly interested and Bomboko followed the campaign step by step. On election night, forgetting the six-hour time difference between Leopoldville and Washington, he began calling me early in the evening to find out if I had information on the outcome. Intrigued by Kennedy's youth and dynamism, Bomboko was a strong supporter of the Democratic candidate. Dayal and some of his sycophants within UN headquarters followed the election with equal interest but for different reasons. They were convinced that Kennedy would change America's Congo policy and that he would follow the Dayal line. This indeed turned out to be case when, during the first few months of Kennedy's administration, his advisers sought out Hammarskjöld for information on the Congo and he, in turn, obtained his views from Dayal.

After the election, the president-elect began to announce his cabinet appointees and Tim became worried about his future as well as the future of our Congo policy. When we heard that Chester Bowles had been appointed deputy secretary of state, Tim commented that it did not bode well for either and probably meant the end of his Foreign Service career. He had served under Bowles when the latter was ambassador to India and believed that Bowles had been greatly influenced by India's non-aligned leaders, and was likely to accept Dayal's views hook, line, and sinker. There had also been personal problems. He and the ambassador had had serious differences concerning a young officer in Tim's department who had done everything to convince both Bowles and Tim that he was not meant to be in the Foreign Service. Bowles demanded that Tim give the officer an outstanding fitness report so that it would be easier to pawn him off on another embassy. Tim, an old Foreign Service hand, would not agree to such a plan and became angry as the argument continued. He gave the officer an unsatisfactory fitness report, but unfortunately Tim completely lost his temper and told Bowles that he was nothing but a moral prostitute. It was not the best way to win friends and influence people.

ON RETURNING to Leopoldville after the welcome break in Katanga, I was back at the old game of serving as an adviser to the commissioners' government and monitoring developments in Thysville, a military camp about a hundred miles southwest of the capital where Lumumba was held a prisoner. We learned that he was often out of his jail cell and sometimes even had dinner with the camp officers. I warned my contacts in the government that both the army and the police were likely to mutiny unless immediate action was taken to increase their pay, but to no avail.

When Louis Armstrong held a concert in Leopoldville a few weeks after we returned from Katanga, I had another brief respite and was able to attend the show with my family. To our surprise,

we found that Louis had no plans for dinner after the concert. So
we invited the Armstrongs to dinner that evening, an event that remains one of our fondest memories of our years in the Congo.

Not long after the Armstrong concert, I drove to the airport one
night to meet Bronson Tweedy, who was making a tour of his
African parish. Bronson was one of our more delightful visitors,
and we would always enjoy his visits. That evening I took my wife's
Fiat sports car to pick him up at the airport. When I arrived, I
found Bronson talking with Stewart Alsop, the well-known American journalist and columnist, and his photographer. For a long time
we stood around waiting for the USIA chief, or one of his assistants, to arrive and drive Alsop and the photographer into town, as
they were scheduled to do. But the airport emptied out and it became clear that there would be no one else coming out from the
embassy and, worse yet, no embassy vehicle. Since most international flights arrived in Leopoldville between one and five in the
morning, there were seldom any taxis available and certainly none
that night.

The two abandoned visitors, clutching their bags, gathered hopefully around my little Fiat. We managed to squeeze the baggage into
the car's trunk and in the small seating area behind the driver's seat.
With me driving and Bronson in the passenger seat, the only place
for Alsop and his photographer to sit was on top of the luggage in
the cramped back seat. This meant that their heads were well above
the windshield so that by the time we got to town they were covered with bugs and smashed insects. They took the discomfort with
good grace, and later, in an article on the Congo, Alsop commented
at length on the good job being done by the CIA. Oddly enough,
his references to USIA were shorter and less generous.

11

THE YEAR'S END BROUGHT NO improvement to the political and military situation in the Congo. Lumumba remained a prisoner at Thysville while Gizenga consolidated his position in Stanleyville, and although his forces had not occupied more territory, it seemed likely that they could do so. The Congolese army and the police were still unhappy and demanding pay increases. I reported this problem to Kasavubu, Mobutu, Bomboko, and other members of the government many times, but no one came up with a solution. Or, if they had one, they did not confide in me.

Matters came to a head on January 13, 1961, when the troops at the Thysville camp mutinied again—the same garrison that had mutinied in July. The difference for me was that I was no longer in the Loire Valley listening to the news on a radio in a cozy French bistro. I was in the Congo in the middle of the action with a role to play.

My sources reported that Lumumba had been freed and was stirring up the troops. I went over to see Mobutu in his military headquarters and found him huddling with Bomboko. They looked up grimly when I came in.

"We're flying to Thysville," Mobutu said.

"We? Who?" I asked.

"Well, all of us. Bomboko, Nendaka, Kasavubu . . . and several others in the Binza group."

I was appalled. "That means all the government's key players will be in Thysville. What if you are killed? Or taken prisoner by the mutineers? And what are you going to do when you get there?" I had never heard of such a harebrained scheme.

Bomboko stared out the window while Mobutu talked. "Halfway measures won't do, Larry. Everything is lost if we don't stop this right now."

"But if you fail, your government will be leaderless." I was really working up a sweat, but Mobutu looked his most resolute, stony self.

"It's an all or nothing situation. All or nothing," he repeated. "Each one of us represents a different tribe. We go there, we talk with our tribal brethren, we ask them to shave back their demands, we keep the mutiny from spreading. It's an all or nothing situation."

And so, without further discussion, they departed.

It was a long day for me. Jeff and I continued with our work, but my mind was on Thysville. It was only late in the day that I received telephone calls from Mobutu, Bomboko, and Nendaka, all assuring me that Lumumba was back in prison and that the mutiny was under control.

After this incident, my primary government contacts—Mobutu, Bomboko, and Nendaka—became unreachable. There was always a "good reason" why they could not see me, and I was unable to learn much about how they had managed to restore order. I assumed that they had promised increased salaries to the garrison. Lumumba, I was told, was to be transferred to another prison, but I did not know where. Given my close and friendly relationship with Mobutu, Nendaka, Bomboko, and other members of the government—normally, they were readily accessible—this stonewalling was worrisome and most unusual.

In retrospect, I suspect that they believed that if they told me of their true plans for Lumumba, the United States would demand that he receive humane treatment or even that he be released. It has been suggested in various publications over the years that I was fully aware of the Congolese government's plans for Lumumba. That is untrue. I assumed, particularly after the Thysville mutiny, that the government would seek a permanent solution to the Lumumba problem, but I was never consulted on the matter and never offered advice. It has also been suggested that Lumumba was assassinated to insure that he was no longer on the scene when President Kennedy took office. I never believed this conspiracy theory rumor, and I never heard it from any of my Congolese contacts or agents.

Naturally, I heard many rumors concerning the Thysville mutiny and the subsequent transfer of Lumumba to Katanga, but they were only rumors, not facts. The first hard information came to me from the CIA officer in Elisabethville. He reported that Swedish peacekeeper troops and others at the Elisabethville airport had seen a plane arrive on January 17 and that someone who looked like Lumumba was kicked down the steps and appeared to have been beaten. He and possibly some others were taken into custody by the Katangan authorities.

The first detailed information we obtained about what had happened to Lumumba came from Nendaka shortly after Lumumba was sent to Elisabethville. Nendaka invited Colette and me to dinner at *La Devinière*, one of the better restaurants in town. It was unusual for him to take us out to dinner so he may well have been designated by the Binza group to tell me the story of Lumumba's transfer to Elisabethville.

When the group arrived at Thysville on January 13, Nendaka said, it was touch and go for some time. But after some initial difficulties, order was restored and the troops listened to Kasavubu, Mobutu, Nendaka, and Bomboko. Kasavubu agreed to study the mutineers' demands and, by the time the discussions ended, Lumumba was back in prison.

It was over so quickly that it was almost as though there had never been a mutiny. Still, the government believed it could no longer hold Lumumba a prisoner in Thysville. On January 17, Nendaka; Ferdinand Kazadi, the defense commissioner; Jonas Mukamba, an influential leader of the Balubas but trusted by Lumumba; and some soldiers drove to Thysville. They told Lumumba that he had won and that they had come to take him back to Leopoldville where he would once more become prime minister.

They had a difficult time convincing the soldiers guarding Lumumba to release him, but eventually they consented. The group drove Lumumba to a nearby airstrip where a small Air Brousse (a private, Belgian-owned company) plane was waiting. It took them to Moanda, on the coast, where a DC–4 awaited them. Kazadi, the soldiers, who were all Balubas, and Lumumba boarded the DC–4 for Elisabethville, and Nendaka returned to Leopoldville on the Air Brousse plane. Nendaka did not provide additional information. I suppose I knew why and did not press him. I had long assumed that the Congolese would resolve their own problems, and Nendaka's story confirmed my earlier assumption.

Shortly after Lumumba was sent to Elisabethville, I received a cable from Dave, an Agency officer in the Katangan capital, which ran something like this: "THANKS FOR PATRICE. HAD WE KNOWD HE WAS A COMIN WE'D A BAKED A SNAKE." Dave was just having fun paraphrasing a song that was popular at that time with the line "if I had knowd you was a comin, I'd a baked a cake."

That bit of humor on Dave's part has bedeviled me ever since. When I testified before Senator Church's Select Committee to Study Governmental Operations with Respect to Intelligence Activities in 1975, I was questioned at length concerning the meaning of Dave's message. One of the lawyers questioning me was convinced that the message contained some secret meaning. Since then, many others have searched for some hidden significance, obviously finding it difficult to believe that it was a perfectly innocent attempt at humor. Dave and I entered the CIA at about the same time and worked together on a number of occasions. He was a highly competent officer who enjoyed the respect of his peers and would never have agreed to play the type of games suggested by those who thought there was a deep, dark meaning in his message.

I have been severely criticized for my role in Lumumba's removal from office and his eventual death. I can understand the repugnance that some people will feel when they learn of the PROP operation. I believed then and I believe now that it was an ill-conceived and unnecessary operation, an operation that demonstrated President Eisenhower's lack of a clear understanding of the situation we faced in the Congo in 1960. I am aware that some people believe I should have rejected the order to implement the operation, but I do not regret the way I handled it.

At the time, I realized that a refusal to obey what I believed to be an order from the president would have resulted in my immediate recall. I believed that we were on the right track operationally, and that our successful efforts to remove Lumumba from power had blocked, at least for the time being, a major Soviet Cold War maneuver. On balance, I thought that it was better to play the time-honored bureaucratic game of stall and delay rather than to return to Headquarters and leave the station chief's position open to some unknown officer who might or might not be able to complete the task that we had begun.

For those who think we should not have attempted to remove Lumumba from power, I can say only that I believed that his lack of understanding of world politics and his dalliance with the Soviet Union made him a serious danger to the United States. We were, after all, involved in a major war, albeit a cold one. Had the Soviet Union succeeded in gaining control of a large part of the African continent and its resources, it could have carried us over the thin red line into a hot war.

In a Hot War, one has to kill one's enemies or be defeated. In the Cold War it was much the same, only one had to remove the enemy from a position of power in which he could contribute to the weakening of the United States' role in the world.

A few days after President Kennedy's inauguration on January 20, 1961, I received instructions to return to Headquarters for consultations, and Ambassador Timberlake received similar instructions from the State Department. This time we were able to take an Air France flight out of Brazzaville's airport across the river. Inside the *salon d'honneur* (the VIP lounge), we found the British ambassador and Daphne Park, my counterpart in MI 6, an absolutely charming young woman and one of the best intelligence officers I have ever encountered. While Daphne and I worked separately and did not have any joint operations, we knew each other well and had come to similar conclusions about Dayal, Lumumba, and the Binza group.

We were chatting amiably when Justin Bomboko walked in. As it turned out, we were all five booked on the same flight, and as soon as we were airborne, we were deep into Congolese politics. We were flying in an old Constellation, a piston-engine plane, which meant that we had ample time to talk. When we stopped in Bangui, capital of the Central African Republic, we all got off to stretch our legs. As we walked, I noticed an unusual number of people, whom I assumed were French officials, observing us.

At our next stop in Fort Lamy (now Ndjamena), capital of Chad, I realized that the presence of the British and American ambassadors, together with the British and American station chiefs (I had been revealed to the French services at a previous post, and I had to assume that Daphne was also known to the French), *and* the Congolese foreign minister had aroused French suspicions. Though pure coincidence brought us all together on the same flight, I was sure that the French security services would devote considerable time to puzzling out why the British and Americans were traveling with Bomboko. They would almost certainly conclude that we were trying to mount some sort of joint operation involving the foreign minister. Also, they would likely assume that it was an urgent matter since we had risked taking the same Air France flight through territory where their security services still pulled the strings. Later, Daphne and I had a good laugh because we knew if we had been in their place, having seen what they saw, we would have sweated over the meaning of such a group of traveling companions.

In Washington, it seemed clear that the new president believed that the Eisenhower administration had lacked imagination in its handling of the newly independent African countries and other members of the non-aligned group of nations. But we soon learned that President Kennedy did not have fixed views on the Congo problem or a plan in place when he took office. He merely believed a better policy could be found. Kennedy and his advisers apparently thought they could woo African leaders such as Nkrumah, Sekou Toure, Nasser, Lumumba (presumably), and other radical figures in the Third World to our side in our struggle with the Soviet Union. Time would demonstrate that strategy to be wrong.

My time in Washington began with reviews of the operational situation in the Congo. I had meetings with Director Dulles, Dick Bissell, Bronson Tweedy, officers of the Africa Division, and other officials who had an interest in the Congo. Evenings were spent with my parents.

When I reached Headquarters the day after my arrival, I learned that there was to be a joint meeting with a friendly foreign intelligence service to discuss the Congo and, presumably, to insure that both services were working toward the same objective. When the meeting was held a few days later, Tweedy, one or two of his staff officers, and I represented the Agency. I recall the meeting well, not because any great decisions were reached, but because of how it evolved. In the morning, CIA representatives sat on one side of the table and the foreign intelligence service on the other. As the meeting progressed, the views expressed by the two Congo-based station chiefs were almost identical while those of the headquarters officers of both services were similar but somewhat at odds with the way those of us resident in the Congo saw things.

The differences were not major but they nonetheless worried me and, as I learned during the lunch break, they worried the other station chief as well. When we met in the afternoon, we two station chiefs seated ourselves on one side of the table and the two headquarters teams sat on the other side. We teamed up to hammer home our views and we finally prevailed. Although the other station chief now lives in Europe and I live in the United States, we chat regularly by phone, and we often chuckle over the day we joined forces against our seniors from headquarters.

During my consultation in Washington, Dick Bissell asked me to accompany him to a meeting of senior officers from all branches of government with an interest in the Congo. Neither Bissell nor the director had chosen to brief me concerning President Kennedy's desire to develop a new and different Congo policy, though I had seen newspaper reports to that effect since my return to the United States. I cannot believe, however, that Allen Dulles and Dick Bissell were not aware that major changes were in the wind.

From what I could gather there were two main factions competing for Kennedy's approval: the liberals and the hard-liners. The liberals were pushing for major policy changes in the Congo such as reconvening parliament and the formation of a broadly based government representing all major parties, to include Lumumba himself or at least his representatives. Without these changes the liberals believed that the UN operation in the Congo might well collapse, in which case a civil war would break out and the Soviets would have a perfect opportunity to intervene and restore Lumumba to power.

The hard-liners, on the other hand, opposed any step that might restore Lumumba to power. They argued that the support of many African and other non-aligned leaders was not worth the political cost. They also maintained that Kasavubu should be given more time to form an anti-Lumumba coalition to replace the commissioners' government created by Mobutu. Harlan Cleveland, the new assistant secretary of state for international affairs, assigned Joe Sisco, his deputy, the task of preparing a draft policy paper, one that, unfortunately from the station's viewpoint, included many of the positions espoused by the liberals. While many of us close to the realities of the Congo suspected that Lumumba might already be dead, the policy argument continued on the assumption that he was alive and waiting to return to power.

Driving to the State Department where the meeting was to be held, Bissell told me that, if I disagreed with anything that was discussed at the meeting, I should not hesitate to speak up. In retrospect, I suspect Dick wanted me to make the criticisms that he believed needed to be made.

I did not have an opportunity to speak to Tim, who was seated on the far side and at the other end of the table, before the meeting started. There were probably twenty or more persons, almost none of whom I recognized, seated around the conference table. I found myself between Bissell and Edward R. Murrow, then the director of USIA. I was delighted to meet Murrow, for his radio broadcasts from Vienna, Prague, and London prior to and during World War II had stimulated my interest in foreign affairs. He had become something of a hero to me at that time, and he became even more of a hero when he became one of the first persons of note, if not the first, to face down Senator McCarthy in the 1950s.

G. Mennen "Soapy" Williams, a former governor of Michigan and one of the early Democratic contenders for the presidency in 1960, was the new assistant secretary of state for Africa and he chaired the meeting. Harlan Cleveland sat next to him with a telephone at hand. Neither Governor Harriman, the ex-governor of New York, and former ambassador to Moscow and London, nor Adlai Stevenson, the former Democratic presidential candidate and the new ambassador to the United Nations, was present. Since no one was introduced, I have no idea whether other officials, who were working with Harlan Cleveland and Soapy Williams to develop a new Congo policy, were present. The meeting began with a number of people asking Williams questions, mostly about the political situation in the Congo. The questions could have been answered easily by Tim or anyone else who followed the Congo on a regular basis. But, when Williams did not have an answer, Cleveland would pick up the phone and call the U.S. Mission to the UN in New York to obtain an answer from the Secretary-General or one of his aides

The replies that came back were obviously based on Dayal's opinions and reports. After the third time that Cleveland picked up the phone to get an answer from the secretary-general, I couldn't stand it any longer. I spoke up and pointed out that the United States ambassador to the Congo was present and could answer their questions. After that, Tim was given a limited opportunity to express his views on most of the points raised, but Cleveland continued to obtain all too many of Dayal's opinions from the American delegation.

The meeting dragged on with a hodgepodge of ill-advised decisions based to a large extent on Dayal's assessment advocating a broadening of the Congolese government to include Lumumba, Gizenga, and other radicals. When it was over, I put on my coat and joined Tim to review the damage over a couple of scotches at a small bar across Virginia Avenue that had, in the past, provided solace to many Foreign Service officers. After reviewing each point with which we disagreed and cursing our inability to influence the direction of the new policy, I suggested one last resort: Director Dulles.

I borrowed a dime from Tim and, using the bar's pay phone, called the director. I told him of our concern and said that Tim and I would like to talk to him. It was already well after seven, but he told us to come straight around to his office.

Dulles received us as though we were old friends. Working as a team, Tim and I reported in detail the decisions of the meeting, and our concern that the new policy would result in a major Cold War defeat in Africa. Dulles listened attentively, asking questions from time to time. When we had finished, he said that he agreed with us and would do his best to convince the appropriate authorities that the projected changes would not be in the best interest of the United States.

With that, he buzzed for his secretary and told her to put in calls to General Lemnitzer, the chief of the joint chiefs of staff; Soapy Williams; the deputy secretary of defense; the deputy secretary of state; and Dean Rusk, the secretary of state, and to wait five minutes between each call. When General Lemnitzer came on the line, Dulles told him that, while the CIA did not become involved in policy decisions, there were serious intelligence *and* military considerations involved in changing the Congo policy. He briefly summarized the arguments that Tim and I had outlined, but did not cite his sources. After five minutes, he spoke to Soapy Williams, repeating almost word for word his statements to General Lemnitzer.

He next spoke with the deputy secretary of defense, again repeating his desire to insure that the intelligence and military ramifications of the new policy were considered.

Before the next five-minute period had elapsed, the director received a call from Dean Rusk. Obviously, the director's concern had made the rounds, just as he had intended. Nonetheless, the new Congo policy was approved. However, it fell between two stools. It was too radical for our NATO allies, particularly Belgium, and not sufficiently radical for the left-wing African states and India. Some governments insisted that Lumumba must be released before they would agree to anything else, and much to the surprise of the liberals, even Hammarskjöld found the new policy inadequate.

Within days, however, the debate was overtaken by events in the Congo. During the first week in February 1961 President Kasavubu announced that he had named a new government, headed by Joseph Ileo, to replace Mobutu's commissioners' government. Happily, Bomboko remained foreign minister and, not surprisingly, Mobutu and Nendaka retained their posts. Kasavubu was probably afraid that the U.S. was planning to support a broad coalition to replace the commissioners' government. Shortly afterwards, news came from Katanga that Lumumba had escaped.

Few, if any, believed the story of Lumumba's escape. The CIA representative in Elisabethville reported that several versions of Lumumba's death were circulating in the Katangan capital, adding that no reliable account was available. Rob McIlvaine, the *chargé d'affaires* in Tim's absence, reported that the story of Lumumba's escape was also viewed with skepticism in Leopoldville. Three days later, after Tim and I had returned to Leopoldville, the Katangans reported that Lumumba had been captured and killed by villagers. Once again, no one believed the story but, equally, no one could prove it otherwise.

Lumumba's death neither resolved the political and military conflicts in the Congo nor the differences between the embassy and the liberals in the State Department and the U.S. Mission to the UN.

After the public announcement of Lumumba's death, Leopoldville remained calm, and there were no reports of disturbances elsewhere in the Congo. Gizenga declared a state of mourning in areas controlled by the Stanleyville forces but there were no demonstrations.

When Headquarters asked why all was quiet, I responded that, in the Congo, nothing succeeds like success and nothing fails like failure. Lumumba had lost the game insofar as most Congolese were concerned, and they turned elsewhere for leadership. Gizenga and his allies used Lumumba's name to advance their own objectives by depicting him as a martyr, but the average Congolese went about his business trying to feed his family and survive.

In Moscow and elsewhere in the Soviet Bloc, Lumumba's death quickly became a *cause célèbre*. There were the usual carefully staged, "spontaneous" demonstrations and propaganda campaigns aimed at the United States, its NATO allies, particularly, Belgium, and Hammarskjöld. Friendship University in Moscow, a school that the Soviets had created to propagandize African and Asian students, was renamed Lumumba University. Communist parties in the West followed orders and organized similar but considerably smaller demonstrations. As Madeline Kalb noted in her book, *Congo Cables*, one might say that Lumumba's martyrdom carried a "Made in Moscow" mark. Nonetheless, these events complicated the station's efforts to avoid a civil war in the Congo and to maintain a government friendly toward the United States.

Our primary responsibility was to provide the United States government with intelligence and to monitor and counter the operations of the Soviets, or any other country or foreign organization whose objectives were inimical to ours. The Soviets used the death of Lumumba as an excuse to multiply their attacks on Hammarskjöld. We naturally assumed their objective was part of a continuing effort to gain support for their troika proposal that would have the United Nations controlled by three secretaries-general: one representing the Western nations, another for the so-called socialist bloc, and the third for the non-aligned states. Such an organizational arrangement would surely have destroyed the United Nations. The Soviet idea was to drive a wedge between the Third World nations and the United States.

The Kennedy administration had come into office hoping to improve Soviet-American relations, particularly those related to the Congo, but the Soviet attack on the United Nations operation there and the Secretary-General changed its tune. President Kennedy warned others against unilateral intervention in the Congo. He did not specifically refer to the Soviet Union but the target of his remarks was obvious, and it met with the Congolese leaders' full approval.

In late February 1961, Ambassador Stevenson pointed out that Khrushchev was attacking the Secretary-General and the United Nations mission because they blocked Soviet efforts to penetrate—and control—Africa, something we had discerned shortly after the Congo's independence but was not always fully appreciated in official circles in Washington and at the United Nations. Had the Congo not turned to the UN for help, the Soviet Union might well have succeeded in its efforts to gain influence in the Congo and eventually in other areas of Africa. The presence of the large UN peacekeeping force made it difficult for the USSR to justify sending men, money, and arms to the Congo. That, in turn, frustrated the Soviets and appeared to convince them that a way must be found to sabotage the UN, and what better way than to replace the Secretary-General with a troika.

About that time, the deep cover agent who worked with Pierre Mulele and who had warned us of the various plans to assassinate Mobutu received word that Mulele wanted him in Stanleyville. Needing to respond immediately to Mulele, he had no time to activate the signal plan for an emergency meeting with us, so he came to my house late at night. I had just returned home and was in the living room when he tapped on the window. Surprised, I took him into my study with its curtained windows. He started to tell me about Mulele's summons when I heard vehicles pulling into the driveway followed by commands in Lingala and the sound of military boots on the porch. My agent turned almost gray, sure that he was about to be shot.

"Here, quickly," I said. "Get down under my desk. Crouch down in the kneehole and wait until I come back."

I hurried to the door and found Mobutu waiting. Two jeeps full of soldiers were in the driveway. He greeted me in his usual friendly manner, said he had seen the lights in my house, and stopped to say hello. I invited him into the living room, poured him a drink, and chatted for a few minutes before excusing myself.

"Rest easy," I whispered to the agent. "And stay under the desk. All is well."

It was a beautiful, balmy evening, full of the night sounds of the tropics, the croaking of bullfrogs, the sighing of the heavy fronds of the palm trees. I was puzzled. A visit from Mobutu at that time of night was most unusual because he did not enjoy late nights and was generally up and about by five in the morning. But, as it turned out, he chose this particular night to follow an impulse for a bit of relaxation over a drink with a good friend. But I was much relieved when he left.

I hurried to my office and rescued the agent from underneath the desk. We agreed that he should join Mulele in Stanleyville. The problem was getting there without being arrested when he left Leopoldville. We finally decided that it would be safer for him to bribe a fisherman to take him across the Congo by pirogue to Brazzaville, rather than to risk crossing the river by ferry with police checks on either side. We assumed that a warrant had been issued for his arrest, but it seemed better not to confirm this the hard way. Once in Brazzaville, he could safely make his way to Stanleyville.

Not long after reaching Stanleyville, this agent pulled off a coup, which so amused Allen Dulles that he gleefully regaled the National Security Council with the story. The agent, while working for Mulele and the other Lumumbist leaders, was used as a contact with the Soviets. On one occasion, he actually accompanied a

Congolese rebel leader to Moscow, and we had to arrange a communications system that he could activate when out of the Congo.

After he left Moscow, he contacted us to report that the Congolese with whom he was traveling had received $500,000 in cash from the Soviets, presumably the KGB, for Gizenga and his allies in Stanleyville. He told us the color of the suitcase containing the money and provided us with the man's return travel plans. When Headquarters learned that the Congolese was to travel via Khartoum, it told the Sudan representative that he would be coming through and instructed him to do everything possible to intercept the money.

Our representative used his excellent Sudanese contacts to have the courier paged when he landed at Khartoum airport. He was told to report immediately to Customs. A CIA officer, who was in the airport lounge, watched as the Congolese left the suitcase containing the money behind a chair and went off to Customs carrying his other bag. The officer picked up the suitcase, jumped in his car, and drove back to his office. Dulles was enchanted by the operation and awarded the case officer a five-hundred-dollar bonus. The director was less enchanted, however, when he learned that the CIA was unable to keep the Soviets' cash because the law required it to be handed over to the United States Treasury. Nonetheless, when in secure company, Dulles happily dined out on the story.

12

MY WIFE AND I GENERALLY GAVE a dinner for ten or twelve people once or twice a week. It was a way to maintain social contact with those I had recruited or who were collaborators, and the dinners provided an opportunity to assess potential agents who I was developing. We rarely gave a dinner that was not operationally oriented.

Mobutu, Bomboko, and Nendaka were our most frequent guests, and it was business for them as well since they invariably accepted for themselves and regretted for their wives. Mobutu—early to bed and early to rise at that period of his life—always arrived on time and managed to leave fairly early. He was an ideal guest, extremely personable, invariably polite, and a treasure trove of interesting stories.

Bomboko, on the other hand, was a wild card for dinner parties. He was one of the most charming and intelligent men I have ever met, full of stories—humorous or serious—always ready to comment on political developments in the Congo or abroad, and a great source of information on tribalism. He was also a notorious ladies' man about town. My wife learned never to serve a soufflé when Bomboko was to be a guest, for we never knew when, or if, he would arrive. If he did turn up, the only sure thing was that he would be late.

After several dinners delayed by Bomboko's tardiness, Colette made it clear that the meal would begin promptly at nine. Monsieur Bomboko would be welcome at any time, but he would have to sit down and eat whatever course was being served. Bomboko, always the gentleman and always gracious, assured her that this procedure would be just fine.

Over the 1961 Easter holidays, I took my family to visit Luanda, the capital of Angola and then under Portuguese control, where we feasted on all the fine seafood and shellfish that was unobtainable in Leopoldville. Several American families from the embassy applied for visas to visit Luanda during the holidays, but strangely my wife, daughter, and I were the only ones to get them. The Portuguese were quite resentful, understandably, over American criticism of their colonial policy. I was surprised at being given the visas and wondered if the Portuguese security service had identified me. A few days after having been told that my visa requests had been granted, I ran into the man I suspected of being my Portuguese counterpart. After a brief conversation, I casually asked how I happened to have obtained a visa when all the other Americans were refused.

"Because you are a nice spy," he replied. "You are the only American who has invited me to his house for dinner, and the only one who has not lectured me on how we handle our colonies."

"But I thought all visas had to be approved in Lisbon," I said.

"True," he said, "but my clerk erred and failed to send your request to Lisbon before issuing the visa. Needless to say, he has been severely reprimanded."

Before we parted, he said: "Just between the two of us, I hope you are really going on a vacation because you will be under surveillance."

With that surprising comment, he jumped in his car and left me wondering why the warning. In any case, he was right. We were placed under surveillance when we arrived at the airport in Luanda and held under surveillance for our entire stay. It was really quite obvious. I was not disturbed by this, as we were truly on vacation, but I have often wondered just why we received visas when the others were refused, and why I was warned that we would be under

surveillance. At first I thought my Portuguese friend might be trying to tell me that he was recruitable, but when I followed up on
that possibility, it became clear that was not the case.

Before leaving Luanda, I arranged to have several lobsters frozen
and packed with ice to take home with us. Shortly after our return,
we invited Bomboko and Mobutu and some other guests over for a
lobster dinner. Colette taught our cook to make *langouste à l'amoricaine* with a particularly spicy sauce. Although everyone knew that
Mobutu was the power behind the government, we followed the
protocol of placing Bomboko at my wife's right and Mobutu at her
left. Mobutu was, as usual, punctual, and Bomboko was, as usual,
late. When nine o'clock arrived, Colette suggested that we go to
the table since Monsieur Bomboko had undoubtedly been delayed
by affairs of state and would no doubt join us during the course of
the dinner. Mobutu found the lobster excellent and had two or
three helpings. Bomboko arrived just as we were starting the next
course, and Mobutu, who knew the secret of Colette's decision to
begin the dinner at nine, teased Bomboko and told him that he had
missed a delicious first course.

Bomboko turned to Colette. "I assume, Madame," he said without batting an eyelid, "that there's still some lobster in the kitchen."

"Of course," she said. "Tomorrow's lunch."

I must confess I felt a little sorry for Bomboko, who loved good
food almost as much as he loved the ladies. Bomboko, however, was
a good sport and played the game by picking up the dinner where
he found it. But the following day, he showed up for lunch, right
on time, with a wide grin on his handsome face, and shared the
spicy and tasty *langouste à l'amoricaine* with us.

Of all my contacts, I enjoyed my time with Mobutu, Bomboko,
and Nendaka the most. They all had excellent minds and were
quick to grasp the political implications of a problem. I realized that
their relationship with me was as much business-related as it was on
my side, but over time we also established real friendships, which I
cherished. I was deeply concerned that the United States might,
under certain circumstances, sacrifice them in an effort to establish

a better relationship with the radical Africans and the non-aligned nations. However, while I was concerned for them, I never allowed myself to forget that I was in the Congo to implement American policy. As with all my contacts—many were not agents but rather sympathetic collaborators—I had to reassure them that their alignment with the United States was in the best interests of their country. The constant meetings, the political and security crises, and the personal problems that many shared with me were fatiguing. But I loved my work and believed that I was making a contribution to the American Cold War effort.

But during that time, we had more crises in the Congo than we had enjoyable dinners. A critical turning point came on February 21, 1961, when the UN passed its toughest resolution on the Congo to date. Its key provision called on the UN forces in the Congo to immediately take all appropriate measures to prevent the occurrence of civil war in the Congo, including arrangements for cease-fires, the halting of all military operations, the prevention of clashes, and "the use of force, if necessary, in the last resort." It also urged the "immediate removal" of all Belgian and other foreign paramilitary personnel and political advisers not under command of the UN.

Kasavubu reacted by turning up the political heat in a radio broadcast in which he sharply criticized the UN operation, specifically singling out Dayal and urging his recall. Kasavubu went on to urge the Congolese people to mobilize to prevent a UN takeover. The perceived threat from the UN also alarmed the governments of the breakaway provinces of Katanga and South Kasai, so much so that their leaders, Moise Tshombe and Albert Kalonji, agreed to meet Prime Minister Joseph Ileo in Elisabethville. All three feared that Dayal would try to disarm their armies, capture and deport their Belgian advisers, and impose a government headed by Antoine Gizenga and the Stanleyville Lumumbists. Ignoring the fact that both Katanga and the South Kasai had declared their independence from the Congo, the three leaders agreed to combine their armies in a military pact directed against communist threats and UN tutelage. They also promised to meet in Tananarive, Madagascar, for a summit meeting on March 5 to discuss the Congo's constitution and invited Gizenga to join them. Much to their relief, Gizenga ignored the invitation.

The UN resolution worried the embassy and the station almost as much as it did the Congolese. Although we liked Soapy Williams personally, neither the ambassador nor I had much faith in his understanding of Africa in general or of the Congo in particular. I had been a great admirer of Adlai Stevenson when he ran for president, but my experience in the Congo made me question Ambassador Stevenson's grasp of the African problems posed by the Cold War.

Tim and I shared the view that the Soviets and the radical African states hoped to use the UN to impose a Gizenga-led government on the Congo. Following Lumumba's death, the Soviet Bloc, communist China, several African countries, and Cuba had recognized the Gizenga regime in Stanleyville. It appeared to us that the Soviets' first objective was to convince the UN that the Kasavubu government and the Gizenga regime were rival governments of equal stature. We were sure that Dayal already took that position and probably favored Gizenga over Kasavubu.

We later learned that President Kennedy shared our views of Dayal. He realized that the man was unable to get along with the Congolese and that they mistrusted him. Thus, some time in early March 1961 he ordered the State Department to do its best to have Dayal replaced. Needless to say, the Congolese were not aware of this request.

Ileo and most of his key ministers flew off to Madagascar for the summit meeting with Tshombe and Kalonji, leaving Bomboko, who was hospitalized with an appendectomy, in charge. We had long feared a clash between the Congolese and UN troops and the violence, when it came, exploded in Banana, a small seaport near Matadi. In the battle, the Sudanese peacekeeping troops were greatly outnumbered and had only small arms in the face of the Congolese artillery. The fighting continued for two days and spread to involve other UN Sudanese troops stationed in Matadi. I found myself constantly running back and forth between Bomboko in Reine Elizabeth Hospital and the embassy. Tim passed on Bomboko's comments and demands to Dayal. On my first visit to the hospital, I found that the guard at Bomboko's hospital room was the tall soldier who had tried to steal my car and was punished by Nendaka. I wondered if he would try to get even, but each time I entered or left Bomboko's room he snapped to attention. Much to my relief, I never met him when he was off duty.

Bomboko could only contact the military in Banana and Matadi by telephone and that, in itself, was quite a feat because the Congolese phone system was deteriorating daily. I remember pointing out to Bomboko that if artillery were used in Matadi, the port installations, on which Leopoldville depended for the importation of food, fuel, and all other necessities, might be seriously damaged. More important, I warned Bomboko that if the battle got out of hand Dayal could call in additional UN troops. The result might be the implementation of the clause in the recent resolution authorizing the use of force, if necessary, to disarm the Congolese military forces. Finally, I reminded Bomboko that it was extremely important to maintain the friendship of Sudan. I wanted to keep the Soviets from obtaining approval to send military supplies through Sudan or from over-flying Sudan from Egypt, one of the countries that had recognized the Gizenga regime in Stanleyville.

Bomboko understood the need for a rapid and peaceful solution, but he was under pressure from the Congolese military to maintain a hard line. He did not control the military so he had no alternative but to negotiate with them. Also, Bomboko disliked Dayal, who treated him like an errant schoolboy, and he found it difficult to accede to Dayal's demands. However, news that Dayal was being recalled to New York for talks with the secretary-general went a long way toward helping us work out a solution that ended the fighting on the second day.

I was able to tell Bomboko that Mekki Abbas, a Sudanese diplomat, had arrived to take over the UN operation while Dayal was in

New York. Abbas, being Sudanese, played a constructive part in the Congolese decision to end the fighting. The Sudanese troops first withdrew from the positions that had originally provoked the Congolese army to attack them and then, the Sudanese government, furious at its troops being attacked, withdrew all its troops from the Congo.

The departure of Dayal and the selection of Abbas as acting chief of the United Nations mission brought a complete change in the atmosphere. He was a fellow African and far more understanding than Dayal. He was easily accessible and was not plagued by the prejudices of a caste system. Tim, his Western diplomatic colleagues, and the Congolese government were delighted by the change, temporary though it turned out to be.

Dayal's consultations in New York dragged on and on, presumably because of Hammarskjöld's insistence or, at the very least, because of American pressure. When press reports suggested that Dayal was about to return to Leopoldville, Adlai Stevenson intervened with a strong protest, reminding Hammarskjöld that President Kennedy was opposed to Dayal's continued tenure in the Congo.

Hammarskjöld's views on most Congo problems, however, continued to be based on Dayal's reporting. The Secretary-General claimed he could not afford to offend India's Nehru, who reputedly held Dayal in high esteem, since the Congo mission needed additional Indian troops to replace those that had been recalled by the African states that had recognized the Gizenga regime in Stanleyville. Hammarskjöld also insisted that Western demands for Dayal's recall made it more difficult for him to implement a change because he did not want to appear to be appeasing or favoring the Western countries.

Hammarskjöld did admit, however, that Dayal had failed to get along with the Congolese and that he had antagonized all the Western ambassadors. Hammarskjöld appeared to be studying the situation to determine if he could risk upsetting the United States by returning Dayal to Leopoldville, and if he did not, what he could obtain in return for recalling his envoy.

What that sacrifice was going to be was revealed in a short item in the "Periscope" section of *Newsweek* magazine. The Timberlakes would not be returning to the Congo after their home leave in June 1961. While Dayal was the wrong man in the wrong job at the wrong time, Ambassador Timberlake was the right man in the right place at the right time. In just under a year, with the support of his wife Julie, he had accomplished more than anyone in Washington, where his good work was never fully appreciated, had a right to expect. Tim knew this and it made the fact that he was being sold down the river all the more difficult to accept. He could have played the Washington game. He could have testified before Congress that he fully supported the new policy favored by Soapy Williams, Chester Bowles, and company. He could have modified his cables in such a way as to tell Soapy and Bowles and Stevenson what they wanted to hear, but he was too honest to prostitute himself. Ironically, American policy was already swinging back in Tim's direction before he left Leopoldville, but the deal whereby we gave the Secretary-General Tim's head in return for that of Dayal had already been struck.

All of us involved in trying to keep the lid on the Congo's political cauldron ran into complications caused, entirely too often, by the State Department and the U.S. Mission to the UN working at cross-purposes with our embassy. Some senior officials in the State Department seemed to believe that Kasavubu, Mobutu, Bomboko, and several other Congolese officials who cooperated with me were controlled agents prepared to act on my orders. Since Dayal could not bring himself to work with the commissioners' government headed by Bomboko, the State Department began as early as mid-October 1960 making plans for us to replace Bomboko with Ileo. Washington apparently thought that the United States could decide who should be the next prime minister. Even though we worked closely with Mobutu and indirectly with Kasavubu, neither of them was prepared to jump through the hoop at our command, but the State Department sometimes failed to understand this situation.

The U.S. Mission to the UN, for its part, could not understand why it could not deal with a parliamentary democracy, which would necessitate the recalling of parliament. In Leopoldville, we felt that the great majority of Congolese had an extremely limited understanding of the democratic process and that recalling parliament would thus not *ipso facto* restore democracy. The most urgent need was peace and a government that would encourage the return of businessmen who would provide jobs. We understood, of course, that outside political pressures would sooner or later require parliament to meet. Although not elected, the commissioners provided what may well have been one of the Congo's best governments to date, but it was always meant to be a bridging mechanism, not a permanent institution.

After Lumumba's death, our efforts were directed toward neutralizing Gizenga, Mulele, Kashamura, and the other Lumumbist leaders who had gone to Stanleyville. We believed then, and I still believe, that their return to power would have opened the way to Soviet influence and possible domination of the Congo and other African countries. Our government certainly understood the broad implications of the Cold War, but it often seemed to lack a clear understanding of the tactical details that confronted people like those of us on the front line.

Washington spent an inordinate amount of time worrying about the reaction of the African radicals and the non-aligned group of nations. Despite all the hand wringing and "what will the Africans think?" our diplomats found, to their surprise, that these countries actually accepted the fact that the United States would not always follow their lead. They understood the realities of the situation in that the United States was a great power whose aid programs were essential to them.

At times, Kasavubu and Ileo, as well as some of our close friends in the Congolese government, took steps that, in our opinion, were not in their best interests. At the Madagascar conference, Tshombe had persuaded the others that the Congo should have a loose federal structure that ensured Katanga's autonomy but gave no guarantees that his province would resume paying mineral royalties to the central government. Kasavubu was not happy about this, and on his return to Leopoldville he signed an agreement with the UN, accepting the February 21 resolution and committing his government to help carry it out—something Tshombe had strongly opposed at the Madagascar conference.

Another meeting to resolve their differences was held in Coquilhatville, a river town in Equateur province, generally known as "Coq" and now Mbandaka, on April 24, 1961. (Coquilhatville was Bomboko's political base, and there is little doubt that he selected it as the venue.) The four main political groups were invited: Kalonji of the South Kasai, Tshombe of Katanga, Gizenga representing the Lumumbists, and the Leopoldville government. All the leaders turned up except Gizenga, who sent a delegation of soldiers to represent him. Tshombe's aim was to secure confirmation of the results of the Madagascar meeting, but the other delegates refused to do so. He left the conference, intending to fly back to Elisabethville, but was prevented from leaving by soldiers who insisted that he remain until unity was restored. Tshombe refused all blandishments, including personal entreaties from Bomboko, to return to the conference, allegedly refusing to eat and drink. He was then placed under house arrest.

For reasons that escape me, Bomboko proceeded to charge Tshombe with high treason and the murder of Lumumba, a move that neither Tim nor I favored. It was clear from the actions of various political groups and Kasavubu's public statements that parliament would soon be called. Prime Minister Ileo was an honest but inept leader and would have to be replaced. We believed the Leopoldville group of parliamentarians would need the votes of Katanga's deputies if they were to defeat Gizenga in the struggle to elect a new prime minister. It was questionable whether Tshombe would be willing to assist the government, but if he continued to be held prisoner the chances of him cooperating would be extremely slim.

I managed to get this idea across to two of our agents in the government delegation, but Tshombe remained a prisoner. The central government delegates returned to Leopoldville, and the Coquilhatville Conference ended without accomplishing anything. Tshombe remained in Leopoldville under house arrest until late June 1961 when he signed an agreement in which he promised to end the Katanga secession.

Those of us who had monitored Tshombe's actions for nearly a year correctly took his statement with the proverbial grain of salt. Nonetheless, we hoped he would find it in his interest to have the Katanga parliamentarians support the candidate of the central government once parliament reconvened. Tshombe was released, but even then the drama was not over. When he boarded his plane at Ndjili, Congolese soldiers guarding the airport blocked the runway and prevented the plane from departing.

Although our government did not hold any brief for Tshombe or his secessionist state, the situation at the airport was ridiculous because it was caused by a group of rebellious, ill-disciplined soldiers disobeying their own government. When I heard of it, I drove to the airport to see what, if anything, could be done to resolve the problem. I found that Tshombe had been sitting in his plane in excruciating heat—there was no air-conditioning—for about two hours. When it became clear that his release would take time, I arranged for ice, sodas, and water to be delivered to the plane. Some hours later Mobutu and Nendaka succeeded in convincing the troops to remove the metal barrels blocking the runway, and Tshombe finally departed for Elisabethville. I am not sure whether we accomplished anything, but we continued to work on the possibility that Tshombe might instruct the Katangan parliamentarians to support the central government's candidate for prime minister when parliament eventually met. In any case, Tshombe, on his return to Katanga, claimed that he had signed the promise to end the Katanga secession under pressure and denounced the agreement.

The issue of reconvening parliament preoccupied us for some months before it actually happened. We were deluged with advice from the State Department and its minions at the US Mission to the United Nations. At first, the priority was to insure that Gizenga did not become prime minister. I fully agreed, but I strongly opposed Washington's recommendation that Gizenga be given a non-sensitive post in an otherwise moderate government. Chester Bowles, Soapy Williams, and other key officials in the State Department continued to believe that we could win over the non-aligned countries and the more radical African countries such as Ghana and Guinea by giving them a stake in the system.

In June 1961, the officers of the embassy met at Ndjili airport to greet G. McMurtrie Godley, Rob McIlvaine's replacement as deputy chief of mission. We knew he would become *chargé d'affaires* as soon as Ambassador Timberlake departed. We assumed he would be leading the embassy during a crucial period, and we were anxious to get a clear impression of him. It was not long in coming. Tim brought Godley down the line introducing him to us one by one. A great bear of a man, Godley greeted each member of the team politely, but much to my surprise he gave my hand a tug as he shook it. "Lunch tomorrow," he said. "I buy, OK?" "Sure," I said, astonished.

He called the next morning to set a time and suggested the best restaurant in town. I will never forget that lunch because it was the beginning of a close friendship that continued long after we had both retired from government service and only ended with Mac's death.

The lunch went well, for Mac, as Godley asked me to call him, was an excellent host. We had the best wines and the relaxed conversation covered everything from life at our previous posts to a review of the Congo political situation. I had assumed that there had to be something behind the lunch invitation, almost certainly something to do with my work, but when that "something" finally came up I was startled, to put it mildly.

As we sat sipping our coffee and cognac, Mac suddenly looked up and said, "What's it going to be, Larry? Are you going to play ball, or are you going to try to screw me?"

"What do you mean?"

"Are you going to introduce me to the Binza Group?"

It had never occurred to me to try to freeze him out of my circle of top-level contacts. While I handled most contacts with the Binza Group and was the American with the closest ties, Tim knew them all and dealt directly with them when it was important to do so.

"Certainly. Would lunch tomorrow be soon enough?" I asked mildly. Mac raised his eyebrows and asked how I could organize a lunch for a group of key government personalities so quickly. I pointed out that the Binza Group was aware that he would soon be the most senior American diplomat in the Congo and that they were just as curious about him as he was about them. Having cast their lot with the United States, the Group realized that our new man was a key figure in their political calculations, someone who could help them achieve their goals or seriously complicate their lives.

Mac had already moved into the deputy chief of mission's residence and wanted to have the lunch at his house—another way of saying that he was his own man and not dependent on me. I contacted all the members of the Binza Group to make sure that they understood the importance of the gathering. The next day, everyone, even Bomboko, arrived on time. It was a long, agreeable meal, and I am sure the Congolese went away with an impression of Mac as a charming and interesting host and a highly capable leader. Nevertheless, I knew they regretted Tim's recall.

The following week, the entire embassy staff was at the airport to see the Timberlakes off. All government ministers were present because Kasavubu had adjourned a cabinet meeting to allow them to bid Tim farewell. Mobutu and his senior officers from the Leopoldville garrison, many senior civil servants, and hundreds of ordinary Congolese were also there. Normally, the chief of protocol, or one of his staff, sees off a departing ambassador, but in Tim's case the Congolese pulled out all the stops. They wanted to demonstrate their appreciation for his help and his support, and some hoped such a show of gratitude would persuade Washington to send him back to the Congo. Mobutu kept repeating that if Tim did not return it could only mean that the United States was no longer interested in the Congo. Tim and Julie were deeply touched by the presence of so many Congolese to bid them farewell, but it could not remove the pain of being dumped.

With Tim's departure, my work continued with little change. I had easy and regular access to Mac. Our two lunches and his introduction to the Binza Group convinced him that he could trust me and that my agents and contacts would prove extremely useful to him. The political problems did not change either. We knew it was just a matter of time before the Congolese parliament would meet again. I concentrated on the parliamentarians from the areas controlled by the Leopoldville government while Frank Carlucci did his best to obtain a reading on their counterparts in the Stanleyville region. The Binza Group, in particular, had a vested interest in whatever new government emerged because they wanted it to be moderate and, ideally, one that they could influence.

As the convening of parliament approached, the need to replace Ileo—an intelligent but weak and vacillating individual—with a competent person at the head of the pro-Kasavubu parliamentarians increased. We began to look around. My personal choice was Bomboko. He had proved a competent prime minister when he led the College of Commissioners, and he worked well with the station and the embassy. But there were drawbacks to his nomination. His role in removing Lumumba from power could not have been well received by the deputies who disapproved of Mobutu's coup and, as head of the commissioners' government, he had made a number of enemies. Finally, it was important to insure that, if he could not lead the new government, he would at least remain foreign minister.

However, we soon came up with our candidate. He was Cyrille Adoula, one of the senators who had helped us when we tried to remove Lumumba by means of a no-confidence vote in early September 1960. Adoula had led one of the three Congolese trade union federations and worked well with Americans; he was popular, well respected in parliament, and had demonstrated leadership ability. We also knew that he was well liked by Kasavubu and thus stood a good chance of winning his nomination. Finally, he was a personal friend of Ileo who, we thought, would be more likely to give way to a friend than someone he did not like. Unfortunately, the last assumption proved incorrect. Ileo refused to step down.

The departure of Dayal vastly improved relations between the United Nations, the embassy, and the Congolese. Hammarskjöld did not appoint a new special representative but ordered Sture Linner, a competent Swede, to continue as the head of the economic and technical aid side of the UN operation while General Sean McKeown, an Irish veteran of UN operations, was to continue as commander of the UN troops.

The selection of Linner could not have been better for the embassy or for the Congo, as he and Mac hit it off immediately. In addition, our objectives were similar. The Secretary-General was determined to have a parliamentary government—one that would include Gizenga—in place before the next meeting of the UN's General Assembly in New York. Washington wanted a moderate coalition government, preferably one that was not controlled by Gizenga. Mac was prepared to accept a coalition, but he favored a government in which the Gizengists were kept to a minimum.

I preferred a government without Gizenga, Mulele, Kashamura, or other parliamentarians who had been cozy with the Soviets, and Mac and I did our best to create a moderate government with Adoula at the helm. It was not easy, and there were many false starts before the various political parties agreed in July 1961 to meet at Lovanium University, set on a hill overlooking the city and the river. (This was where I had been sent to remove the rods from the atomic reactor a year earlier.) The university, rather than parliament in the center of the city, was chosen for security reasons. An agreement between the Congolese parties and the UN called for the parliamentarians to be confined to the university grounds while UN troops kept out all unauthorized persons. There would be no liquor, money or other valuables, firearms, or women allowed on the campus. The agreement also called for the disarming of the Congolese troops in the Leopoldville area. Although that clause was not implemented, Linner decided to go ahead with the meeting.

As the opening day approached, Washington grew increasingly worried. When Tshombe announced that his parliamentarians would not attend, the State Department began to consider the possibility of postponing the meeting. The Secretary of State instructed Mac to meet with Kasavubu to ask him to delay the session, but Mac stood his ground and reminded his superiors that plans had progressed too far to delay. It took considerable courage for Mac to do this, particularly since Timberlake's recall for opposing Washington was fresh in his mind.

Mac's judgment that an acceptable government would emerge from the Congolese palavers at Lovanium was based on information given him by Sture Linner, as well as on assessments provided by Frank Carlucci and my clandestine sources. Prior to the opening of the Lovanium conclave, I met daily with Bomboko, Nendaka, and Mobutu. Bomboko had a radio installed in his automobile to insure communications between us during the meeting. I saw Adoula regularly to discuss ways of insuring that Kasavubu would name him prime minister, and I met with as many parliamentarians as possible. I arranged for all our agents who were in direct or indirect contact with Kasavubu to drive home the fact that Ileo was incompetent and to recommend that Adoula be chosen to lead the next government.

Working through Jacques, one of our best agents, we arranged to have the editor of the main newspaper review the potential candidates for prime minister. The editor's conclusion was that Gizenga would be a disaster for the country, Ileo was not fit for the job, and Adoula was best qualified to head the new government.

The period before the reconvening of parliament was extremely active and full of worry. As anticipated, the meeting was delayed by the failure of some parliamentarians to appear, particularly those from Stanleyville. During this period, two alleged journalists from communist China arrived in Stanleyville. Although we were unable to identify them, we assumed that they were intelligence officers operating under journalist cover. A Soviet delegation of nine people also arrived. The delegation was led by Leonid Podgornov, a member of the Soviet embassy who had been expelled from the Congo when Mobutu declared all Soviets *persona non grata* in September 1960. Although we did not have the identities of all the Soviets, experience had taught us that as a general rule a large percentage of the personnel of any Soviet embassy were intelligence officers. We assumed that the size of the delegation meant the Soviet Union had decided once again to make a major effort in the Congo. Through our agents, we learned that Podgornov and his associates were trying to convince Gizenga to go to Lovanium to take charge of the Lumumbist group. They apparently believed that he would be elected prime minister if he were present. They worked on him for more than two weeks with no success.

About that time, Sture Linner, at the urging of Mac Godley, visited Kasavubu. He pointed out that Ileo lacked leadership qualities, had failed to persuade the moderates in the Stanleyville group to join the Leopoldville deputies, and was even unable to hold his Leopoldville supporters together. Linner also urged Kasavubu to visit the conclave, offering to put a helicopter at his disposal. Linner's arguments coincided with the recommendations of a number of our agents and tilted the situation in our direction.

Kasavubu finally obtained Ileo's resignation and appointed Adoula prime minister. He then formed a government with Gizenga in his old position of deputy prime minister, Christophe Gbenye, a leading Lumumbist, became minister of the interior, and Bomboko remained as foreign minister. To our surprise, Adoula managed to obtain a near unanimous vote of confidence from both houses of parliament. Gizenga's refusal to attend the Lovanium conclave in person may have tipped the scales in Adoula's favor, but Gizenga managed to secure key positions for himself and his ally Gbenye.

I would have preferred a government without Gizenga or Gbenye but, considering all that we had been through, I was not unhappy with the outcome. Given Gbenye's position, I immediately set out to establish a clandestine relationship with him, one that would keep him on the reservation without undercutting Adoula. Soon Gbenye was meeting with me secretly and apparently taking me into his confidence. Although I never fully trusted him, I did get a foot in the enemy camp.

Adoula's success must have surprised Moscow as well as the other countries that had recognized Gizenga as the legal head of the Congo government and established diplomatic missions in Stanleyville. Perhaps most surprised of all was Gizenga himself who pleaded ill health as an excuse for not attending the conclave. Khrushchev, a political gambler, probably sensed that Gizenga's presence in Lovanium might have provided a knockout victory for his protégé and must have been disgusted with him for not having had the courage to exploit the opportunity. The Stanleyville press and radio made no mention of Adoula's election until several days after the fact. It was only after Gbenye visited Stanleyville in early August and met with Gizenga that the local media announced the formation of the new Congolese government in Leopoldville.

One can imagine the disappointment of the thirty-six foreign diplomats, all of whom had only recently arrived in Stanleyville, when Gizenga's government announced it no longer existed. Gizenga, however, still refused to go to Leopoldville so Adoula flew to Stanleyville in mid-August to meet him. After two days of talks, Gizenga made his first public appearance in months. He announced his recognition of Adoula's government but still did not say when he would depart for the capital.

Khrushchev, ever the activist, officially gave up on Gizenga on August 31, 1961, when he sent a letter of congratulations to Adoula. He said the Soviet Union was prepared to "continue to maintain diplomatic relations" with the Congo, ignoring the fact that relations between the two countries had been severed almost a year earlier. Presumably, Khrushchev had finally realized that Gizenga lacked Lumumba's political appeal and decided that it would be better to try his hand in Leopoldville where a well-funded embassy might be able to achieve his objectives. He seemed to think he could use Gizenga and Gbenye to influence the new government's policies, and with Soviet support and the passage of time these two might be able to gain control of the government.

After his election, Adoula described his government as "non-aligned," but he continued to maintain our close relationship. He and his wife used to come to my house regularly for drinks or intimate dinners. The couple came from a simple background. Adoula's formal education was limited, but he was intelligent and had learned a great deal about people and politics in climbing the trade union ladder. Knowing that I was able to provide him with an assessment of how the shifting trends in Congolese politics were likely to be viewed in the West, Adoula confided in me about his political problems. I also suspect he hoped that I would warn him if Mobutu or Nendaka turned against him. He had long been a member of the Binza Group and thus was aware that Mobutu, Nendaka, and Bomboko were more influential than the others.

Adoula suffered from enormous bunions on both feet and wore shoes only when absolutely necessary. When he arrived at my home, he would immediately take them off, noting with appreciation that he could do so without embarrassment because he considered me a friend as well as an adviser. The poor man must have been in pain much of the time when he was receiving ambassadors or indeed in his everyday working life when he could not slip off his shoes.

Adoula worked so hard during the month of August at polishing his non-aligned image that Washington, once again, became alarmed. The same men who had been prepared to accept a coalition government with Lumumba, Gizenga, and other anti-American politicians began to worry that Adoula was going too far and might make major concessions to Gizenga and his allies. Secretary of State Dean Rusk decided to send a letter to Adoula assuring him that he could count on American aid for his moderate government, hoping that this would encourage Adoula to stand up to pressure from the Gizengists.

Rusk's emissary was Soapy Williams, the assistant secretary of state for African Affairs, who was on a swing through the continent. I will always remember Soapy's visit. He arrived from Rhodesia with a large black eye, given to him as he was leaving Salisbury airport by a white Rhodesian who resented American support for that country's black nationalist aspirations. Soapy had a habit of greeting everyone within reach, introducing himself, and giving the person one of his trademark green polka-dot bow ties. As a four-term popular governor of Michigan, this was his style, but it seemed strange to see him doing it in the Congo where few, if any, of those he greeted had the faintest idea of what he was saying in English. Unfortunately for Soapy, the Rhodesian had understood him, and the story produced an interesting sequel. Friends took up a collection to help pay the assailant's fine. Apparently, the total amounted to twice the amount of the fine, and the Rhodesian sent Soapy a message inviting him to return and to give him a chance to have a go at the other eye for another collection.

Soapy and Mac Godley were scheduled to have breakfast at my house. I made sure that I had an icepack for the assistant secretary's splendid black eye. Despite his shiner, Williams called on Adoula to deliver Dean Rusk's message and came away with the impression that while Adoula would adhere to his non-aligned policies, he would also continue to cooperate with the United States and other Western states.

Many of the non-aligned countries were highly suspicious of Adoula. They had assumed that Gizenga would be elected prime minister and found it difficult to believe that the Lovanium conclave had produced a fair result. In September 1961, the non-aligned states held a summit in Belgrade hosted by Marshall Tito, the head of the Non-Aligned Movement. They invited Adoula and Gizenga, who was still in Stanleyville since he remained fearful of going to Leopoldville. Gizenga was reluctant to go to Belgrade, too, but was eventually persuaded to do so by Gbenye and the UN. He joined Adoula in Leopoldville first, and then flew with him to the Yugoslav capital. Adoula was anxious to have Gizenga at his side because he believed the latter's presence strengthened his own legitimacy as Lumumba's successor in the eyes of the non-aligned states.

Adoula had worked hard to obtain an invitation to the meeting for, even after his election as prime minister, many of the non-aligned states were not prepared to recognize him as the legitimate head of the Congolese government. Some even urged the Secretary-General to delay recognition of the Adoula government. Hammarskjöld did not accept the recommendation, but the fact that it was made by India and supported by a number of radical African states reveals the limited understanding of the Congo political situation that prevailed at the time.

Although many foreign leaders viewed Gizenga as Lumumba's successor, he lacked Lumumba's political popularity, his charisma, and the ability to move quickly to exploit a situation. Moves to delay the recognition of Adoula's government, however, were bound to influence the Secretary-General and to be carried back to the State Department, where they were viewed with concern.

Adoula and Gizenga arrived near the end of the summit conference, but since the participants were curious about Gizenga's relationship with Adoula, both men were invited to speak. Each stressed national reconciliation, yet their speeches were quite different. Madeleine Kalb in *The Congo Cables* noted that one observer at the conference commented that the speeches sounded as though they had been "drafted by NATO and the Warsaw Pact."

Just before the summit began, Khrushchev announced that the Soviet Union was about to resume nuclear testing. The immediate reaction of the non-aligned leaders to Khrushchev's statement was highly critical, but in no time they also took the United States to task, urging *both* superpowers to negotiate and resolve their differences. Even Adoula failed to see that the Soviets had caused the problem by resuming nuclear tests, and joined the other leaders in calling on the Russians and the Americans to find a peaceful solution to their differences.

President Kennedy noted this double standard and he began to question the policies advocated by the liberals in his administration—notably Chester Bowles, Adlai Stevenson, and Soapy Williams—toward the Afro-Asians in general and the Congo in particular. We were to see more of this new realism at close quarters with the arrival of our new ambassador.

13

E DMUND GULLION, our new ambassador, arrived in early
September 1961, having been personally selected by President
Kennedy for the job. He represented the greater degree of realism
that was shaping U.S. policy toward the Congo but, like all ambassadors, had his own way of running his embassy. A man of keen in-
tellect, he was a career Foreign Service officer who had climbed the
promotion ladder rapidly until he was named deputy chief of mission in Saigon well before the United States took an active role in
that area. At that time, the American ambassador followed the
French line, regularly advising Washington that the communists
were losing the struggle. Gullion, on the other hand, was convinced that they were winning and made his view clear in Washington. As a result, Gullion fell out of favor with his superiors and
was not offered another important post. While biding his time,
Gullion met Senator John F. Kennedy and became one of the senator's foreign policy advisers. Gullion told me that he had even introduced Kennedy to Jacqueline Bouvier.

After the establishment of Adoula's new government, the focus
of our efforts turned to Katanga. Conor Cruise O'Brien, an Irish
diplomat and the UN's senior representative in Katanga, shared
Hammarskjöld's opinion that Tshombe would never end Katanga's
secession as long as his army was led by Belgian military advisers
and hundreds of mercenary troops.

The mercenaries came mainly from South Africa, Belgium, and Rhodesia, although Ireland, England, France, Spain, Germany, and a number of other countries were also represented. Many were men with a questionable past and were not the best their countries had to offer. Some, however, were gentlemen adventurers like Mike Hoare, a South African dubbed "Mad Mike" by the press, and others were professional soldiers such as the Frenchman Bob Denard. The French provided some of the more competent mercenary officers, many of whom had been involved in the paratroop rebellion in Algeria against the French government. When their short-lived revolt failed, Jacques Foccart, the head of French intelligence for Africa in the Elysée Palace in Paris, offered some of them an eventual pardon if they would fight for Tshombe in Katanga. This led some American insiders to believe that the French hoped to displace the Belgians in Katanga and to obtain control of the province's great mineral wealth.

On August 28, O'Brien, acting under the tough Security Council resolution that had created such concern for the Leopoldville government when it was passed on February 21, launched a surprise operation in Katanga to expel the mercenaries. It took less than one day, and many mercenaries were arrested. Tshombe and his ministers were taken by surprise and agreed to cooperate with the UN by terminating the contracts of all foreign soldiers and expelling them from Katanga. The Belgian consul promised to insure the departure of the Belgian military personnel. Unfortunately for the UN, neither Tshombe nor the Belgian consul kept his promise, and most of the mercenaries were back in Katanga within a few days.

Hammarskjöld sought to resolve the problem by recommending that Adoula issue an order calling for the expulsion of all mercenaries and foreign military advisers from Katanga, and that the UN should implement the operation. In late August, Adoula complied, without consulting the station or the embassy, and provided O'Brien with warrants for the arrest of Tshombe and Munongo, the hard-line minister of interior.

On September 13, O'Brien launched a second operation against the mercenaries. O'Brien's plan included occupying the Elisabethville post office (to control the telephone exchange), the radio station, the headquarters of the Katanga *Sûreté*, and the ministry of information, raising the Congolese flag on all public buildings, and installing a central government representative to take control of the province. UN personnel offered differing interpretations of their actions, but it was clear to anyone who followed the matter that the object of the operation was to put an end to the Katanga secession.

O'Brien and his staff believed they could complete the operation in a day, but both Tshombe and Munongo eluded capture, and the fighting continued for several days. In the embassy, most of us believed that the use of force was necessary to expel the mercenaries, but Washington did not share that view. After supporting the first UN operation in Katanga, the administration—as was so often the case—wound up straddling the fence.

The embassy was instructed to tell Adoula and Linner that while the United States favored the removal of Belgian military personnel from Katanga, it did not believe that all peaceful means to do so had been exhausted. Washington believed that the UN should not destroy Tshombe and his political organization but should persuade him to cooperate with Adoula. Anyone who had dealt with Tshombe and with Union Minière, the Belgian mining conglomerate that supported Katanga's independence, knew that there was no chance Tshombe would yield to friendly persuasion. Washington must have known this, but it was torn between what was really happening in the Congo and an old habit of remaining in step with the African policies of its NATO allies.

Secretary Rusk sent an unofficial message to the secretary-general urging him to get Adoula and Tshombe together for talks. Rusk also reminded Hammarskjöld that the U.S. government was paying a large part of the costs of the Congo operation, and thus believed it should be consulted on major developments such as the Katanga operations.

Hammarskjöld flew out to Leopoldville to study the situation for himself and to meet the leading players. Ed Gullion urged him to remain in the Congo until the fighting ended, but Hammarskjöld had already decided to go to Ndola in Northern Rhodesia, close to the Katangan border, to meet Tshombe. The night before his departure I attended a reception for him given by Linner, and I recall wondering how this man could appear totally relaxed when he was under attack from all directions.

I was in the station's communications center the next day when we received a flash message reporting that Hammarskjöld and all but one of his entourage had been killed in a plane crash near Ndola. There are many theories about his tragic death. His plane was delayed in its departure from Leopoldville, and I was told that it was because one of the engines needed replacing. The plane, however, had not been test-flown because the secretary-general was in a great hurry to leave. Another unlikely story was that the plane, which had returned from Elisabethville the previous day, had been damaged in an attack by one of Katanga's French-built Fouga Magister fighter planes.

I also picked up numerous reports about the two pilots' fatigue. I heard from several people that the pilots had had little sleep during the two days before the flight. There have been many unconfirmed reports about the plane being sabotaged, that a bomb was smuggled on board, or that it was actually shot down by a Katangan jet fighter. Most of us at the embassy concluded the crash probably resulted from pilot error or a mechanical failure that may have occurred when the plane was preparing to land.

One possibility, suggested by our air attaché who visited the crash scene shortly after the wreckage was found, appeared credible to me. He noted that a chart for landing at Ndolo, Leopoldville's old airport, was on the deck of what remained of the cockpit. This chart raised the question of whether the pilot was reading the wrong chart when he was preparing to land, and had confused *Ndolo* in the Congo with *Ndola* in Northern Rhodesia, there being a considerable difference in altitude between the two places. The commission of inquiry that studied the evidence failed to reach a definitive conclusion.

Additional information concerning the crash has become available since the period immediately after Hammarskjöld's death. Major General Egge, a Norwegian who was the first UN officer to see the body, stated in an interview on July 29, 2005—the one hundredth anniversary of Hammarskjöld birth—that he had noted a hole in the secretary-general's forehead. It had been airbrushed out of the official pictures taken at the scene of the accident. The size and appearance of the hole was not, to the best of my knowledge, further described. Such a wound could have conceivably been caused by the explosion of a bomb or by the plane crash itself.

The general also reported that he found leaves and grass in Hammarskjöld's hands, as though he had been thrown from the plane and attempted to crawl away from the plane. Presumably, Egge reported his observations to the commission of inquiry.

In August 1998, Archbishop Desmond Tutu, the chairman of the South African Truth and Reconciliation Commission, revealed that recently uncovered letters had implicated South African agents in the crash. One letter said the bomb in the aircraft's wheelbay was set to detonate when the wheels were let down for a landing.

While the archbishop's report would appear to confirm the many reports that circulated at the time of the crash, I do not know enough about the details of the letter in question to accept it as factual evidence. Did it refer to a plan to kill the Secretary-General? Or was it a report on the success of an assassination plot? I know only too well from my own experience how one can be falsely or erroneously accused of a crime. It raises a question concerning the commission's report, for the investigators at the scene of the crash reported that there was no evidence of a bomb. Thus, until I know more about the archbishop's evidence, I will continue to believe that Hammarskjöld's death resulted from pilot error that may have resulted from fatigue.

The death of Hammarskjöld put an end to the UN's Katanga operation, and the conflict shifted to New York where the Soviets unsuccessfully revived their demand for a troika of secretary-generals to replace the single office-holder. The Congo problem remained in limbo for nearly seven weeks before U Thant was finally elected acting secretary-general for the balance of Hammarskjöld's term.

America's Congo policy also changed with the death of Hammarskjöld. Before, Washington—influenced by its NATO allies—had been reluctant to have the UN employ force to terminate the Katanga secession. With the renewed Soviet efforts to replace the position of Secretary-General with a troika, the United States feared that such a change would result in the end of an effective international organization. In return for American support of effective action against Tshombe, Washington hoped the Afro-Asian neutralists would oppose the Soviet Union's efforts to impose a troika leadership on the UN. The change was not precipitous. It had its starts and stops, but with the help of the UN leadership, our policy slowly changed. Our number-one priority became the need to take a firm stand on Katanga in order to convince the Afro-Asians, who were almost all anti-Tshombe, that the United States shared their position. In turn, the United States expected them to oppose the Soviet-sponsored troika, and most of them did. Washington's support for Adoula greatly facilitated my efforts to work closely with members of his government and influence its decisions.

Before his death, Hammarskjöld had proposed that the U.S. put four large transport planes at the disposal of the UN to help move troops and supplies within the country. President Kennedy had initially rejected the plan but changed his mind after the secretary-general's death. The main purpose of the planes was to facilitate the build-up of the UN's forces in Katanga, but a cease-fire agreement with Tshombe put the plan on hold. The truce pleased the British but enraged Adoula, who declared that he was prepared to use his own forces to bring Katanga back into the Congo fold. Bomboko, Mobutu, and the other members of the Binza Group supported him, even though they realized that the Congolese army was incapable of mounting and successfully implementing such an operation.

The ambassador and I urged Adoula, Bomboko, and Mobutu to continue to take a tough line with Katanga. I also made the same point with Nendaka and other members of the Binza Group. As part of this strategy, Mobutu announced in early November that his troops had crossed into Katanga. Our government preferred a negotiated settlement, but Ed Gullion did his best to make the State Department and the White House realize that Tshombe would not give up the independent status of the Katanga as long as he felt militarily secure. Ed and I stressed in our cables that if Adoula was unable to settle the Katanga crisis, Gizenga or some other extremist might take over the government and turn to the Soviets for help in ending Tshombe's secession.

We were also working to help solidify Adoula's political base by providing him with a public relations adviser and launching a campaign to denigrate Gizenga through our Congolese press contacts. This became easier when Gizenga returned to Stanleyville and ousted the moderate governor of Orientale province, replacing him with one of his own men, and laying himself open to charges that he was an extremist.

By this time, the Soviet Union appeared to realize that Gizenga was a loser. It did not embrace Adoula publicly, but its policy appeared to rest on the possibility that the failure of the UN to reunite Katanga with the rest of the country would eventually force Adoula to move his government to the left, or it would collapse and he would be replaced by a leader who would be more amenable to Soviet blandishments. While Ed Gullion and I stood firmly behind Adoula, Washington often let its desire for a negotiated settlement get in the way of its desire for a successful conclusion to Katanga's secession.

Tshombe had few friends in Washington, but he was represented by Michel Struelens, one of the most effective lobbyists who ever worked the halls of Congress and the ranks of the press corps. Struelens was usually one step ahead of the State Department and stories with a pro-Katanga slant appeared regularly in the American press. Taking advantage of the Cold War atmosphere that permeated all facets of our lives in those years, Struelens painted Tshombe as the lone anti-communist leader fighting to prevent the Congo from slipping into the hands of the Soviet Union.

For reasons that escaped us, Senator Thomas Dodd of Connecticut, a senior and influential Democrat, appeared to accept Struelens's propaganda hook, line, and sinker. Dodd's speeches on the Congo upset my agents and contacts, for they could not understand how one of the most powerful figures in the U.S. Senate could fail to understand that they, not Tshombe, were the ones holding the line against the Soviets.

There were rumors that Dodd found it financially profitable to support the Tshombe bandwagon, but since there was no hard evidence, I looked forward to meeting Dodd when he announced his intention to visit the Congo in November 1961. I thought that Ed Gullion and I might be able to set him straight, but Dan Margolies, the embassy's economic counselor, warned me to be extremely cautious and to weigh every word carefully in dealing with the man. Dan, who had worked for Dodd at the Nuremberg trials of the Nazi leaders, described the senator as a tough prosecutor prepared to trample anyone with an opposing opinion. I thought Dan was overstating Dodd's menace, but I kept his warning in mind.

The senator and Dave Martin, one of his staff, came to my office the day after his arrival and asked if I could spare them a little time. Needless to say, the answer was yes. Dodd began the conversation by saying that he held me in the highest regard and, turning to Martin, described me as a true patriot in the fight against communism. He also referred to me as a World War II hero, an obvious exaggeration since I was just one of many young Americans who fought in the war. I do not recall his exact words, but they were extremely flattering and were, presumably, intended to put me at ease.

Dodd then threw out easy, non-controversial questions about Lumumba, Mobutu, Bomboko, Adoula, and others. My phone kept ringing and interrupting us and Dodd suggested that we adjourn to the ambassador's residence where we could sit in the garden and have an uninterrupted talk. When we arrived, Dodd asked if I enjoyed a good cigar. I admitted that I did, whereupon he sent Martin to his room to bring down a box. Martin returned with the cigars, and Dodd, seemingly annoyed, looked at them and told him to go back and get the *good* cigars because I deserved the best.

With these little courtesies, Dodd set the tone for our talk, which lasted well over an hour. Throughout, he exuded friendship and admiration for me and for my work. He listened attentively as I spoke of Adoula, Bomboko, Mobutu, and other key players in Congolese politics. From time to time, he would stop me and say something to the effect that if he understood me correctly, I meant such and such, but he never seemed to have it exactly right. If it had not been for Dan Margolies's warning, I might have agreed with him or not have corrected him as precisely as I did. Each time he would thank me for my clarification and ask more questions.

Toward the end of our meeting, Dodd asked my opinion concerning Tshombe and the Katanga problem. I gave him a detailed response, carefully outlining my views and those of Ambassador Gullion. I stressed that any re-drawing of the map of Africa would open Pandora's Box. I explained that when the European powers had formalized the division of Africa at the Congress of Berlin in 1885, they had ignored tribal boundaries, and any attempt to redraw them would lead to endless conflict. Such an outcome would not only result in great suffering and chaos, but it would also provide an opening for the Soviet Union to gain the foothold on the continent that Khrushchev was seeking. Moreover, Katanga provided some fifty percent of the Congo's foreign exchange earnings. If it were to become an independent state, it would leave the rest of the Congo without the means to support itself. That dynamic would also work to the advantage of the Soviets.

As I finished speaking, Senator Dodd stood up to light his cigar and took a step or two toward me, almost standing over me as I sat in a low garden chair. The *bonhomie* that had accompanied our conversation vanished. I was no longer Larry. I was Mr. Devlin. He was the prosecutor. He began by pointing his cigar at me and recapitulated what I had said, misquoting me on almost every point. I did not enjoy having him standing over me, pointing his cigar at me, and misquoting me. It put me at a great disadvantage as I tried to correct his statements. So, I pushed back my chair and stood up and faced him. I did my best to defend my position and to correct any misunderstandings that might remain. I knew, however, that I was not getting through to the senator.

As I left, I thanked God for Dan Margolies's warning, being fully aware that I had not made a friend in Senator Dodd. He had begun by playing the good cop and then had unsuccessfully tried to put words in my mouth. When that failed, he tried to frighten me into accepting his own warped interpretation of what I had said. Dodd is a good example of some members of Congress who, when they travel overseas, feel they have to exercise their egos and browbeat embassy officials. Some years later, when I was chief of the Africa Division, I was to have another difficult session with Senator Thomas Dodd.

The senator and his wife next visited Katanga. Lew Hoffacker, the newly arrived U.S. Consul in Elisabethville, accompanied them to a dinner given in their honor. On their way, they came across two senior UN officials, George Smith and Brian Urquhart, who had been arrested by Katangese soldiers, badly beaten, and loaded onto an army truck. Lew took in the situation at a glance, jumped out of his car, and waded in. He managed to rescue Smith and a Belgian banker, who had also been mistakenly arrested, but he was unable to reach Urquhart before the soldiers drove off with him in the truck. While Hoffacker was fighting to save the prisoners, Mrs. Dodd, according to George Smith, was heard to say, "Why, if it isn't that nice Mr. Smith."

Urquhart was rescued the next morning by UN troops, but both he and Smith suffered broken ribs and contusions. Notwithstanding this raw example of Katangan democracy in action, Senator Dodd returned to Washington to preach the Tshombe gospel.

In November 1961, two UN transport planes flown by Italian crews landed in Kindu, Kivu province, with supplies for the Malayan UN troops. Unfortunately, Congolese soldiers loyal to Gizenga had occupied the town. A squad marched into the UN mess where the Italian air crews were eating, arrested the airmen, beat them, and took them away without meeting any resistance from the Malayan soldiers. A joint Congolese-UN delegation flew to Kindu to try to negotiate the release of the Italians but without success.

General Victor Lundula, commander of the troops in Orientale and Kivu provinces, barely escaped with his life when he tried to reason with the soldiers who were theoretically under his command. Colonel Pakassa, the commander of the mutinous unit, was also unable to control them, and refused to help the UN, Lundula, or any other Congolese authority.

Gizenga, we heard, was in the Kindu area at the time. If the reports of his presence were correct, he made no effort to control the troops. We soon learned that the thirteen Italian airmen had been killed almost immediately after their arrest. Their bodies were dismembered and parts were eaten. Body parts were later found wrapped and packaged in a Greek merchant's freezer that the soldiers had commandeered.

Secretary-General U Thant ordered his representative, Sture Linner, to demand that the Congolese arrest Colonel Pakassa and punish those responsible for killing the airmen. The Secretary-General's desire for action was admirable, but his decision to call on the Leopoldville authorities to implement the demand was a mistake. UN troops did move to seal off the Kindu area, disarmed hundreds of Congolese troops in the area, and sought the killers, but as with so many crimes committed in the Congo, I do not recall that the guilty soldiers were identified, let alone punished. As for Colonel

Pakassa, he went on to become one of the military leaders of the rebellion in the eastern Congo. However, if the reports that I picked up many years later were correct, he was killed in a bar fight in Cairo. Justice was slow, but at least he finally met the end he deserved.

14

I HAD HEARD A GREAT DEAL about Equateur from Bomboko and Mobutu, both natives of that province. Located along the Congo River between Stanleyville and Leopoldville, it played a key political role in blocking the Gizengists, based in Stanleyville, from moving south toward the capital. The station had mounted an operation in Coquilhatville, the provincial capital, involving support for several local leaders. The operation appeared to be going well, but I had never personally visited the area, and I wanted to determine whether the operation was worth the time and effort. As I had a brief period of relative calm in Leopoldville, I decided to visit "Coq"—as everyone called it—to obtain an assessment of the political situation. I decided not to advise Mobutu or Bomboko of my visit, for I did not want them to alert their political allies that I was coming. Instead, I treated the visit as a vacation for Colette who rarely had an opportunity of getting out of Leopoldville and traveling in the interior of the country.

As luck would have it, who should be at the airport but Mobutu. He immediately said he must arrange a proper reception for us in Equateur—exactly what I was trying to avoid. I kept insisting that I just wanted to get out of Leopoldville for a while for a change of scene. Mobutu muttered a few protests and then we were off in an old crate of a DC–3 that had seen better days.

As we approached Coq, I looked down from the plane and saw a jeep followed by a sedan racing toward the airport. Here comes that reception, I said to myself. When we got off the plane, sure enough, we found the officer commanding the garrison and a major waiting for us. Both men saluted and addressed me as "*Monsieur le Consul Général.*" I took this to mean that Mobutu had promoted me from *Consul* for our stay in Coq. The officers assured me that every effort would be made to make our visit agreeable and added that the city officials planned a lunch in our honor that very day. They also told us that we were to be lodged in the governor's guesthouse, noting that it was the same guesthouse in which King Albert of Belgium had stayed when he visited the Congo.

All of this totally defeated my plan for a low-key visit to Coq. The officers accompanied us to the guesthouse located in a large park that surrounded the governor's mansion, once the residence of the colonial governor of Equateur. The province was appropriately named for the equator, which runs directly through the city of Coquilhatville and is marked by a line painted in the streets and in the park near the guesthouse. It was the custom for first-time guests to have a hokey picture taken standing with a foot in each hemisphere.

At lunch, served in Coq's best hotel, we met all the provincial ministers, with the exception of the governor and his minister of interior who were enjoying a "working vacation" on a lake in southern Equateur. The mayor and other town notables were also present. The meal was typical Congolese fare: boiled river fish—head, bones and all—and a meat stew of ambiguous origin. The stew was highly spiced with generous amounts of *pili-pili*, an extremely hot pepper sauce, and was accompanied by fried plantains and manioc. Delicious tropical fruit came as the dessert. Wine and local beer lubricated the speeches, all of which dealt with the topic of Congolese-American friendship. The people were friendly, more so than would normally accompany a formal welcome. We had the impression that we were dealing with real Congolese, not superficial politicians seeking our support. After the last speech, we were escorted back to the guesthouse for a siesta and told we would be picked up in the early evening to visit the city.

At first light the next morning the governor's secretary arrived and announced that he would be taking us to the lake resort where the governor was staying. In colonial times, the Belgians had required each village to maintain its section of the road, but all that had ended with independence. In the short time since independence, it had become more trail than road. The ride through the deep rain forest was an unforgettable experience; the trees formed an arch over the road, a shadowy, dark green tunnel with only occasional rays of sunlight coming through the thick foliage. We stopped at a village and drank palm wine with the village chief and some of the elders. It was our first experience with this beverage and one we decided not to repeat if at all possible, suspecting that a palm wine hangover would be as rough as the road.

The governor and the interior minister welcomed us like old friends, confirming my suspicion that everyone in the province had been instructed to make a fuss over us. (The resort turned out to be an experimental station for raising fish built by the Belgian colonial administration.) While the dinner of lake fish and manioc left something to be desired, the governor and his minister proved delightful hosts and regaled us with stories about life in Equateur. The next day, we accompanied our hosts on a boat ride to the end of the lake and a hike through the deep jungle to visit two villages. We walked for miles on narrow, dark trails listening to the jungle sounds of birds and monkeys.

At one village the children from a bamboo, one-room schoolhouse sang and danced for the governor and spent a lot of time simply staring at Colette and me. The governor told us we were probably the first white people the children had ever seen.

When it came time to return to the fish station, the boatman cast off and then tried to start the motor. He tried repeatedly and hopelessly until someone from the village paddled out and helped get the motor running. That evening we joined the governor, who was invited to dine at a plantation that belonged to a White Russian who had settled in the Congo in the 1920s. As we were to cross the lake in the fisheries boat, we incorrectly assumed that someone would have checked to see that the motor was now in working condition. When we cast off, the motor refused to start, and we drifted for nearly an hour before the governor—shouting and gesticulating like a man on fire—was able to attract the attention of some villagers who put out in pirogues to help us.

The governor decided that we should go ashore in the pirogues and use a car that was available to drive to the plantation, but before we got into the pirogues, he sent for chairs for Colette and me. We appreciated the gesture but feared it would result in us taking an unwanted bath in the lake. Pirogues are narrow canoes hollowed out of a single log and not designed to carry passengers sitting in chairs that dangerously raised our center of gravity. Happily, we reached the village without being dumped in the water.

The village automobile was a vintage Dodge that seemed to be running on two cylinders with no lights. Nevertheless, guided by a full moon, we chugged along jungle trails to our destination. We found the old Russian sitting on his veranda strumming a balalaika and singing Russian songs, evidently having already helped himself to an ample supply of vodka. He spent much of the night recounting stories that were far from politically correct and making brutally frank comments on the incompetence of the Congolese government officials. I thought that the governor would either be angry or embarrassed, but at one point he whispered to me that the old man had a right to say what he wished because he had been in the Congo a long time, having arrived well before the governor himself had been born.

The next morning, we were breakfasting with the governor beside the lake when some local hunters arrived and presented him with a baby chimpanzee. The governor gave them a small amount of money and some cigarettes and told us that the hunters killed the adult chimpanzees for their skins. He offered the baby chimp to Colette, but she politely declined, saying that the chimpanzee should not be removed from its natural habitat.

Later that morning, we heard on the Congolese radio news that an unidentified American attaché had been murdered in Leopoldville.

This was unsettling news, and I was anxious to return to the capital to find out who it was and what was going on. We flew back as soon as we could. When I checked into the embassy, Mac Godley called me into his office and told me that it was the assistant army attaché who had been murdered. Mac said he wanted me to drop all other duties and to find out who had killed the man.

The attaché had been shot in the head through his bedroom window at exactly 10:00 p.m. the previous evening. The embassy had been able to pinpoint the time because several people in the neighborhood had heard a shot just as the ten o'clock BBC world news came on. Mac wanted me to interrogate all the embassy staff to determine their whereabouts at the time of the shooting. He asked if I knew anyone in the diplomatic community who might have reason to murder the attaché. Although I knew of no enemies, I was aware that the man's personal life was complicated with a wife and children in the United States and a female companion who had accompanied him to Leopoldville. I reminded Mac that CIA officers are prevented by law from investigating American citizens, other than in counter-espionage cases, and suggested that he request the Pentagon to send a Criminal Investigation Division team to investigate the murder.

The Pentagon did exactly that, but it turned out to be a waste of time and the government's money. For a start, the team failed to ask the right questions. On the night of the murder, someone had given the attaché's watchman the night off, but the investigators failed to determine who told him not to come to work. When they later looked for the watchman, they found that he had returned to his village, and they dropped him from their inquiry. Oddly enough, the security lights in the attaché's garden were not on that night. The neighbors said they could not remember a time before when the lights were turned off at night, but I was told the team did not probe this curious occurrence. Further, one thousand dollars in cash appeared to have been thrown across the attaché's dresser but, according to Mac, the team failed to ask the attaché's female companion for an explanation. Even stranger, she called the embassy's marine guard to report the murder approximately forty-two minutes after the shot that was presumed to have killed the attaché was heard. The team never obtained an acceptable explanation for the delay. A Canadian captain and his girlfriend had dined with the attaché and his companion that night, but the captain refused to take a polygraph test requested by the investigators. He was recalled to Canada shortly thereafter, and I am not aware that the American authorities ever questioned him after he left the Congo. In short, the investigation seemed to be handled by the team that couldn't shoot straight.

Since Nendaka was chief of the Congolese *Sûreté*, he became involved in the case. He asked to speak to the attaché's companion only to be told that she was sleeping. I heard later that one of the embassy wives had given her Valium to help her sleep. When he next asked to speak to her, the same woman had given her another Valium and she was again unavailable for questioning. Stymied, Nendaka contacted me. He said he could understand if the United States had, for reasons of state, found it necessary to eliminate the attaché. If that were the case, he said, he would not interfere. If not, he was prepared to arrest the woman and hold her in jail until she recovered from her deep sleep so that he could question her.

I assured him that the attaché had not been killed by our government but, strangely enough, I do not believe that Nendaka ever tried to question the woman again. Perhaps the way the Pentagon's investigators had handled the case convinced him that I had not been telling the truth. In any event, the woman was allowed to return to the United States and, to the best of my knowledge, the murder of her lover was never solved.

15

ADOULA AND NENDAKA TOLD ME separately that Gbenye was causing problems within the government. Gbenye, as minister of the interior, was technically Nendaka's direct superior, but they were old political enemies from Orientale province, and Nendaka kept him at arm's length, shutting him out of the *Sûreté's* plans and operations. Nendaka and Adoula began to plan to get Gbenye out of the government, eventually, by having Nendaka pick a fight with his boss, which was not difficult given their long-standing rivalry. The matter would be allowed to fester until Gbenye turned to Adoula, demanding that he remove Nendaka. Adoula would agree to study the matter and finally take Nendaka's side and fire Gbenye.

Shortly after Ambassador Gullion's arrival, I briefed him on my relationship with Nendaka. It was my habit to give ambassadors more information than was necessary, and I explained in some detail Adoula and Nendaka's plan to remove Gbenye at some time in the future. Unfortunately, I was unaware that Ed could give the appearance of listening while his mind was actually on another matter. I eventually learned that I had to watch his eyes. When Ed's eyes were not looking at me, he was not listening, and his mind was somewhere else.

Sometime after that briefing, Ed put his head in my door and said: "I've just told the prime minister to get rid of your boy." That grabbed my attention. I slammed my desk drawer shut and followed him to his office.

"Wait a minute, Ed. What was that you just said? Who's to be fired?"

"Nendaka. He never should have picked a fight with Gbenye," Ed said, as cool as can be, settling back in his chair.

I was so furious, my ears were singing.

"If one of them has to go, it's got to be Nendaka," he continued. "That's what I told Adoula. Gbenye is the one with political clout. Nendaka is just a civil servant."

"Ed, don't you remember that I briefed you, in some detail on this plan? It was a setup to get rid of Gbenye!"

Ed looked vague and stared past me. "You never briefed me on any setup." Neither one of us spoke for a moment. "Anyway, it makes no difference. Nendaka has to go. I've already advised Adoula."

I was so pissed off that I was spluttering. "Nendaka is pivotal. He has more political clout than almost anyone in the government. You just don't get it." I could see that Ed had tuned me out, but I was stubborn and kept going. "Nendaka, Bomboko, and Mobutu are the central power figures here. If we attack one, the other two will support him. You'll see. If Adoula tries to oust Nendaka, Mobutu might use the army to remove both Adoula and Gbenye. You and I wouldn't be sitting here today without Nendaka. He has been a tremendous ally."

I was wasting my breath. "Okay," I said, reaching for the door. "I'll tell Adoula there's has been a misunderstanding, and he should go ahead when he is ready with his plan to get rid of Gbenye."

I immediately drove to Adoula's office. His *chef de cabinet* was aghast at what had happened and wanted to know why the ambassador chose to defend Gbenye at the expense of Nendaka. I assured him it was all a misunderstanding and went into Adoula's office.

Adoula's first question was should he interpret Gullion's advice as a change in American policy? I assured him that there was no change in policy, there had merely been a misunderstanding, and that he should carry on with his plan when ready, which is what he did. Some time after our conversation, Adoula dismissed Gbenye from the government.

Ambassador Gullion and I had picked up where I left off with Tim and Mac. We met, if only briefly, almost every evening to review the day's events and to brief each other on the day's developments, often over a drink at his residence. We had been on a first-name basis, but after the Adoula/Nendaka incident, we abruptly returned to a "Mr. Ambassador" and "Mr. Devlin" basis.

I assumed that Ed would request that I be replaced, as was his right, and each day I expected to receive a cable recalling me to Headquarters. I had not reported my actions because there seemed little use in stirring the pot until I knew what action Ed would take. We continued to meet and work together, but our discussions were formal in contrast to our earlier relationship. Things rocked along like that for several weeks until one evening at his house after our customary drink and day's round-up. I was about to leave when he said, "Have another, Larry."

I noted the use of my first name, but I declined the invitation because I knew he had some social engagements ahead of him. However, he insisted, saying he had time before going out to dinner and asked me to pour him another Scotch as I poured mine. We sat sipping the second drink, not saying anything. Then, to my surprise, he said, "Hey, I nearly screwed up rather badly, I know that now. And you saved me from making a serious mistake. What I want to know is, can you still work closely with me?"

"Except for that one incident I think we have been working well together," I said. After that, it was the Ed-and-Larry team. We were never as close, personally, as I had been with Tim and Mac, Ed being more reserved than either of them, but we worked quite well together. I think he came to respect my abilities as an intelligence officer, and I know that I felt lucky to work with him. There was never another serious problem between us, and when we had a difference of opinion, we worked it out.

In late 1962, Ed suggested that I resign from the CIA and accept a commission as a Foreign Service officer. He said he had discussed his recommendation with Secretary Rusk and with the inspector general of the Foreign Service and both had agreed that I could transfer in grade. Ed believed I would eventually become an ambassador if I were to make the change. I was flattered, but after some consideration I decided to remain in the CIA. I believed that so long as the Cold War lasted I could accomplish more in the CIA than I could in the Foreign Service.

And, Lord knows, I had my hands full in the Congo. Dave, our Elisabethville representative, reported that the situation in the Katanga was worse than it had ever been. The Katangans had set up roadblocks, opened fire on the Indian troops who tried to remove them, and surrounded the airport, preventing the UN forces from moving freely along the road between the airport and Elisabethville. They had also hit a UN helicopter with ground fire and arrested UN personnel.

Dave kept trying to obtain intelligence on Katangan plans, but each time he went out to meet his agents he came under fire. Though most of the shots came from Katangan troops, I was to learn from personal experience that UN troops sometimes regarded any white man as a likely mercenary. Dave kept the intelligence flowing, but since he was no longer able to send messages through the post office telex machine, Dave's communications officer began sending them to us via Morse code.

This worked fine for a time, but one day while sending his dots and dashes the message broke off with a long, uninterrupted dash. Our communicators tried to re-establish contact with Elisabethville but there was no response. There had been no telephone contact with the city for some time, and we were completely cut off. The embassy asked Sture Linner, the UN chief, for information but learned only that the military situation was highly confused.

I feared that Dave's offices had either been hit by a mortar round or his communicator had been felled by a stray bullet, so I decided to fly to Elisabethville immediately. Taking a communicator and a replacement radio with me, we got a ride on a United States Air Force C–130 that was transporting supplies for the UN.

On reaching Elisabethville airport, the pilot put the plane into a sharp dive, pulling up and landing at the very last minute. He later explained that it was an "attack landing" to minimize the risk of being shot at by the Katangais as he came in to land. It was, no doubt, an effective means of avoiding ground fire, but it took the communicator and me by surprise and gave our hearts a pretty fair jumpstart.

Once on the ground, I contacted the senior United Nations officer, an Indian, to ask how we might get into town. I also wanted his assessment of the military situation.

"There are roadblocks and roving bands of Katangan troops on the airport road," he said. "We have an armored column that goes into town once a day. It's the only safe way. Unfortunately, it has already gone so you'll have to wait until tomorrow."

For me, waiting a whole day was out of the question. The Indian officer refused to loan us a vehicle, so we began checking the large number of abandoned cars at the airport parking lot. We eventually found a Peugeot that was unlocked with the keys in the ignition.

Everything went as smooth as silk until we approached a roadblock manned by Ethiopian UN troops. I slowed down and gave the Ethiopians a friendly wave. Either I failed to appear friendly or they took us for a couple of mercenaries for, just as I slowed down to show them our American passports, one of the soldiers opened fire. I floored the accelerator, and we shot through the roadblock knocking aside the barrels that were supposed to stop vehicles. From then on, it was clear sailing until we reached Dave's offices.

Dave greeted us and explained the sudden break in communications. Stray mortar rounds aimed at Tshombe's palace had been landing near Dave's offices. Fed up with the situation, Dave's communicator had moved his emergency generator inside to protect it. He had assumed that with all the windows in the room open it would be safe to operate, but when Dave returned to the office, he found the communicator unconscious, slumped over his telegraph key, done in by the carbon monoxide fumes from the generator's motor. Dave rushed him to a Belgian doctor, who was able to revive him, though he was still not in fighting trim and needed rest and treatment in Leopoldville.

After Dave gave me his verbal assessment of the military and political situation, I left the replacement communicator with him and headed back to the airfield with the sick man, returning by the same road I had come in on. When we reached the Ethiopian roadblock, we showed our American passports and were waved through without further ado. Either the troops had changed or they had realized their mistake.

At the airport, I returned the automobile to its original parking place and left my card together with a note stating the United States government was responsible for any damage and would pay to have it repaired. As far as I know, no one ever presented a claim.

While I was trying to keep communications open between Elisabethville and Leopoldville, the ambassador was doing his best to come up with a compromise between Tshombe and Adoula. In order to keep Britain and our other NATO allies happy, the United States opted for a political compromise between the two sides rather than having the UN settle the problem militarily. Our government was fully aware that something had to be done to end Katanga's secession. If the Western powers failed to act, it was feared that Adoula would be replaced by Gizenga or another leftist who would then turn to the Soviets for help to defeat Tshombe and re-integrate Katanga into the Congo.

One of my jobs was to work in the shadows supporting Ed's efforts. When Ed was not meeting with Adoula and Bomboko, I was pressing them and several other members of the Binza Group to take our advice to meet with Tshombe and try to work out a compromise. While our objective was to end Katanga's secession, we wanted to preserve the province's relatively stable government and its rich mines.

Adoula finally agreed to meet with Tshombe, who consented when it appeared that the UN was prepared to resort again to force.

The meeting was to take place at Kitona, a former Belgian military base in the western Congo controlled by the United Nations. Ambassador Gullion flew to Ndola in Northern Rhodesia to meet Tshombe who was accompanied by the American, French, and British consuls from Elisabethville. Tshombe initially expressed his reluctance to go to Kitona but eventually consented.

The negotiations at Kitona were long and difficult and broke down several times only to be saved by Gullion and the UN representatives. Tshombe finally gave in and agreed to recognize the unity of the Congo with Kasavubu as chief of state, to place the Kantangan military under central government control, and to send Katanga's deputies and senators to the parliament in Leopoldville.

Washington was elated over the agreement, but its joy was short-lived. Tshombe reneged soon after his return to Elisabethville. A statement issued by his office claimed that Gullion had written the Kitona agreement and forced him to sign it. He agreed, however, to send his parliamentarians to Leopoldville for the next parliamentary session. But what he really wanted to do was to stall UN military action and, disappointing though it was, the Kitona meeting came to nothing. Knowing Tshombe's delaying tactics well, neither Gullion nor I were greatly surprised.

The next problem was purely a station matter. Jacques, the European who had volunteered his services in the early days, had become an invaluable agent through his many contacts with Congolese ministers, parliamentarians, and newspaper editors. But, one fine day, he received an expulsion order giving him thirty days to leave the Congo. Every effort by his influential political friends to have the expulsion order annulled was useless. Even Kumoriko, the president of the senate, who was from the district where Jacques had his plantation, claimed he could not get the order revoked.

I could have gone to Nendaka or Mobutu for their help but that would have blown Jacques's cover, something I did not want to do unless as a last resort. I asked Jacques to make one last effort, and his solution, as it turned out, was entirely African. He went back to his plantation and sent the local *feticheur* (a medicine man) a case of beer three days in a row. On the third day, the *feticheur* came to see Jacques and asked him why was he was sending him beer. Jacques explained that he was being expelled from the country and that even the president of the senate, a local man no less, could not help him. He had decided to return to his plantation for one last visit, and the beer was his way of saying thanks for all the favors the *feticheur* had done for him in the past. The *feticheur* nodded thoughtfully and said he would return later that day.

When he came back, he was carrying a fetish made of dried bat skin, feathers, and leaves pierced by several needles. He told Jacques to see Kumoriko once more and give him the fetish with the message that the *feticheur* had sent it because Jacques was being expelled.

Jacques promptly called on Kumoriko and presented him with the fetish. Kumoriko, who was sitting behind his desk, began flailing his arms and screaming in terror. He fell over backwards and, from the floor, begged Jacques to take the fetish away. Jacques picked it up and walked out. The next day, his expulsion order was cancelled. Later, the *feticheur* told Jacques that Kumoriko had planned to take over his plantation. Jacques was not entirely surprised.

Jacques remained in the Congo for some years until he was transferred, for medical reasons, to a European post where he could obtain proper treatment. He was one of our more productive and capable agents, a man who was sometimes frightened by the dangers involved in his work, but one who never failed to try to carry out whatever task he was assigned.

On the political front, we could not rest easy so long as Gizenga remained in the wings. He had been out of sight since he had returned to Stanleyville, but he was certainly not out of mind. Projecting himself as Lumumba's political heir, he was a rallying point for Adoula's opponents. In retrospect, he probably was not as great a danger as we Americans and Adoula considered him to be. He lacked charisma, almost never left his house to meet people, and, from my personal observation of him, seemed a dull person of limited intelligence. At the time, however, we were concerned that Adoula's failure to resolve Katanga's secession would provide an opening for Gizenga to move in and take over the government.

I doubtless contributed to some of this fear by my reporting on Gizenga's efforts to return to power. While no one considered physical action to eliminate him, we were fully committed to opposing him politically. Our efforts were focused on parliamentary support for Adoula's government to impress on the non-aligned nations that he had the backing of the Congolese parliament and people. The first victory came in early January 1962 when parliament voted sixty-six to ten to give Gizenga forty-eight hours to return to Leopoldville to defend himself against a charge of secessionist activities. Gizenga responded by saying that he would return only when the government had forced Katanga to abandon its secession. At the same time, he tried to arrest General Lundula, the commander of the Stanleyville garrison. When that move failed, he reversed course and said he would return to Leopoldville on January 20 to resume his duties as deputy prime minister. But on January 15, parliament voted sixty-seven to one to censure him, automatically removing him from office, and Adoula, somewhat unnecessarily, declared he had dismissed Gizenga from his government.

While Adoula and the Binza Group were congratulating themselves on their success, we found ourselves facing another problem. To everyone's surprise, Gizenga flew to Leopoldville, spent the first night at the Royale, the UN headquarters, but told Sture Linner the next day that he planned to move to his official residence. I will never understand why Gizenga took this step because he was not a man to take chances. Meanwhile, Adoula told us that Gizenga was going to be arrested for having caused the deaths of Congolese soldiers when he tried to arrest General Lundula.

The UN, however, made it clear to us that Gizenga was neither under arrest nor under its protection. Adoula assured Linner that the government would provide security for Gizenga, but a few days later Gizenga was arrested and moved to the army camp in

Leopoldville. Adoula said he was being held in protective custody, rather than house arrest, and would be safer there than in his residence. But it did not stop Washington from feeling terrified that Gizenga would meet Lumumba's fate. The death of Lumumba had resulted in a political fire storm in many parts of the world that surprised Washington. The United States was not involved, but much of the world believed it was responsible. Thus, the United States did not want a repeat performance. The ambassador and I received strict instructions in our separate channels to prevent any such action, and were also instructed to avoid giving the impression of American participation in deciding Gizenga's future. Nendaka told me that Gizenga would be held incommunicado but would be allowed to meet with his lawyers. I warned him of the need to ensure Gizenga's safety and also pointed out the dangers of delay in resolving the crisis. If there were to be a trial, the sooner it was held the better.

While Gizenga had never won any popularity contests, many Lumumbist deputies, who had voted to censure him, were concerned about his situation. Gizenga's tribal support came from eastern Leopoldville province and the capital where his tribal brothers accounted for a considerable portion of the population. After Gizenga's arrest, they demonstrated in front of our embassy to show their displeasure at what they saw as American involvement in the move against their leader.

Gizenga's imprisonment placed the Soviet Union in a quandary. The Soviets did not want to offend Adoula because they still hoped that the reluctance of the Western nations to use military means to end Katanga's secession would force Adoula to turn to them for help. On the other hand, they could not ignore his imprisonment. Khrushchev's response was to orchestrate a campaign for Gizenga's freedom by rallying communist parties and their allies throughout the world. The campaign ostensibly had no connection with the Soviet Union, but anyone familiar with communist tactics knew that the Kremlin was the mastermind. The campaign was not as massive or successful as those that the Soviet Union had mounted on behalf of Lumumba, but it served to demonstrate that the Soviets were doing their best for an old friend. As a second string to its bow, the Soviet Union called for a UN Security Council meeting to discuss the Katanga problem. No mention was made of Gizenga, but the Soviets, or one of their stooges, would undoubtedly raise the subject.

I pointed out to Adoula and Bomboko the trap that the Soviet Union was preparing. Ed tried a little later to do the same with Adoula, but the prime minister had already left for an African summit meeting in Lagos, Nigeria. Instead, Ed sent a private message warning Adoula that the Soviets would use the Security Council meeting to raise Gizenga's imprisonment and criticize the Congolese government. Ed suggested that he tell the secretary-general that a special Security Council meeting was unnecessary because he himself would be explaining the situation to the General Assembly. U Thant agreed with Adoula, and the Soviets never got their Security Council meeting.

In February 1962, Ed flew to the United States to prepare the way for Adoula's visit to Washington and the United Nations in New York. Before leaving the Congo, he asked me to impress on Adoula that it was important to be in Washington on time for his meeting with President Kennedy. One afternoon, shortly before he was scheduled to leave, Adoula asked me to tell President Kennedy that he would have to postpone their luncheon engagement by one day because his wife wanted to do some shopping in New York before going to Washington. I told him that one does not arbitrarily postpone meetings with the president of the United States. Besides, I continued, the president almost certainly had a full schedule and might well not be available for lunch a day later than planned. Adoula accepted my argument, but I could see that he found it hard to take. After all, although he was a prime minister, people were always canceling or changing appointments with him.

Adoula duly turned up on time and during the lunch with Kennedy, he looked around the table and asked, "Où est Carlucci?" (Where is Carlucci?) He had known Frank, then a second secretary at our embassy, and assumed that he must be influential in policy matters concerning the Congo since he had been recalled to Washington. Kennedy, who had never heard of Carlucci, turned to Soapy Williams and asked who Carlucci might be. When he was told that Carlucci had been at the Leopoldville embassy and was now assigned to the Congo Task Force, Kennedy quietly told Soapy to get him to the table as soon as possible. In no time, a somewhat surprised Carlucci was having lunch with Adoula and President Kennedy in the White House.

While Adoula was in New York, he met with African and Asian diplomats at the United Nations and assured them that Gizenga was in no danger. Meanwhile, back in the Congo, Gizenga was moved from Leopoldville to the small island of Bula Bemba located just off the Congo's narrow coastline in the South Atlantic. Nendaka said that it was done because Gizenga was having too many visitors in the military camp. Nendaka also said that Adoula had approved the move before leaving for Washington.

I do know that Mobutu, Nendaka, and many other government leaders strongly favored placing Gizenga on the island. The only way to reach the island was by a small boat controlled by the Congolese army, which did not mean it was escape-proof, but it was more secure than where he had been kept in the capital. Gizenga remained a prisoner for a considerable time, but eventually, as a result of pressure from abroad, he was released and lived for some years in Egypt before returning to the Congo.

The eclipse of Gizenga complicated Khrushchev's efforts to gain a foothold in the Congo. He did not want to antagonize Adoula and risk having his embassy closed once again. The Soviets had returned to Leopoldville in September 1961 with Leonid Podgornov as *chargé*. He had been a member of the original Soviet embassy that had been closed down by Mobutu a year earlier. He got down to business immediately and started passing out money a bit too obviously to Adoula's opponents. Adoula was not amused.

Since the Congolese are not secretive people, Nendaka's *Sûrêté* quickly spotted what was going on and provided Adoula with an excuse to refuse Khrushchev's invitation to visit the Soviet Union. Undeterred by Adoula's lukewarm attitude, the Kremlin sent an ambassador, Sergei Nemchina, to lead the Soviet mission in September 1962. Nemchina's mission appeared two-fold. First, he made every effort to provide assistance to Adoula in an effort to undermine the Congo's dependence on the UN and the Western powers. At the same time, he wooed Adoula's leftist opposition, providing money and advice. It was not an easy assignment, and it was one that soon came to our attention.

When the Soviets had returned to Leopoldville a year earlier, they began looking for a large building to serve as office space and housing for the new embassy, a search that we heard about from one of our agents. It appeared that the Soviets had found a large, ten-story apartment building and were negotiating to buy it. We immediately went into action and arranged to have one of our agents express an interest in purchasing the building. Our man negotiated with the owner, a Belgian, who claimed that he did not want to sell his property to the Soviets, but would be forced to do so if our agent could not meet his price. Our man stalled as long as possible, claiming he had to obtain the agreement of partners and arrange financing through his bank.

Our objective was to get into the building in order to bug as many of the apartments as possible. Our primary targets were the apartments on the top floors where we believed the ambassador's office, the communications center, and the offices of the senior KGB and GRU officers would be located. Once inside, we made plans of the configuration of the building and requested audio technicians. We were short of time because the Belgian owner had finally agreed to sell his building to the Soviets.

The technicians arrived, but there was a major problem. Murphy's Law was at work against them—what could go wrong did go wrong. They failed to bring a drill. We requested one immediately, but it took two days to arrive. By that time, the Soviets had placed two guards in the building and even the so-called silent drill is a noisy machine. Suffice it to say, some installations were completed but not as many as we had planned.

Once the Soviets had moved into their new embassy, Jeff thought of a plan to make life difficult for them. We contacted a *feticheur* through Jacques and paid the man to place a curse on the embassy and anyone who entered the property. In order to insure that his curse became well-known in the community, Jacques had him dance in front of the embassy for hours chanting the curse. We had no idea what it was all about, but we knew that most Congolese were extremely superstitious, as Jacques's tactic for saving his plantation had revealed. The cost, anyway, was minimal and we felt it was money well spent, even if it only prevented one potential Congolese agent from falling into the hands of the Soviets.

16

TSHOMBE AND KATANGA PROVINCE continued to preoccupy the Adoula government throughout 1962 and into 1963, and the issue increasingly concerned Washington. It was clear to us in the embassy that Tshombe was still stalling. He was obviously hoping that either the UN would withdraw from the Congo or the United States would tire of trying to force him to abandon secession.

Khrushchev, ever the gambler, placed his wager on the flagging interest of the United States. Actually, it was not a bad bet. Belgium, Britain, and France opposed the use of force to bring Tshombe into line, and the United States government was sharply divided. Rusk and his under secretary, George McGhee, generally went along with the British and Belgians while Soapy Williams and a number of the State Department liberals had come round to support the embassy position.

Ed and I believed that if Tshombe were allowed to stall indefinitely, Adoula would either lose control of parliament or he would turn to the Soviets and African radicals for help in ending Katanga's secession. We made these views clear to our superiors in Washington, but the stalemate continued month after month.

Tshombe was supported by one of the best lobbying organizations in Washington, ensuring that his case was heard in Congress and the media. President Kennedy, who found himself between the contending forces, often called Ed on an open telephone line to discuss his reports. This was bad for security, but it insured that Ed's views reached the pinnacle of the political pyramid.

I once found myself involved in the dialogue. Mac Godley had been recalled to Washington to serve as head of the Congo Task Force in the Department of State. His replacement as deputy chief of mission had not yet grasped the nuances of the Congolese political situation when, in the absence of Ambassador Gullion, President Kennedy called. The DCM asked me to take the call, and I answered the president's questions, apparently to his satisfaction. Another time, Ed came to my office to say that President Kennedy had called him around three in the morning. Ed had been at a party that night and had had more drinks than he could carry comfortably. He told me ruefully that he could not remember what he had said to Kennedy, nor could he remember whether he had received any instructions from the president. He asked me if I could try to find out without drawing the attention of the president or senior State Department officials. I sent a back channel (an unofficial message that is not disseminated) to a friend who reported that the president seemed satisfied with the conversation and that he had not given Ed any new instructions.

In addition to the cable traffic, Kennedy and Ed exchanged letters via the diplomatic pouch when a courier was available. One day, Ed asked if I could rush a letter to Brazzaville where a courier was leaving for Washington that night. By chance, Jeff wanted to go to Brazzaville to do some shopping so I told Ed that he would take it. Jeff was given a letter identifying him as an official diplomatic courier, picked up the sealed courier bag, and left for the beach to catch the ferry. At the Congolese customs, he was told to open the pouch. Jeff refused and presented the courier's letter. But the official insisted he open the pouch. When Jeff refused again, the man pulled out his revolver, pointed it at Jeff, and ordered him to open the pouch. Jeff refused once more, picked up the telephone on the desk, and called Nendaka on his direct line.

Luckily, Nendaka was in his office and came to the beach immediately. Nendaka lectured the Congolese customs officer on the sanctity of diplomatic pouches and departed. Jeff headed for the door to get on the next ferry, when, suddenly, he was stopped by the same officer who again pointed his pistol at Jeff and demanded that he open the pouch. Astonished, Jeff reminded him of Nendaka's statements, only to be told that Nendaka was no longer present. At that point, Jeff simply ignored the man and boarded the ferry.

Ed's correspondence with Kennedy continued well into 1963 as the Katangan crisis dragged on and Tshombe proved himself a master of stonewalling. Exploiting the divisions within the United States political community, he suggested a meeting with Adoula at Kamina, a large former Belgian military base in Katanga occupied by UN forces. Adoula countered, offering to meet in Leopoldville and, after much haggling, Tshombe agreed. This small step raised the hopes of Secretary Rusk and the Washington and European factions that favored a peaceful solution. Our view in Leopoldville was that Tshombe saw the meeting as another delaying tactic designed to head off the UN from taking action against him.

Tshombe did come to Leopoldville, the talks stalled, and Adoula had to leave on a previously scheduled visit to the interior. Tshombe decided to return home for what he described as a brief stay while Adoula was absent. But, once again, he was prevented by Congolese soldiers from leaving the airport, a situation similar to the one that transpired at Coquilhatville where soldiers had prevented Tshombe from leaving.

I worked hard on Nendaka, Bomboko, and Mobutu that day and into the night, trying to convince them that, by preventing Tshombe's departure, they were only helping his supporters in Europe and the United States. Ed and UN officials did the same, and Tshombe was finally allowed to leave in the early hours of the morning. The fact that some soldiers decided to prevent Tshombe from leaving after the Congolese authorities had agreed to his departure made the Leopoldville government look weak and incompetent. That, in turn, provided Tshombe with an argument for why it had been necessary for Katanga to separate from the Congo.

The long delay in resolving the Katangan crisis contributed to serious political problems for Adoula. As the months passed, we noted a sharp drop in his parliamentary support. Adoula lost favor with many of the Lumumbists who had supported his dismissal of Gizenga. Some believed he had not shown sufficient determination in trying to end Katanga's secession. Others had succumbed to the financial blandishments of the Soviets, or were unhappy that he had not rewarded them with government positions. Whatever the reason, Adoula faced the danger of losing a vote of confidence, which would have forced his resignation. In the embassy, we felt sure that a successor would come from the Lumumbist group and would be either Soviet-leaning or openly pro-Soviet.

But Secretary Rusk was reluctant to act on Katanga. Once Adoula's negotiations with Tshombe had failed, Ed recommended that economic sanctions against Katanga should be considered. One plan called for Tshombe to hand over fifty percent of Katanga's tax and foreign exchange revenues to the central government. Economic sanctions, including the most extreme option with the UN blocking all Katanga's copper and cobalt exports, would be backed up by the threat of military action.

Ed and I flew to Washington in July 1962 to support these initiatives. We briefed everyone of importance in the Africa policy community, stressing our belief that failure to end Katanga's secession would sooner or later bring down the Adoula government. We were not successful: the sanctions' option was watered down by Secretary Rusk and President Kennedy. In short, they were no longer sanctions, merely pious recommendations that played into Tshombe's hands. On the return flight, I concluded that the only things of value on the trip were some useful meetings with my CIA colleagues and a visit to my parents on their wedding anniversary and my mother's birthday.

In mid-October 1962, I received an "eyes only," not-to-be-discussed-with-anyone cable. It was short, but alarming. I was instructed to remain within a fifteen-minute drive from the embassy until advised to the contrary. It did not take great imagination to guess what was going on. The Voice of America and BBC radio broadcasts, to which I listened every morning while shaving and showering, had been full of reports of the newly discovered Soviet missile sites in Cuba. Reading between the lines, I could see that the United States was about to respond.

I normally made it a point of knowing exactly where the ambassador was—which receptions and dinners were on his calendar—and I always told the communications duty officer and Jeff where I could be reached. After receiving the cable, I was even more careful than usual to check with the ambassador's secretary every evening and sometimes to ask Ed himself about his plans.

One night, when Ed's secretary assured me that he was free that evening, I decided to double-check because it was most unusual for him to have a free night. American ambassadors are much sought-after guests for receptions, dinners, and parties, and politics was Leopoldville's life's blood. Ed's office was only a step away from mine, and around seven in the evening, as I was preparing to leave, I dropped in and casually asked whether he had plans for the evening. Yes, said Ed, quite positively. He was going home to split a bottle of champagne with his wife, Pat, and enjoy a quiet evening with her.

I returned home late when, shortly before eleven o'clock, my communications chief called to say that I was needed immediately at the embassy. I made the drive through the dark and deserted streets of Leopoldville in less than four minutes. A fourteen-part cable was still coming in with instructions for me. The first section stated that Ed and I were to brief Adoula at exactly midnight on U.S. plans to counter the Soviet missile threat. From the specific time mentioned, I realized that ambassadors and chiefs of station the world over would be briefing chiefs of friendly nations at exactly the same time. The details of the U.S. action were coming in the remainder of the message.

I telephoned Ed's residence at once. The phone had rung many times before a sleepy houseboy answered and said the ambassador was out. I called Jeff and told him to go to the residence immediately to confirm that the ambassador was not there. If he happened to be there, Jeff was to ask him to come to the embassy and then join me in the office. Five minutes later, Jeff phoned to say the ambassador was not home. I told him to call our station officers and to assign each a section of the city. It was vital, I told him, to find the ambassador.

While Jeff and his crew were beating the bushes, I read the full message. Part thirteen of the fourteen-part message was missing, but I made notes on the other parts. I thought I could guess the general drift of the missing section and quickly ordered my thoughts for I realized that I might have to brief Adoula alone if Ed could not be found. As I finished writing, one of the junior communicators ran in to say that he had just seen the ambassador's car parked in front of a nearby restaurant.

It was nearly 11:45. I rushed to the restaurant where I found Ed and Pat having a liqueur with their coffee.

"We have to be at the prime minister's by midnight, Ed."

Pat put down her glass and stared at me in disbelief. "You're joking, Larry. We're having dinner."

Ed had already pushed back his chair.

"Ed, where are you going? Ed?" Pat asked.

Ed smiled wearily and buttoned his jacket. "Do you have enough money to pay the bill?" he asked, patting her on the back.

I briefed Ed as we drove to Adoula's residence. I looked at my watch as we rang the doorbell. Midnight. There were no soldiers guarding the house, and the night watchmen had long ago found a quiet nook to sleep in. Adoula came padding to the door in pajamas and bare feet. We explained that we had an urgent message from President Kennedy and outlined the decision of the United States to impose a naval blockade against Cuba. After we had provided a full justification of the move, Adoula rolled his eyes, as was his wont when nervous or excited.

His first words were, "This could mean war."

"True enough, but only if the Soviet Union tries to break the blockade," Ed said.

We went over the details of the policy and stressed that President Kennedy counted on the Congo's support in any UN debate on the matter. Adoula immediately promised the Congo's full backing and said he would tell Bomboko to instruct the Congolese ambassador to the UN to work with the U.S. delegation and to do his best to rally as many African nations as possible to the United States' side.

Ed and I returned to the embassy where we sent off cables reporting on our meeting and Adoula's assurance of Congolese support. I then drove to Bomboko's home, briefed him on our meeting with Adoula, and made sure that he would send the necessary messages to his UN mission, as well as to all Congolese embassies. I finally returned to the embassy and found that the missing thirteenth section of the message had come in and that my guess concerning its contents had been correct.

Jeff, who had remained in the office, and I got home at about five in the morning but were back in the embassy by eight. We had to contact our agents to insure that they clearly understood and supported U.S. policy on this critical matter. We continued with our regular work but also kept Headquarters advised of the reaction of our agents and other key Congolese contacts.

When it was all over, we discovered that Kennedy's successful gamble raised our stock with the Congolese. Even some of those who leaned far to the left congratulated me on the president's successful handling of an extremely delicate matter.

The Cuban missile crisis in October 1962 erased the Congo from the minds of Kennedy and most of his key advisers. The president was reluctant to take or support any action against Tshombe that was likely to upset any of the nations that had supported the American blockade of Cuba. Many of our NATO allies opposed stiff measures, and President Kennedy believed he owed them a debt of gratitude for their support during the Cuban missile crisis. As we had expected, Dean Rusk's diluted plan of action vis-à-vis the Katanga accomplished little or nothing. The Katangan problem, however, would not go away.

The same senior advisers, namely Soapy Williams and Harlan Cleveland, who had been prepared to deal with Lumumba and who had contributed to the removal of Ambassador Timberlake, were now hell-bent to support strong United Nations action designed to whip Tshombe into line and to end the Katanga secession.

While Washington was trying to resolve its policy differences over Katanga—and failing—we were compelled to step up our political action operations to counter a new Soviet effort to expand its influence in the Congo. Ambassador Nemchina and his intelligence crew were providing financial support for the parliamentary opposition, but at the same time Nemchina was offering to provide the government with assistance in ending the Katanga secession. Although our official policy supported the maintenance of a moderate government in the Congo, the failure of Secretary Rusk to accept the fact that negotiating with Tshombe was pointless insured the situation remained precarious. Operating against the Soviets and the Congolese left-wing political groups was not easy. Around this time I was handling twenty-two agents and/or collaborators.

The Soviets were trying to forge a closer relationship with Adoula and depict the U.S. as a half-hearted supporter of his government. We picked up intelligence that the Soviets had told Adoula that, after the UN had withdrawn from the country, Moscow would provide sufficient military equipment to enable the government to end Katanga's secession within a few months. The Soviets were playing the same old Cold War game as they had done in Lumumba's time. Khrushchev had not forgotten his objectives in Africa. His failures in the Congo in September 1960 and in the Cuban missile crisis made success in this new initiative all the more important.

Fate rather than careful planning in Washington eventually resolved the Katanga problem. On Christmas Eve 1962, Katangan troops shot down a UN helicopter and wounded several UN soldiers. After failing to obtain a cease-fire, UN troops rapidly removed the roadblocks, captured the Katangan Gendarmerie headquarters, and occupied Elisabethville. They took Kipushi, a key border town with Northern Rhodesia, two days later.

We were delighted, but Washington dithered once again, urging the Secretary-General to prevent his forces from going too far. U Thant assured the United States that he was not seeking a victory, but by January 2, 1963, UN troops had occupied Jadotville, site of the *Union Minière* headquarters and the mines. They were in a position to cut off all exports of Katangan copper and cobalt, a situation that almost certainly motivated *Union Minière* to encourage Tshombe to seek a peaceful end to the secession.

Nonetheless, Tshombe did not give up easily. He desperately tried to negotiate a compromise, but the UN made it clear it would only deal with him as a provincial president and that officials from the central government would be sent to Katanga. Britain, having long opposed a military solution, changed tack and urged Tshombe to cooperate. However, Britain's continued involvement with Tshombe so infuriated Adoula and the Binza Group that they considered breaking diplomatic relations. I had to work hard to convince them that such a step would hurt the Congo far more than it would punish Britain. Persuading Adoula to proclaim an amnesty for Tshombe and all the members of his government posed another major problem, but he finally agreed.

On January 21, UN forces entered Kolwezi, Katanga's last major town, and Katanga's independence, which had lasted two and a half years, was finally over. There were, however, innumerable problems facing the government, and Ambassador Nemchina and his KGB team were there to exploit them. The economy in the areas outside Katanga was nearing complete bankruptcy. The army remained a disorganized mob incapable of fighting, but its support was necessary to insure that an Adoula government, or at least a moderate pro-Western government, would remain in control of the country. A large number of parliamentarians were for rent to the highest bidder, thus posing a constant threat to the government. We continued working with the same intensity as before Katanga's re-integration, but the sense of crisis had eased.

The last months of my three-year tour as station chief had more ups than downs. But although I had lost the habit of being arrested, a habit I never learned to enjoy, I had to go through that experience one last time. Early in June 1963, I was awakened by a phone call about six in the morning from George, a junior case officer who had been assigned to the station on his first operational tour.

"I think I've killed a man," he said, in a low, strained voice.

"What?"

"I think I've killed somebody. Someone has been trying to break into my house several times over the past few nights. Last night he tried again. I couldn't find a flashlight, so I took a lantern and my pistol and went out to scare him away." At that point, George ran out of breath.

"And did you scare him away? What happened?"

"Well, we ran into each other in the carport, and, without thinking, I fired a shot at him. Just like that. No aiming, no nothing. And he ran away into the garden, so I thought that was the end of that."

"Then what?"

"I went back to bed," George said. "I went back to sleep. Then this morning my wife looks out the kitchen window and sees this man lying on the ground near the fence."

"Is he alive?" I asked.

George hesitated a minute. "I think he's dead," he said finally. "But I haven't actually gone close enough to the body to check."

"Get your wife and children to the embassy," I said. "Wait there until you hear from me."

I instructed him to take his wife and children to the embassy because a white man killing an African could result in demonstrations, even riots. I called Jeff and a Canadian doctor of Jeff's acquaintance and asked them to join me at George's house. When they arrived, we found that there was no question about it: George, who was far from a marksman, had drilled him right through the heart. The doctor departed, and while Jeff took photographs of the body, I called the police. After carefully explaining that I was merely acting in my consular capacity, I told the police sergeant that there was a dead man in the garden and gave him the address.

Jeff left to mind the office, and, expecting the police to arrive at any minute, I found a sheet in the house and covered the body. After half an hour or more, I heard a man outside shrieking like hell. I looked out to find that a guy had come along, had tried to steal the sheet, and was scared out of his wits when he found a body underneath. I recovered the sheet and covered the body once again, but the man continued to shriek at the top of his lungs, and in no time at all there was a crowd of Congolese in the street just outside the fence.

The crowd was muttering and shouting and raising their fists. They assumed that I was the killer. Realizing that things were turning ugly, I again phoned the police, only to be told that they could not come because they had no transportation.

Leaving the body in the garden, with the crowd still in the street, I drove to the police station and picked up a sergeant and another policeman. Back at George's place, I again explained that I had had nothing to do with the man's death and was there in my consular capacity. The sergeant assured me that he understood, but when we uncovered the body, he pulled out his pistol and, looking directly at me said, "Don't anyone move."

I realized that I was "anyone" and tried once again to explain that I was only doing my duty as the American Consul. He placed me under arrest in the house.

The sergeant then called what he referred to as the technical police; the body could not be moved, he said, until the technical police had photographed the scene of the crime. It appeared that the technical police were also without transportation; so the sergeant told me to go and get them in my car. "Sorry. I can't go," I told him. "I'm a prisoner. I'm under arrest."

He repeatedly ordered me to get them, but each time I pointed out that I was a prisoner and thus could not go. He finally got the point and told me I was no longer a prisoner and again ordered me to get the technical police. I did as he asked and found that the technical policeman was armed with a Brownie box camera. When we returned to George's house, the sergeant, as I expected, again declared me to be a prisoner.

Once the man with the Brownie box camera had taken a few pictures, the sergeant said he had to call the magistrate before we could move the body. And, lo and behold, guess what, the magistrate was without a car, and I was again told that I was no longer a prisoner and ordered to go fetch the magistrate.

When I picked up the magistrate, I found that he seemed to be intellectually a step or two ahead of the police sergeant and, better yet, he was a Mongo tribesman. I told him that I was a close friend of Justin Bomboko, the Mongo chief and foreign minister, and I revealed that I had been initiated into the tribe and made an honorary Mongo by Bomboko at a ceremony held at the Zoo Restaurant.

With that bit of information the magistrate assured me that he would guarantee that I would have no more problems with the police, and we drove off to George's house. When the magistrate removed the sheet, he let out a scream: the man was a fellow Mongo and one of his friends. I was a prisoner again.

The sergeant and the magistrate discussed my case and decided that they should take me to Makala Prison, but—same old problem—they did not have a car. So, we loaded the body into the trunk of my Peugeot 403. By this time, of course, *rigor mortis* had set in, and one of the man's arms was frozen up by his head. We all worked and sweated, trying to get the hand inside the trunk with the body. We finally had to give up. Someone pulled off his belt, and we tied the trunk down. The sergeant and his assistant, the technical policeman and the magistrate all piled into my car, and I got behind the wheel and drove off, with the dead man's hand sticking out of the trunk.

Instead of going to Makala Prison, I drove directly to the foreign ministry. When I arrived in front of the ministry, I swerved the car, drove up onto the lawn, jumped out of the car, and ran as fast as I could into Bomboko's office. Bomboko sat there bug-eyed as I blurted out my story of the dead burglar and my on-again, off-again arrests. Then he started to laugh.

When he stopped laughing, he went outside with me, ordered the police to remove the body from my car, and told them that they could not arrest a consul who was merely performing his duties. After that solemn harangue, I drove off leaving the foreign minister, the magistrate, the police sergeant, his assistant, the man with the Brownie box camera, and, last but certainly not least, the dead burglar on the lawn in front of the foreign minister's office.

We sent George and his wife and children to Brazzaville because we were afraid the police might take it into their heads to arrest him. We arranged with Headquarters for his recall, and Bomboko made it possible for George and his wife to return to their home to pack their personal effects. I later learned that George resigned from the service shortly after his return to the United States. He reportedly obtained a Ph.D. and went on to teach political science in a college somewhere in the western states.

ONE OF MY LAST major efforts as Chief of Station involved trying to obtain an air force for the Republic of the Congo because, up until then, it didn't exist. Adoula, Mobutu, and most of the government officials in Leopoldville recalled how Tshombe had employed his fighter aircraft to threaten the UN forces, and they asked me to obtain planes for the Congo. They believed that planes would prevent them from ever being at the mercy of some African state or a rebel movement. I told them that a few planes, even new ones, would not guarantee such protection, but they looked on airplanes as some sort of a talisman that would guarantee victory. Adoula insisted that, without planes, his government would fall.

Neither Ed nor I believed that for one minute, but we knew that planes, used properly, could prove useful in putting down a rebellion. The first signs of trouble instigated by the Soviets and radical Africans were beginning to appear. The situation was not obvious to the uninitiated onlooker, but Ed and I could see the early signs. We believed that a few planes would provide the government with a psychological weapon that would strengthen their resolve and, if properly employed, would be of use in case of rebellion or civil war. God knows, their army was a weak reed to lean upon.

I started the ball rolling by submitting a recommendation that the United States provide the Congo with a small number of planes. Ed endorsed my recommendation by sending supporting cables through his channels. The State Department was not convinced, and CIA Headquarters was not prepared to act without the approval of the Department. Neither of us was surprised, but we continued pressing our case.

Washington finally agreed to provide six unarmed World War II vintage T-6 training planes on the understanding that their use would be primarily psychological. Ed and I agreed that the planes should be unarmed, for we knew it would not be difficult to mount arms on the planes if the need arose. Since there were no Congolese pilots at that time, Headquarters agreed to locate pilots and maintenance personnel to work for the government of the Congo.

The planes arrived in the first half of 1963 and were ready for combat by the time Pierre Mulele launched his rebellion the following year in the eastern part of Leopoldville province. The government of the Congo and the station were one step ahead of the game, and although I was no longer Chief of Station when they were needed, I understand that it did not take long to arm the planes. They were slow but well suited for the Congo, where the enemy was not armed with modern weapons. This nucleus of an air force proved extremely useful when civil war broke out in earnest in 1964. Without the preparation that the T-6 planes provided, the conflict might have ended differently.

Sometime in the early spring of 1963, I received word that the man who had replaced Jeff as my deputy would assume my functions in June and that, after vacation and home leave, I would be assigned to Headquarters in Virginia as Chief of the East Africa branch (Jeff departed at the end of his two-year tour of duty in August 1961). At the same time, Headquarters advised me that I had been promoted to the grade of GS-15. Since I had been promoted to GS–14 in the spring of 1961, the promotion came as a surprise, an extremely agreeable one.*

The balance of my tour was, by Congo standards, a relatively calm period. While we were sometimes called upon to prop up the government, we concentrated primarily on developing new intelligence agents. The Devlin family also enjoyed numerous farewell parties. We had attended many dinners and receptions throughout our time in Leopoldville, but at last we were able to relax for perhaps the first time in nearly three years. It was not easy, however, to leave the Congo, for we had made many good friends among the Congolese and expatriate communities, some of whom remain in contact with us to this day.

*At that time, grades ran from GS-1 to GS-18, but to the best of my knowledge, there were few, if any, persons in a grade less than a five. Much depended on one's education, experience, and the needs of the service. A GS-15 is roughly the equivalent of an army colonel or a navy captain. I was surprised to be promoted so soon, as it normally required three years as a GS-14 before one could be considered for promotion to GS-15.

17

DURING THE TWENTY MONTHS that I was Chief of the East Africa branch at Headquarters, army mutinies occurred in Uganda and Kenya along with a coup in Zanzibar. I was also drawn back into the Congo where Kasavubu and Adoula struggled to keep the country from fragmenting as armed rebellions, fractious politics, and tribal conflicts sprouted like mushrooms after rain.

On one of my visits, rebels seized the U.S. Consulate in Stanleyville. The consul and four other members of his staff locked themselves in the communications vault and sent us a message that attackers were trying to beat down the heavy, reinforced door. I relayed the consul's message flash to Washington and called Mac Godley who was at a dinner in Binza. (Mac had replaced Ed Gullion as ambassador after a tour in Washington as head of the State Department's Congo Task Force.) While waiting for him to return, I drafted a message for him outlining four possible courses of action. The first was to take no action. The second was to call on the Congolese government to take action. (I noted that this scenario would have the same result as the first choice.) The third course was for the embassy to put together a small task force to try to rescue the consular staff. The last was to drop a unit of American paratroops on Stanleyville.

Washington's reply was, as I recall, ambiguous. None of my CIA or State Department colleagues can remember the message itself, let alone its contents. Left to our own devices, Mac, his DCM, Bob

Blake, and I began organizing a small force composed of embassy personnel to do the job, and we called it "Operation Flagpole," which was ironic because none of us could remember where the consulate's flagpole actually was. Its location was critical, however, for we planned to land a helicopter on the lawn in front of the consulate, load the personnel on the chopper, and be off in a matter of seconds. Unfortunately, the rebels moved more men into the area around the consulate, and the consul sent a message recommending that the operation be cancelled. The consul in Stanleyville and his staff were taken prisoner and finally rescued 111 days later by Belgian paratroopers flown to Stanleyville by the U.S. Air Force.

Some time in mid-1964, Glenn Fields, Chief, Africa Division, informed me that the director had received information that Christophe Gbenye, the then-leader of the Stanleyville rebellion, would soon be leaving Moscow to return to Stanleyville. As this was the same Gbenye with whom I had established a relationship when he was minister of interior in the Adoula government, President Johnson wanted me to try to contact the rebel leader. The object was to try to obtain the release of the American consular personnel being held hostage in Stanleyville. Glenn added that this mission was of the greatest importance and took precedence over all other operational duties with which I was involved. He stressed that it was expected that I would take up this temporary duty assignment immediately.

Glenn did not need to stress the importance of this assignment. I knew that the CIA was already devoting an enormous effort to achieve this objective. I also knew that President Johnson had a political interest in obtaining the release of the hostages.

In reply to my question, Glenn confirmed that no one knew Gbenye's specific itinerary. I noted that there were three likely itineraries that he might follow: to Cairo and then on over the Sudan to Orientale province; to Dar-es-Salaam, across Lake Tanganyika, and then up the rebel-held areas to Stanleyville; or fly to Burundi, cross into the Congo, and drive up to Stanleyville.

"You know the area; which route would you take?" Glenn asked. After a brief reflection, I eliminated the Dar-es-Salaam alternative, explaining that it was the longest and posed the greatest danger for Gbenye.

When I halted, Glenn, in his Georgia drawl, said: "You've got to pick one. You have to get a move on if you're going to fly the Atlantic tonight. Just do you're best, boy. That's all anyone can do." That was Glenn's way. He made you think, and if you seemed to be on the right track, he let you work out the details. I liked and respected him. He was a great boss, just as his predecessor, Bronson Tweedy, had been.

I was on my feet as he finished. "I'll put my money on the Burundi route. It is the safest. The Chicoms practically own Burundi. Also, Gbenye will likely want to talk to the rebel officers in the Bukavu area. They have been carrying the rebels' ball in the most recent fighting. He will want to insure that they are on his side in the infighting that plays such a role in the rebel leadership struggle. I'll cable you from each stop. Send me any new info that may come in."

I called Colette to tell her of my travel plans and to ask her to pack a travel bag. Poor woman, she was used to unscheduled departures and delayed returns. She had my travel bag ready when I reached home and was ready to drive me to Dulles airport. Maureen, our daughter, came home from school just in time to go with us. Maureen's education had not been that of the average American girl. Born in Paris, kindergarten in Washington, first through the third grades in Belgium, and fourth through sixth grades in Leopoldville. Now, she was enrolled in an American middle school. Luckily, she spoke and wrote English and French with bilingual proficiency, sailed through her classes, but was just learning about boys, softball, and American football.

As our travel office had told me that there was a daily Air Congo flight from Leopoldville to Bujumbura, I had booked a flight via Leopoldville in the hope that I could contact some of Gbenye's friends who might have information concerning his plans. That proved as wrong as the travel office's assurance that there was a daily flight to Bujumbura. It was a weekly flight, and it was not leaving until two days after my arrival in Leopoldville. Unable to find anyone who knew (or would tell me) Gbenye's plans, I booked myself on the next Air Congo flight and, at the same time, explored other means of speeding up my arrival in Burundi. Glenn had cabled that no one in Washington had info on our man's travel plans.

Late in the afternoon, I found that an American C–130 was transporting some Congolese military equipment to Bukavu and was told by the air attaché's office that it would be easy to get a flight from there to Bujumbura. Wrong. It took several early morning hours, but with the help of a fellow from our consulate, I found a Congolese pilot who was willing to fly me to Bujumbura in a Piper Cub for a price that I knew would upset the Agency's audit staff. It was the only way, as I was not about to try to drive through rebel territory.

It was only when we were in the air that the pilot proudly told me that he had eight hours solo time. It occurred to me that shooting my way through rebel ambushes might have proved a safer method of travel, but there was not a damn thing I could do about it.

We made a beautiful, one-wheel landing, but my hands were too busy holding on for me to bite my nails. The pilot finally managed to get both wheels on the ground, and I deplaned with pleasure. There was only one immigration/customs man to be found in the airport, but he was asleep. I borrowed his stamp, thus more or less legalizing my arrival in Burundi. As there were absolutely no vehicles in sight, I walked to the main road, thumbed my way into town with a friendly truck driver, and arrived at the American Consulate looking most undiplomatic.

Henry, our man in Burundi, was busy trying to close his diplomatic bag that would reach Washington in a few weeks. I found it rather difficult to get his attention concerning my need for his help. He had no information concerning Gbenye. He was one of those guys who believed he was doing his job when he sent a routine dispatch to Headquarters. I did, however, convince his administrative assistant to rent a car for me under the false name on a false driver's license that I had brought with me. While waiting for the young lady to return, I began calling all of the hotels in town. It was an easy job as there were only a few. A desk clerk in a hotel in the native district first said Gbenye was out, but revised his statement when I was unable to reply to a question he put to me in Swahili. He then said he had never heard of Gbenye.

With my newly rented Peugeot 404, I drove to the Paguidas Hotel, an old establishment that had seen better days, but it was still the best hotel in town. I gave the hotel telephone operator a small tip to place a call to my "old friend Christophe Gbenye," explaining that I could not speak Swahili. I would have given a thousand dollars if he could have found Gbenye for me, but big tips sometimes result in unwanted attention. He made the call and was told that Gbenye would return in about an hour. I went out for a short walk, telling the operator I would return in an hour.

Anxious to reach Gbenye, I returned after forty minutes. The operator demonstrated an unusual interest in me. He began by asking if I were an American. "No, Canadian," I replied. He then asked for my name, and I told him Joseph Smith, the name on my false driver's license. With that, he became very excited and said, "A friend, who is looking for a Canadian by the name of Joseph Smith, came to see me just after you went out. I told him you would be back in an hour. He should be back any minute."

I was afraid that was the case, for I wanted to get away before the man, who I presumed to be a member of the local service, returned. "I will wait in the bar," I said casually as I walked toward the bar. The bar was graced with enormously tall windows that were kept open and ran from the floor almost to the ceiling. I stepped through the nearest one into the garden and kept moving until I had reached my car. I next drove to what passed for a yacht club in Bujumbura. I recalled there used to be a pay phone there, and I immediately put through a call to Henry, the CIA man, who said he had to see me soon. We agreed by indirection on a meeting place.

When he arrived, he told me he had just met his best agent, a senior member of the Burundi service. The agent reported the Chicom intelligence representative had told him that Lawrence, a.k.a. Larry Devlin, a senior CIA officer, was scheduled to arrive two days hence on the Air Congo flight from Leopoldville. The Chinese had requested that Devlin be arrested at the airport and transported to a safe house used by the Burundi service for meetings with their Chinese counterparts. The agent had added that the Chinese had warned him that the government must be prepared to deny that Devlin had ever arrived in Burundi. The agent explained that a request of this sort was the equivalent of an order, as the Chinese communists controlled the Burundi government.

It was the agent's opinion that the Chinese might wish to move Devlin to the Congo for additional questioning. Once the interrogation was completed, Devlin could either be disposed of in the Congo or moved to China if he proved to be a useful source. Our conversation then went something like this.

"It's obvious that the Chicoms have a source in Air Congo, as I made that reservation only yesterday," I commented, feeling a bit weak in the knees at the thought of being *disposed of in the Congo*. The idea of becoming *crocodile bait* did not appeal to me.

I then told Henry that Gbenye appeared to be at the hotel in the native quarter of Bujumbura. When I told him about the phone operator's alleged friend who wanted to meet a Canadian by the name of Joseph Smith, he interrupted me to say: "That must be the hotel man for the Burundi service. He handles information on foreigners staying in the local hotels. It also means you can't stay at a hotel here, and you can't stay at my house. My houseboy is probably recruited by the locals. You will have to get out of town before they realize you are here."

"You forget one thing. I am here to see Gbenye. I will have to stay until I see him," I replied a bit sharply.

"Well sure," he said, "but where the hell are you going to stay?"

"In one of your safe houses, if you have one that is not blown."

"There is a house out by the lake that some of the consulate people use when they have beach parties. It has a toilet and running water."

"If that's the best you have, I'll have to take it," I said. "I will try to see Gbenye tonight or tomorrow morning early. I don't want him to have time to talk to any of his local contacts about me before I see him."

Henry looked rather pessimistic as he asked, "Do you trust him?"

"Hell no, I don't trust him, but he is the only chance we have at this time of trying to get the hostages out of Stanleyville."

Henry's eyes were dull with pessimism when he said, "I have a personal weapon, a small .38 revolver. I will loan it to you. You may need it. I'll go home and get it, and then show you the house out by the lake."

He was gone only a short time, and when he returned I followed him to the shack by the lake. It was not up to Hilton standards, but I had slept in a lot worse places when in the military.

Henry left me as fast as he could. "I'm sorry not to be able to put you up, but I know you understand." When I said it would be helpful if he would cover me when I went to see Gbenye, he mumbled something about having to think of his own security.

I replied that "I would like someone to know if the Chicoms picked me up." He replied that "he was sure I would not take unnecessary chances." He then wished me luck, ducking his head, and urged me to keep in touch.

After checking out the pistol to insure it was loaded, I slipped it into my pocket and set out for Gbenye's hotel. I thought it better to render him a surprise visit rather than give him time to think about it and, perhaps, consult the local authorities. Our relations had been friendly when he was minister of the interior, but both of us had been trying to use the other. I hoped that old relationships had left a favorable memory.

The area in which the hotel was located was reasonably well-lit, and the sound of music came from a nearby beer hall. The band was playing "Independence cha cha cha," the old standby of the Congo in 1960. Perhaps it was a good omen.

I parked and locked the car in a well-lit area around the corner from the hotel entrance; I wanted my wheels available if I had to make a hurried departure.

As I entered the modest reception area of the hotel, I came face to face with a Congolese that I recognized as one of the twin torpedoes who had served as bodyguards for Gbenye in Leopoldville. They were also alleged to be his hit men and enforcers. I could not remember his family name, but he was either Joseph or Jean. The twins were identical. I had never before felt the need to be able to greet them.

The other twin sat at a table by the hotel desk drinking beer. I greeted them both using their first names as though I had just found my long-lost brothers. Their response was anything but effusive, but I pretended not to notice. I saw the hardness of their eyes and the slight tightening of their facial muscles. It was my move, and they were ready for anything. In reply to my question as to whether le chef was available, they said "no," but one added he was not expected back until very late.

I was anxious to get out of the hotel and their presence; instead, I casually sat down, insuring that my back was to the wall and ordered beer for myself and for the twins. Careful not to ask questions that might upset them, I talked about Leopoldville, how much I missed it, and other generalities. The twins appeared to relax slightly, one of them even laughed when I mentioned a parliamentarian who had the reputation of a drunk and had fallen into a swimming pool at a reception given by the Italian ambassador.

My mind was racing as I sipped my beer. Should I ask them to give Gbenye a message? And what should I say? They would surely tell him I was in town and looking for him. I decided to say that I would return at nine the next morning to see Gbenye. When I asked them to deliver that message, I observed the quick glances they exchanged. I knew they would tell their friends of this meeting. I could only hope that it did not precede my meeting with their boss.

As I stood and paid for the beers with some local money that Henry had provided, they stood and walked out of the hotel with me, one on either side. That made me rather nervous, as I recalled that one brother was known for his dexterity with a knife and the other with the deadly use of his hands. Apparently they worked only on instructions. They saw me to my car, offered a perfunctory *bon soir*, and turned away as I pulled out. I did not turn on my lights immediately as there seemed no reason to facilitate their reading my license plate, if indeed they tried.

I spent the night among a cloud of mosquitoes, alternately cursing myself and Henry for having failed to obtain or provide a mosquito net. I realized that in the rush of my departure, I had failed to pack a supply of malaria suppressants. Having "enjoyed" bouts of malaria, after the Tunisian campaign, that returned annually for some seven years, and after being stationed in the Congo, I should have known better.

I was up with the sun and enjoyed a swim in the lake rather more than washing and shaving in cold water. I had decided to arrive at the hotel at eight rather than nine. If they were setting a trap, it might not be ready. I had decided not to carry Henry's pistol; the twins would likely shake me down. If I was found to be armed, it might upset Gbenye, and it might lead to the twins taking preventive action. If the locals were involved, five rounds of pistol ammunition would not do much good.

I walked into the hotel at exactly eight. My arrival clearly surprised the twins who were sipping coffee and staring into space. Bulges under their left arms told me they were packing iron, and I suspected that at least one also had a knife and the other a garrote chord. Almost in unison they demanded to know why I was there so early.

"I'm not early. It is eight o'clock. The time I told you last night." Looking confused, they insisted I had said nine. I smiled and replied: "I'm sorry. I was sure I had said eight. I will, of course, wait if this time is not convenient for my friend, *Monsieur Gbenye*. After a brief exchange in Swahili, one of them ran up the stairs, presumably to consult with their chief, and the other placed himself between me and the stairs.

Jean or Joseph, whichever twin he might be, reappeared and told me to follow him. I did as I was told, but I felt my flesh creep as I heard the footsteps of the other twin close behind. Was the twin behind me the one with the knife or the garrote chord? We climbed the warn runners of the stairs to the third floor (second floor, European) where the leading twin patted me down to ensure that I was not armed. I pretended to be offended and asked in a loud voice—that I hoped Gbenye would hear—why I, a friend of *Monsieur Gbenye*, would carry a weapon to a meeting with him.

I was shown into Gbenye's room, an eigh-foot by five-foot box, with a rug that had not seen a vacuum in recent years and a small window that had not seen soap and water since the building was constructed. The furniture consisted of a straight chair, a wash stand, and a bed.

Gbenye, who was standing near the head of the bed, planted wet kisses on my cheeks as he welcomed me. Speaking in French, he instructed the twins to wait for him in the lobby. He suggested that I sit on the unmade bed. He then asked to be excused for receiving an august representative of the United States in such a poor setting, adding that the role of a man fighting for the freedom of his country was not easy. He insisted it must have been the same for George Washington and Thomas Jefferson.

Seeming to accept his identification of himself with Washington and Jefferson, I said I had missed his friendship and guidance when he had withdrawn to Orientale province. I asked him why he had joined the rebels rather than remaining in Leopoldville where he wielded great political influence. I said he had had an excellent chance of becoming prime minister. His response was unexpected. With tears suddenly welling into his eyes, he said: "It was my turn to be prime minister, and they gave it to Adoula."

Caught off guard, I said something about positions being important, and, for the purpose of my mission, I promoted myself as now being responsible for half of Africa in the Department of State. He congratulated me, saying that he was happy that a man of my experience held such a post and launched into a long justification of the Congolese rebellion. I listened attentively until he ran out of breath. I then assured him that I would present his views personally to the Secretary of State and to President Johnson. As I had not expected to see him on my trip, however, I explained that I was not prepared to negotiate with him concerning the legality of his role, but as the United States government officer responsible for Stanleyville, I wished to discuss the fact that our consular personnel were unable to carry out their mission, and other American citizens, to include missionaries, were being mistreated.

Gbenye showed his true colors at that point, saying: "I utterly reject your claim that your consulate cannot function. If they are not meeting your needs, it is their fault, not mine."

I replied that "perhaps his officials had not kept him advised," but that I had incontrovertible evidence that they were being held under house arrest in the Stanleyville SABENA guest house.

Gbenye looked at me for nearly a minute, and then, shaking his head, said, "I can assure you that your people are as free as you are at this very minute. Why don't you come to Stanleyville with me and see for yourself that they are free and well-treated. Or, are you afraid to come?"

The gloves were off. I had been playing along with him in an effort to obtain the release of our consular personnel, but I could not show fear or accept his veiled threat that they were as free as I at this very minute.

I responded immediately: "No, *mon cher Christophe*. I am not afraid to go to Stanleyville with you. Why should I be afraid? In the first place, you are my friend. You would never allow anyone to hurt me. Secondly, you are an educated man who knows international law. You know that all diplomats are protected by international law." I put in the part about international law to remind him that he would be held responsible if something happened to the members of our consular staff.

I thought for a moment and mentally added a third reason. I had to report my conversation with Gbenye. The report would go to the director, and he, in turn, would take it to the Secretary of State, to McGeorge Bundy, the president's national security adviser—the man who had recruited me—and to President Johnson. He was the one on the political hook. The Stanleyville hostages were becoming a political problem for the administration. You could never be sure how a politician would react when he was under fire. I had to offer to go to Stanleyville with Gbenye. If my meeting was to achieve anything, I had to convince him that he was responsible for their safety. Despite all my talk about his being a friend, I did not trust him worth a damn. I had to take out insurance for myself in case the president or one of his minions decided that I was expendable, that it would be good politics to be able to show that he had gone so far as to send a personal emissary to Stanleyville in an effort to save "our boys." If the emissary died in the process, he could be awarded a posthumous medal and buried in Arlington.

With a sardonic smile, I looked at Gbenye and said, "You and I know there is a third reason you would protect me and protect those Americans you hold in Stanleyville. You know that I know, and the office for which I work knows, where your wife and children reside in Europe. You would never do anything that would place them in danger."

I knew that threat would shake him, for he would believe it as it was the kind of revenge he might exact. I also knew that I would be sharply criticized by some people in my own government for employing such a threat. I knew full well that the United States would never seek such revenge, but Gbenye did not know this.

Before ending the meeting, I reminded Gbenye that I was prepared to go to Stanleyville with him. He told me that he would visit his troops in the Bukavu region, but said he would return to Bujumbura. We could work out the details of the trip at that time.

As I recall, he did not sound all that eager to take me along with him, but I asked him to have someone advise our consul in Bujumbura when he wanted to see me once again.

I reported my meeting with Gbenye in some detail while remaining at the house by the lake. Headquarters happily instructed me to meet with Gbenye once again if he returned, but said I was not to go to Stanleyville as I would just become one more hostage. I remained in Bujumbura for about two weeks, but Gbenye did not return, and no one contacted the consul seeking a meeting with me.

I was involved in one more failed effort to win the release of the hostages. I was assigned on temporary duty to advise and support the American ambassador to Nairobi, who was named to negotiate the consular hostages issue with Thomas Kanza, the foreign minister of the rebel government. I had known Kanza in July 1960 when he was Lumumba's ambassador to the United Nations.

The negotiations went absolutely nowhere. Kanza was either not serious about resolving this issue or he was not given the authority to do so by his so-called government.

Most CIA operations officers begin trying to line up another field assignment almost as soon as they return to Headquarters. I had set my sights on Morocco, but on finding that the division chief had already promised the post to an Arabic- and French-speaking officer, I lined up Algiers as my next assignment. It appealed to me because it was totally different from the Congo. Algiers was a small post in a country with far more educated people than the Congo. There were no political or paramilitary operations, only normal intelligence operations. It offered an opportunity to go back to my first love: operations directed against the Soviet Union.

One morning, I heard through the office grapevine that the person scheduled to become station chief in the Congo, in July 1965, had just announced that he would not accept the post. The news spread like wildfire because it was most unusual for an officer to back out of such an important assignment at the last minute, a step not likely to prove career enhancing.

I was not surprised to receive a phone call that morning from Elizabeth, Richard Helms's secretary, informing me that Dick wished to see me. Dick had replaced Richard Bissell as deputy director of operations. (The title had changed from deputy director of plans, but it was the same job.) Dick greeted me in his usual, friendly manner and suggested that we sit down and chat. He was an experienced operations officer who knew how to handle people, but I had never heard of him inviting an officer to take a seat for a chat.

He soon got to the point. He was sure, he said, that I would love to return to the Congo. Knowing that he was keen to find a replacement for the Leopoldville post, I told him that I had many fond memories of the place but that I had plans for Algiers and was not interested in going back to the Congo. That did not stop him from fishing for me to volunteer for the assignment. I finally told him that if he wished me to go, he would have to give me a direct order. I would not volunteer. With that, it was agreed that I was to return to the Congo.

I remained Chief, East Africa for the time being. Fortunately, I had an extremely competent deputy and an equally competent chief of operations (Jeff, who had been with me in the Congo), which enabled me to focus on Congolese developments. In 1964, a rebellion led by Pierre Mulele, backed by the Soviets, launched a major offensive against the central government. Adoula's position became precarious, and Nendaka was dispatched—by the Binza Group—to see me, in order to determine whom the United States favored as Adoula's replacement.

Since this was State Department territory, I told Soapy Williams about Nendaka's mission and arranged for them to meet. Soapy refused to discuss the matter, stating that the U.S. continued to support Adoula, and Nendaka came away frustrated and empty-handed. He contacted me after the meeting to say that Adoula had lost his parliamentary majority and that his government was sure to fall soon. He added that the Binza Group was not prepared to go down with Adoula and would take action to insure that whoever took over would not be a Stanleyville leftist.

Shortly after Nendaka's visit, Adoula resigned and President Kasavubu named Tshombe—the man who had led Katanga's secession for two and a half years—to be his successor. Notwithstanding the irony of the situation, Kasavubu's choice proved popular with the great majority of the Congolese people. One of Tshombe's first acts was to recall the mercenary leaders who had fought for him in Katanga to help drive the rebels back and forestall the creation of an independent state based on Stanleyville.

The United States found itself in a position where it had no alternative but to work with Tshombe. It replaced the old T–6 planes with thirteen T–28 fighter-bombers, five long-range B–26 attack bombers, three C–46 transport aircraft, and two small twin-engine liaison planes. The latter were to be used by CIA personnel for rapid movement within the Congo. All of the planes were World War II vintage aircraft, but they were adequate for the needs of the Congo. The T-28s could carry more armaments and had a greater range of action than the T-6s.

It was clear that I was going back to a much larger and different kind of war than I had encountered in Katanga and that the political situation was likely to become increasingly volatile. With this in mind, I selected Dick to serve as chief of paramilitary operations, Ken to supervise the air operations, and began working with Frank, who was to be my deputy.

Dick knew military operations from the ground up. He had enlisted in the marines in World War II, reached senior noncommissioned rank, and prepared the way for major landings by American forces. He completed his college education after the war, accepted a commission in the marines, and held the rank of major when he transferred to the CIA. He was an outstanding intelligence officer, served as a chief of station, and held a number of other key assignments. Ken, who had been one of the youngest American fighter pilots in Word War II, left the service in 1945 to attend the

Chicago Institute of Art. He was called back to duty for the Korean War and remained in the service until 1965 when he retired. He had flown almost every kind of aircraft from B–52s to helicopters, and was a natural leader and manager. Frank had considerable experience as an operations officer and had served as a station chief in West Africa. He spoke French with native fluency and was extremely personable. We all became good friends and have remained so into our retirement years. Dick and Frank are still around, but Ken died of a heart attack while on a clandestine mission.

I knew that Tshombe owed his position to the Binza Group, and I suspected that Mobutu had played a key role in his selection. It was obvious that Tshombe was suspicious of the old guard of the American embassy, and I wondered how he would react to working with me. He surely knew that I had always taken a strong stand against him when he was in Katanga.

It was soon clear that Tshombe had it in for Mac Godley, whom he knew had played a major role in the UN's efforts to crush Katanga's secession. During one of my visits to Leopoldville, I learned from one of our sources that Tshombe planned to give Soapy Williams, who was visiting the Congo, a letter asking for Mac's recall. I warned Mac of Tshombe's plan. At the end of Soapy's visit, Tshombe offered him a letter, saying that he hoped that Soapy would act on its contents. Mac swiftly put out his hand, took the letter, pocketed it, and assured Tshombe that Soapy would give the matter careful consideration.

When we were having drinks that night, Mac produced the letter and translated its contents for Soapy's benefit.

"Mac, I'm so terribly sorry," Soapy said. "All you were doing was carrying out our policy."

Mac, clearly not prepared for this mealy-mouthed response, growled that if Soapy allowed himself and the U.S. government to be maneuvered in this way, he would resign immediately and go to the press. It would make a good story, Mac said, how Tshombe could simply hand over a letter to the assistant secretary of African affairs, ordering him to dismiss a United States ambassador. Soapy looked shocked. He urged Mac to do nothing of the kind and assured him of his full support.

I visited Belgium during one of my trips to Africa and spread the word among key Belgian figures that I looked forward to working closely with Tshombe. In particular, I met a Belgian professor, who I knew from my penetration of Tshombe's entourage had long been Tshombe's *éminence grise*, and suggested that we work together to support Tshombe in his new position. While the professor was smoothly agreeable on the surface, we soon heard that he had advised Tshombe to avoid me at all costs. I suspect the man did not want to share his close access to Tshombe with anyone else, though he may also have been on *Union Minière's* payroll, or perhaps it was simply that he did not trust me.

Glenn Fields, who had replaced Bronson Tweedy as chief of the Africa Division, believed that Tshombe was the key to the new situation in the Congo, and that most of my close contacts, including the key members of the Binza Group, were on the way out. However, I found it difficult to believe that people like Mobutu, Bomboko, and Nendaka were on the skids. I recognized the current importance of Tshombe, but I believed that the last hand of the political game had yet to be played and that this formidable trio would be at the table when it was.

Frank and I arrived together in Leopoldville on July 1, 1965, five years and a day after the Congo gained independence. The CIA office was considerably larger than the one I had left two years previously. Paramilitary operations inevitably mean expansion. I had selected some of the men, and I had studied the files of those I did not already know personally. All had volunteered for this assignment, a good sign, given that Africa is not exactly the garden spot of the world.

Returning to Leopoldville was like a homecoming for me. Mac Godley was the ambassador, the same locally employed Congolese were on duty at the embassy, all of my closest Congolese friends were in town, and many were in high office. As before, plenty of work awaited me. I had been warned by CIA paramilitary colleagues that the air program was rudderless and needed fixing. The problem was pressing, and I replaced its commander with Ken three days after my arrival.

The next job was to meet the two key mercenary leaders, Colonel Mike Hoare, a South African of Irish origin and British demeanor, and the Frenchman Colonel Bob Denard. Both officers had played important roles working for Tshombe in Katanga, were well-known figures in the Congo, and we had recently provided air support for their ground operations. I had met Denard shortly after Katanga's collapse, but I had never met Hoare. Washington insisted on having no overt relationship with the mercenaries, but since our objective was to prevent the rebels from taking control of the country, I could not realistically ignore the men selected by Tshombe to carry out the mission.

Ken flew me to Albertville on Lake Tanganyika in one of our small twin-engine liaison planes to meet the senior air operations officer and Hoare. Neither Ken nor I had ever been to Albertville. We knew the airfield was north of the town, but we did not have a chart showing its exact location and the heading of the runway. Although we had refueled in Luluabourg, we were forced to make a long detour around some enormous thunderheads. As a result, we were running low on fuel as we approached Albertville. To make matters worse, night had fallen and the airfield tower was not responding. We knew we did not have enough fuel to circle the area. Fortunately, just as one motor began sputtering, a truck down below turned on its lights and drove down the runway. Ken managed to line up on the runway. The second motor quit as we touched down and we made a bumpy but successful landing. As the aircraft coasted in silence to a halt, Ken reached for a cigarette. "Any landing you can walk away from is a good one," he said. I noticed, though, that his hands shook slightly as he lit his cigarette.

I had not met the senior air operations officer before but he was a competent man and had arranged a meeting with Hoare. Well-educated, articulate, a man of tremendous charm, Mike had proved himself to be a serious and capable soldier, a far cry from the "Mad Mike" image created by the media. Mike had dash and pizzazz. He read Christopher Marlowe and Shakespeare, he told great stories that made your hair stand on end, and he was a man of integrity and dignity. We became good friends, a friendship that has lasted over the years.

Back in Leopoldville, I arranged a meeting with Tshombe—with Mac's approval—to brief him on our understanding of the rebels' plans and personalities. I was shown into a room in his living quarters located above his offices, a room that I knew well from the days when Adoula was prime minister. I waited for a few minutes until Tshombe arrived. He took in the scene immediately, and exclaimed, "They haven't even provided you with a drink." He took my drink order, hurried into the next room and returned almost immediately with a drink and a tray of small sandwiches.

Tshombe, with the charm and warmth of a practiced politician, was putting on a show for me, which I interpreted as a sign of his intention to cooperate. Later I realized that he could turn the charm on and off at will but, happily, he always kept it turned on for me. I also discovered that Tshombe had the knack of appearing to agree with others without fully committing himself. On more than one occasion, I left him believing that he had agreed to take some specific action only to find that he had no intention of doing so. I could understand the problems the UN had encountered in dealing with him. However, I liked him as a person and appreciated his ability to influence people.

A few weeks after my return to the Congo, I had my first problem with the Congolese army. I arrived at the office one morning to find Frank and Dick waiting for me.

"Trouble in Orientale province," Dick said. "Big trouble." Both of them looked grim.

"What's going on?" I asked.

"We received a message from one of the senior air operations officers. The air unit is surrounded by a howling mob of Congolese soldiers. They could attack at any time."

"Yeah, some of the boys got drunk last night," Frank said. "On their way back to their quarters, they disarmed a Congolese soldier on guard duty. They decided to have some fun with him. They tied him up and threw him into the bushes. When the poor guy finally worked himself free, he went back and told his commanding officer and fellow soldiers what had happened. In no time, furious Congolese soldiers were on the rampage at the airfield."

"They want to punish the pilots and mechanics," Dick said.

Frank and Dick, both new to the Congo, had attempted to resolve the problem by instructing the air group to abandon the airfield and to pull back to another one a safe distance away.

"Yeah, well, if the air group pulls out, the Congolese troops are going to retreat, too," I said. "The government will lose control of a large part of Orientale province."

I realized that they had acted on their own initiative in order not to wake me in the middle of the night. But they had not understood that, no matter how angry the Congolese troops were, they would interpret the air group's departure as a sign that the region could no longer be held and would abandon their positions immediately.

"Cancel the withdrawal order," I said. "And tell them to alert the Congolese commander that I'm on my way to Orientale to talk to him."

I left immediately in one of the liaison planes for a long flight over savanna and tropical rainforest. After some six hours, I touched down and was met by a contrite air operations officer and a Belgian civilian. The latter, an ex-colonial administrator who had stayed on after the Congolese army mutiny, was acting as a go-between and peacemaker in an effort to prevent an attack on the air group. The Congolese insisted that the men responsible for the incident be handed over for punishment. From personal experience, I knew enough about Congolese methods of punishment to refuse, point blank. The air operations officer stressed that his men had disarmed the Congolese sentinel only because they were drunk. And being drunk, they had meant the whole thing as a joke, not as an insult to the Congolese army.

I gathered all the pilots and mechanics together. Pulling no punches, I told them that the actions of a few irresponsible men had been stupid and had put all our lives in danger, as well as jeopardizing military operations in Orientale province. I asked the Belgian to tell the Congolese commander that I believed it was important to punish the guilty men with the loss of three months' pay and to take them back to Leopoldville with me. The men, I said, would be replaced immediately so that air support for the Congolese military would continue uninterrupted.

The Belgian intermediary did his job well. After several hours of negotiation, he told me that the Congolese commander had agreed to my plan but with one reservation: the loss of pay had to be for six months. I had expected this and agreed immediately. I departed at first light with the culprits in tow after making certain that replacements would soon be on the way to Orientale. I later met the Congolese officer who, it turned out, was a Mongo. When he learned that Bomboko had initiated me into the tribe making me an honorary member, we drank to eternal and fraternal friendship.

Politics remained as volatile as the military situation. Kasavubu's term as president was due to end in 1965, and it was clear that he wanted another term. Tshombe showed signs of opposing him, and it was clear that he might defeat him. The State Department had never viewed Tshombe favorably since the days of Katanga's secession and firmly supported Kasavubu. The Department seemed to forget that both Kasavubu and Tshombe were on our side insofar as the Cold War was concerned, for neither showed any liking for the Soviets. To me, this was a win–win situation, but Washington was afraid that a tough campaign would work to the advantage of Soviet-supported rebel movements. Although bound by the State Department's decisions, I tried to persuade Tshombe and Kasavubu and their supporters to concentrate on winning the war against the rebels.

I met Mobutu almost daily, often over breakfast on the terrace of his home in the paratrooper camp. (As I ate my omelet smothered in *pili-pili*, I occasionally reflected that I had only one stomach to give for my country.) Mobutu and I had picked up where we had left off two years earlier, and we talked easily in a friendly, open way. We were technically dealing with military matters but, being political animals, the approaching struggle for the presidency often crept into our conversations. I gradually came to suspect that Mobutu himself had presidential ambitions. He did not say anything specific; it was more a gut feeling based on several years of friendship and cooperation in difficult times.

Each time I mentioned the idea of him throwing his hat into the ring, he would dodge the question with a comment that he was a soldier, not a politician. That reply, of course, did not eliminate the possibility of a military coup, but I had to be careful there. The wrong question, or too many questions, might imply that the United States favored such a step. Yet, as time went by, I became increasingly convinced that he had his eye on the prize. Once, as I was leaving his study, I noticed a book on a small table. It was Machiavelli's *The Prince*.

"Interesting reading for a busy general," I said.

He smiled and shrugged. "It's one of my favorite books."

Knowing that he was a great admirer of de Gaulle, I said, "I would have thought you might prefer a biography of General de Gaulle."

But Mobutu changed the subject and ignored my implicit invitation to explain his interest in *The Prince*.

Perhaps I did not stress sufficiently my suspicion of Mobutu's desire to be president in my reports to Headquarters. Moreover, the State Department continued to focus on the developing conflict between Tshombe and Kasavubu and did not seem to regard Mobutu as a contender. I believe they thought of him only as a military man and not as a man with political ambitions.

In any event, I received instructions, originating from the State Department but delivered via CIA channels, to tell Mobutu that the United States favored Kasavubu's re-election as president, with Tshombe remaining prime minister. I imagine that the Department wanted to insure Mobutu's continued support of Kasavubu, and I will never forget Mobutu's response.

"So, the United States favors a Johnson-Goldwater ticket," he said, laughing. (Johnson and Goldwater, politically miles apart, had contested the 1964 U.S. presidential election.)

Kasavubu made the next move in the political drama by firing Tshombe and appointing another prime minister. I made a point of continuing to see Tshombe because I believed he was likely to return to the political scene. I met him in a house in Binza where I found him absolutely terrified that he would be assassinated. I repeatedly told him that I did not believe he was in danger. I even offered him temporary lodging in my home where I assured him he would be safe and under diplomatic protection. I later learned from our penetration of Tshombe's group that his *éminence grise,* the Belgian professor whom I had met in Brussels, had warned Tshombe that I wanted him under my control so that I could kill him. I knew that this man distrusted me, but he did no service to Tshombe by feeding him such paranoid nonsense.

18

I HAVE BEEN CREDITED in numerous books and articles with
having organized and supported Mobutu's 1965 *coup d'état*. The
fact is that I first learned of it when Frank, my deputy, called me
about six o'clock in the morning on November 25, and said
Leopoldville radio had just reported that Mobutu had ousted the
president and prime minister and taken over the government.

Mobutu's security had been excellent, and I had failed to penetrate his protective barrier and warn Washington with any hard intelligence. I had reported my suspicions and was not totally
surprised by Mobutu's move, but suspicions are not hard facts. In an
effort to redeem our reputation, we sprang into action. Frank went
to the office to supervise reporting on the coup, and I set out to try
to see Mobutu and the other members of the Binza Group, who
remained my best sources.

I drove to Bomboko's house first, but he said he knew nothing
about it. Nendaka arrived while I was there but he, apparently, was
similarly in the dark. I went next to the paratrooper camp above the
Congo rapids where Mobutu resided. Mobutu was in conference
with his senior military officers, but he broke off shortly after my
arrival to see me. I chided him in a friendly way for having failed to
advise me of his plans. He, in turn, reminded me that he could not
say anything to me because he knew that Washington opposed a
change of government. He also insisted that the decision had only
been made on the eve of the coup. I did not believe that for a mo-

ment because I knew from experience that such matters take time and planning. However, I made no comment.

It was clear that Mobutu was anxious about the American reaction. Mobutu read from a hand-written list the names of persons he planned to name to his new government, discussing the pros and cons of each one. He took my advice when I suggested two changes. He seemed buoyant and extremely self-confident. I was happy to see that Colonel Mulamba, one of the more competent army officers, was his choice as the new prime minister, Bomboko remained foreign minister, Ndele continued as governor of the country's central bank, and Nendaka retained his job as head of the security service. The other members of the government appeared satisfactory.

I used Mobutu's telephone to call a report to the station, relaying the composition of the new government and an explanation of how the coup had been organized. Apparently, senior army officers had spent the night at Mobutu's home and concluded that an army takeover was essential to save the country from a dangerously divisive election pitting Tshombe against Kasavubu. The group allegedly insisted that Mobutu assume the presidency, which he accepted. Mobutu drove to Kasavubu's residence, told him of the military's decision, and recommended that he resign. The transition went smoothly with Kasavubu and Tshombe going quietly. Tshombe later left for exile in Spain and never returned to the Congo.

I assumed Mobutu had been the real instigator of the coup and had planted the idea in the minds of his senior military colleagues. There was no point, however, in voicing my skepticism. It was a *fait accompli*, and it was in our interest to maintain friendly relations with the new regime. In Cold War terms, the new government would be on our side and unfriendly to the Soviet Union.

I visited Mobutu several times a week, usually for breakfast. As in the past, we sat on the terrace of his house with its magnificent view of Stanley Pool, the rapids, and Brazzaville across the river. Mobutu used me as a sounding board for our government's reaction to his policies. These sessions yielded good intelligence, but they were also a conduit for Washington's views and recommendations. Ostensibly, I acted unofficially, although I doubt if Mobutu was fooled because he must have understood that, as a senior intelligence officer, I was speaking for my government. While Washington did not want a coup, there was little it could do once Mobutu had taken over. In a profound sense, the Cold War played into his hands. The United States could not afford to withdraw its support for him because, if it did, the still restive Soviet-backed rebels in Stanleyville would surely have taken over the country. We were back to where we had been in 1960. Washington wanted to prevent the Soviet Union from controlling the Congo and thus had to work with whomever was in power and could keep the Soviets' surrogates at bay.

Shortly after Mobutu took power, there were reports of others planning coups—so many, in fact, that we dubbed them the "coup-of-the-month club." Nendaka managed to nip these plots in the bud, and it was several months before a serious attempt came to light. In late April 1966, one of our agents reported that the minister of defense had asked him to join in a plot to overthrow Mobutu. We instructed the agent to cooperate with the minister whose aim, not surprisingly, was to take Mobutu's place. A well-known senator, one of the two who had voted against Lumumba in 1960, and a former minister were also involved. We told our agent to stay engaged since their plans seemed to be well-advanced and constituted a credible threat to Mobutu's regime.

As the plot thickened, I got less and less sleep because the agent was generally unable to meet me until midnight or later. By the time I had debriefed him and sent a cable summing up the results, it was often two or three in the morning, and I was back in the office some five hours later. I did not want to get the plotters into trouble as long as they did not move from the planning stage to action. But it was clearly not in the interest of the United States to have the central government collapse or be debilitated to the delight of the Stanleyville rebels.

The plotters, however, went ahead and set a date for the coup. As they were about to move, I reported it to Mobutu. Apparently, he was already aware of the plot but thanked me for trying to save his life once again. He also said if any of the men involved worked for me, they would be spared. Consequently, the four key members of the group were arrested, tried, and condemned to death by hanging. I knew three of them who were involved in the anti-Lumumba movement in 1960, and urged Mobutu to commute their sentences. He refused, saying that he had to take harsh action to put an end to the plotting against him. He added that eventually somebody would evade the *Sûreté's* vigilance and there would be fatal consequences. I argued with him up to the last minute, but he was adamant, and the four coup leaders were hanged in public as a warning to others that planning coups was no longer a safe sport.

Desmond Fitzgerald, the new deputy director for operations, who had replaced Dick Helms, paid us a visit. (Helms had been promoted to deputy director of the Agency and within a year he had become director.) Des proved to be as fine a houseguest as he was an outstanding chief of operations. We introduced him to the junior officers, several of our key agents, and had ample opportunity to discuss our operations.

Frank and I drew up a detailed schedule for his visit with backup plans in case of some unexpected change. There was one development, however, that we had not considered. On his last evening, Des surprised me by asking if it would be inconvenient if he extended his visit by one day. We said we would be delighted but, in fact, I was at a loss as to what we were going to do with him. We needed to resume our normal work schedule.

I lamely asked if there was anything special he would like to do. He replied that he was a bird-watcher and asked if I knew a good place where he could watch tropical birds. Never having been a bird-watcher, I suggested the ambassador's garden, which was full of birds. Mac was away so Des would not be disturbed. Armed with his binoculars, Des studied the birds in the garden for nearly four hours while I sat beside him. While he was watching, he began asking me questions, keeping his voice low. He wanted to know my opinion of the Agency's Soviet operations, what I thought we could do to improve our paramilitary operations, whether Headquarters could improve its support of field operations, and, if so, what changes I would make if I were in his shoes. The questioning went on and on. I knew I was being assessed for some job or special operation, but I had no idea what it might be.

Mac returned and almost immediately found himself in hot water with Mobutu. For reasons that escaped me, Mobutu had never fully appreciated Mac. He dealt with him because he was the U.S. ambassador and, thus, in a position to be friendly or hostile to Mobutu and influence the direction of American policies in the Congo. I had recently organized a luncheon, with the help of Bomboko and Nendaka, to try to establish a better feeling between the two men but without much success.

One morning, I received a call from an extremely agitated Mobutu asking me to come to the paratrooper camp immediately. I could tell from his tone of voice that he was angry. I found him pacing up and down in front of his residence, and when he began to speak he stammered. It was unusual because Mobutu was a smooth, articulate speaker. I had never seen him so furious. Over the past few years, he had put on a good bit of weight, and as he strode back and forth, he was the image of a powerful and very angry man.

"I want him out of here!" he almost shouted. "Godley is *persona non grata!* He has forty-eight hours to leave the country. NO MORE!"

The entire city of Leopoldville must have heard him bellow "no more!"

I knew better than to say anything. I stood there and watched him whip back and forth.

"When one is the official ambassador in a country," he said softly and sweetly in a mincing, prissy manner, "one does not make disparaging remarks about a close friend of the president." He stopped and glared at me.

"What kind of ambassador does that? *Hein?* A moron? A stupid bastard? Who dares to ridicule the president's close friend? *Hein?*"

I was beginning to get the drift. Mac had, apparently, made some kind of offensive remark about Mobutu's mistress.

"This is the last straw!" Mobutu raged on. "Understand me? The last straw. Tell Washington. I want him out of my country within forty-eight hours. How can I work with a *salaud* like that?"

I spent the next hour coming up with every argument that I could think of to persuade Mobutu to change his mind. I reminded him of Mac's role in marshaling American support for the Binza Group when he was *chargé* in 1961. I pointed out that expelling Mac would be regarded as an unfriendly act by the United States and could result in a change in American policy toward Mobutu's government. It could even mean the end of American economic aid. I argued with considerable heat for I considered Mac to be one of my closest friends. I was also convinced that it would be impossible to find a replacement who was as well-qualified.

Moreover, I was afraid that Mobutu was about to take a step that would endanger everything for which I had worked since my arrival in the Congo in 1960. Finally, Mobutu agreed not to expel him. His alternative, however, was not much better. He said that, henceforth, I was the only member of the embassy with whom he or any of his ministers would meet or speak as long as Mac remained in the country. I reminded Mobutu in no uncertain terms that he was jeopardizing everything that he had worked for, and I told him he was placing me in one hell of a spot because Mac was my friend. He remained adamant, however, and I could not persuade him to compromise any further.

I went back to the office, my head pounding. I knew that I had to break the terrible news to Mac. I had no intention of cabling the news to Washington, as Mobutu had requested. I had to tell Mac first. After that, it was up to him how he wanted to handle the matter. I told Frank what had happened and went to Mac's office and told him about Mobutu's decision.

Mac was stunned. He admitted that he might have made some foolish remark about the president's mistress at a private dinner party, but he insisted that he had not meant it to be offensive. Only friends had been at his table and he could not believe any of them would carry tales to Mobutu. He had to admit, however, that someone must have talked. Mac's weakness was that he expected his friends to treat his friendship the way he treated theirs. When he told me who had been at the dinner, I immediately identified the person who I was convinced had spilled the beans. It was almost certainly a Belgian officer who circulated widely in the diplomatic community and worked closely with Mobutu. I had known him since 1960 and had never fully trusted him.

Mac said he would inform Washington of Mobutu's request immediately. In his message he stated that our government should not give in to Mobutu's whims and tantrums and recommended that he remain one month before departing. Washington agreed and during that period I was the only official American in contact with the Congolese government. When Mac finally left, the United States and the Congo lost the services of one of the best ambassadors in the Foreign Service. Happily, this unfortunate incident did not prevent Mac from going on to serve with great distinction in other posts.

And, as has happened so often, the professional foreign service carried on. Robert O. Blake, Mac Godley's DCM, became the *chargé* and, seconded by Monteagle (Monty) Stearns, the very able chief of the political section, implemented American policy in the Congo. They continued in their new functions until well after I had completed my tour of duty and left the Congo in June 1967. Both men were later promoted to the rank of ambassador and served with distinction.

19

ONE NIGHT IN MAY 1966, I was awakened from a sound sleep by the voice of my fourteen-year-old daughter, Maureen, and the lights suddenly going on in my bedroom. Still half-asleep and partially blinded by the lights, I jumped out of bed thinking she was ill. I took a step or two before I saw a masked African holding her with a knife at her throat. Another man held an iron bar ready to hit her on the head.

I panicked and did everything wrong. In a desperate but stupid move, I tried to reach a small pistol that I kept in my bedside table drawer. "Don't do it, Daddy," Maureen said in English, "the other one has you covered." I suddenly realized there was a third masked man in the room. He was aiming a Browning 9mm pistol at me and could have shot both Colette and me before I could have reached my gun. Meanwhile, Colette was telling the Congolese in very idiomatic French that they should be ashamed of themselves, to get out and not come back, and any number of other things that I no longer recall. The man with the gun seemed flabbergasted, as though he could not understand why she was not terrified.

I asked them what they wanted. "Money," they said. I told them I would not give them a franc until they released my daughter. "Then we will kill her," the masked man said, scratching her on the throat with the point of his knife. "Well, if you do that, you won't have anything, will you?" I countered, trying my best to bluff and sound indifferent.

They started arguing among themselves in Lingala. The man with the knife, apparently the leader, ended it saying it did not matter, they were going to kill us before they left. My Lingala was shaky but that came through loud and clear and then he pushed Maureen toward me. I yelled at them to get out of the house.

"Daddy, these guys mean it," she said, picking up the money that was on my dresser and throwing it at their feet. As they moved to pick it up, I leapt at them.

"Shoot him!" the leader yelled.

I saw the man coming at me, I saw the gun, and felt the barrel as it hit my head. Then Maureen began speaking to him in Lingala in a steady but calm voice. She looked at the man standing over me with his raised gun and said that she felt sorry for him. While the three of them stared at her, she began a long speech on what a wonderful father I was, and concluded by explaining why she was sorry for the gunman.

"We have a *dawa*," she said. He knew his black magic well enough to know that she meant a magic talisman that could protect us and do pretty ghastly things to anyone who harmed us. "Our whole family has a *dawa*." She said that anyone who hurt or killed us would die, as would all his wives, children, mother, father, grandparents, aunts, uncles, nieces, nephews, and cousins. The *dawa* would kill them all. The gunman was beginning to look extremely solemn. And maybe a little anxious. Maureen kept talking, going over and over the litany of family members who would be eliminated by our *dawa*.

The leader looked skeptical, but he was listening. He suddenly interrupted her, shouting, "Shoot him! Shoot him!" Maureen turned to him and asked if he believed anyone who hurt or killed us would die and that his family, to the last relative, would die. He shook his head. "Put your knife in my stomach, not my heart, and I will see you die first," she said. "Shut up," I yelled ungraciously. But Maureen was in command. "You shut up," she said. "I know what I am doing." The leader, who had no idea what we were saying, looked at her but didn't move. Maureen turned to the others. "You see, he wants you and your families to die."

"We have already stolen things from you," the gunman blurted out.

"Our *dawa* does not protect our things," Maureen said. "Only us. Only our bodies."

By then it was clear to Colette and to me that everything depended upon Maureen. There was nothing more we could do and I kept my mouth firmly shut.

Suddenly, the leader seemed to make up his mind and ordered us into the bathroom. I thought, my God, this is the end of us. Recently, a number of families in Leopoldville had been found murdered in their bathrooms. Colette and Maureen went in but I delayed in the hope of a lucky break. Colette reinforced that possibility when she said, "Larry, the key is on the inside of the door."

Inside, I kicked the bathroom door shut and threw myself against it. At first I pushed too hard and the door would not lock. It seemed an eternity but it must have been only a few seconds before I realized the problem, eased my pressure, and the lock clicked shut. I expected the burglars to shoot through the door or to try to push it open. There were two Johnnie Walker whisky bottles of boiled water for drinking and brushing teeth on a shelf over the sink. Maureen and Colette dumped the water into the sink and gave me one to use as a weapon. I stood on the ledge at the end of the bathtub, ready to break the bottle over the head of the first person who tried to smash down the door.

Outside the bathroom, there was not a sound. We waited and waited. It was still pitch black outside. We started to yell for help, hoping that Daniel, our houseboy who lived in the *boyerie*, or a neighbor would hear us. Fortunately, Daniel heard us and came along the hallway, calling out, and asking where we were. He assured us that there was no one else in the house and we unlocked the door. I picked up my pistol and checked the house. The burglars were gone. I went out to the garden and street while Colette called Frank.

He arrived a few minutes later and we walked through the neighborhood looking for the men without success. We were walking back to the house, guns in hand, as the sun rose. I was still dressed in my pajamas. On the way, we met a man taking an early morning walk with his dog. He looked at us—two men strolling by with guns in their hands, one still in pajamas—and without batting an eye asked, *"Alors, on se promène?"* ("Out for a little walk, are we?")

The police were with us much of the day. A UN adviser to the local police force took fingerprints, but no one had any idea about the burglars' identity. The police assumed, however, that they were the same people who were responsible for a dozen recent robberies and murders. Some of the "usual suspects" were rounded up but, since the intruders had all been wearing masks, we could not identify anybody. We handed over a list of all our missing items, and I distributed small sums of money to the policemen and told them to let me know if they obtained any leads.

Although we were aware of locking the barn door after the proverbial horse was stolen, we put a heavy bolt on Maureen's bedroom door and installed an intercom system between our bedrooms that enabled us to hear sounds and movements in her room. We told her to refuse to open the door no matter what I said unless I used a specific code word that we agreed upon. I took her out to show her how to fire a small revolver, a Smith & Wesson, five round air weight. I discovered that she was an excellent shot, and I gave her the weapon to keep in her room for the rest of our stay in the Congo.

A few weeks after the robbery, a policeman told me that he had heard that a radio similar to mine was on sale in Thysville, the town between Leopoldville and Matadi, where two army mutinies had begun. We set off in my car and found the store where everything from second-hand shoes and clothes to used electrical appliances were sold. There were several radios on a shelf at the back. One glance was enough to discover my Zenith but, before picking it up, I looked at some others as though searching for the best deal. When I came to the Zenith, I looked at the number on the back and identified it as mine. The owner of the store claimed he could not remember where he had got it but, after we applied a bit of persuasion, he remembered. We loaded him into my car and visited the man who had brought the radio to the store.

He, too, suffered a temporary loss of memory about the provenance of the radio but, again with a little persuasion, he recalled that his brother-in-law in Leopoldville had given it to him to sell. We returned to the capital, and the police arrested the brother-in-law when he returned home. He denied any knowledge of the radio, but his fingerprints were one of the sets of prints found in my house by the UN police adviser. In due course, the man identified his partners in crime but, before they could go to trial, they reportedly escaped. One story had them killing two guards. I was told that they resisted when apprehended and were killed in a gunfight by the police.

All CIA personnel who are the object of a criminal act are required to report the fact and to indicate whether there were security implications. I reported the burglary to Headquarters and did not go into details except to say that there were no security problems. But when Jerry, our logistics officer, returned to Washington, he described Maureen's role in saving all of us from being killed to Glenn Fields, the Africa division chief. Glenn was so impressed that he took Jerry to see Desmond Fitzgerald, the deputy director of operations who had visited the Congo a few weeks before the incident, had stayed with us, and knew Maureen quite well. Des ordered that she be awarded the Intelligence Star, the CIA equivalent of the military's Silver Star.

I later heard that one of Desmond's assistants cautioned him that this medal was reserved for heroic acts by CIA personnel only and that Maureen was thus not eligible to receive it. Des went ahead anyway, and Maureen received the decoration from Dick Helms when we returned to Washington at the end of my Congo tour. Most of the Agency's senior officers turned out for the ceremony. Poor Maureen, the girl who had calmly faced down three armed men, not to say killers, was chalk-white and terrified standing in front of all those eminent people while the citation for her award was read. Sadly, Des was not present. He had died on the tennis court of a massive heart attack only a few days before our return. His successor, Tom Karamessines, hosted a lunch for Maureen after the ceremony.

A FEW MONTHS AFTER Mobutu's coup, he began expressing dissatisfaction with what he described as *Union Minière's* failure to pay the central government its royalties and taxes for Katanga's copper and cobalt. Mobutu claimed that *Union Minière's* payments were ten or eleven months in arrears, and he began talking of nationalizing the mines. Around that time, Colette and I started receiving social invitations from a *Union Minière* representative. The dinners were enjoyable, and I found it useful to get to know the Belgian group who frequented the representative's home.

In mid–1966, after one of those dinners, I found myself alone with a Belgian gentleman whom I had not previously met. After talking about the dangers of nationalization and the importance of setting Mobutu straight on that matter, he got down to business. He said that the man who could persuade Mobutu to forget nationalization would be doing the Congo and Belgium a favor as well as doing himself a good turn. He added that such a person could expect to be handsomely rewarded if he were successful. He mentioned the sum of three million dollars, which would be placed in a tax-free, numbered Swiss account. After a short delay to let the offer sink in, he commented that it was well known that I was close to Mobutu. After another slight delay, he asked if I would be interested in such an arrangement? I replied that I would under no circumstances be interested and suggested rather crudely what he might do with the money. Colette and I left the party and, come to think of it, we never received another invitation from our host.

It was a crude attempt at bribery. When I thought about it afterwards, I was convinced that they would never have given me the three million dollars. Signing up for a numbered Swiss bank account would have made me their prisoner. They probably would have put a much smaller sum into the account but, with proof of my venality, they would have made me jump through the hoop.

Despite strenuous opposition from *Union Minière*, the mines were nationalized in 1966. *Union Minière*, however, continued to manage them and provide personnel under a contract with the government. But as the government took an increasingly active role in managing the mines, copper and cobalt production dropped rapidly.

One evening after sundown, while we were still in the Congo, Maureen returned from the riding club. She was alone in the house with Daniel, our cook. She began her homework but, missing one of her books, she wandered into the living room to look for it. Daniel had turned on the security lights in the garden, but the living room was still dark. Maureen, with a clear view of the illuminated garden, saw two men with rifles climb over the wall. Moving from window to window, she followed them to the back of the house where she saw them take up a position less than twenty feet from where I normally parked my car. She immediately called my office but it was well after seven in the evening and no one was there. She called Frank who told her that I had been at his house but that Colette and I had already left for home. He said he would try to catch me but doubted he could do so before I reached the house.

Maureen told Daniel where the armed men were hidden. She knew the direction I was coming from and told Daniel to go to the corner and stop me from pulling into the driveway. Next, she got the pistol I had given her a few weeks previously. While she would have had little chance of hitting them in the dark, the shots would have served as a warning for me and might have confused the assassins.

I almost hit Daniel when he ran out in front of my car. He was so excited he began speaking in his village dialect that was unknown to me. Little by little, he calmed down enough to give me Maureen's warning. Fortunately, one of our agents had picked up a rumor that an unidentified group had issued a contract to have me killed. While the report had seemed vague and raised more questions than it answered, I had started to carry a small pistol.

I told Colette to wait in the car until I called her. I ran the short distance to our house and jumped up on the low wall directly behind the two men. By the time they heard me, I had them covered. I called Colette and we put the two men in the back seat of the car with Colette driving and me covering them from the front passenger seat. We took them to a nearby police station and turned them over to the police.

All of us were shaken by the incident, and I called some of my more influential Congolese friends. Mobutu immediately sent a squad of soldiers to protect us. Nendaka excitedly told me to hold the men for him. When I told him that I had turned them over to the police, he said that he, too, had received a report late that afternoon of a plan to have me killed. He had no proof, but he thought that the police chief, who had previously served in Katanga under Tshombe, was involved in the plot. Not long afterwards, Nendaka came to my house to say that the police had reported that the men were killed while trying to escape. This convenient elimination meant that we never obtained hard evidence linking the projected attempt on my life to anyone or any organization. I was left with my suspicions, only suspicions.

20

MIKE HOARE HAD DEVISED a plan to attack a rebel force under Laurent Kabila (a gold smuggler and rebel leader in the eastern Congo) and supported by a group of Cubans led by Che Guevera. The Cubans and the rebels were receiving large amounts of supplies from Tanzania on the other side of Lake Tanganyika. (Decades later, Kabila would lead a successful rebellion that deposed Mobutu, become president himself, and, later still, be assassinated.) The plan called for Hoare's unit, 5 Commando, to mount an end run attack by boat on the rebel positions in the Fizi-Baraka area at the northern end of the lake. Hoare planned the operation but Colonel John Peters, a former non-commissioned officer in the British Army who had served under Hoare, had taken over from him when it was put into effect.

Washington was adamant that no CIA officers were to be involved in the attack. But Murphy's Law once again prevailed: anything that can go wrong will go wrong. Mick, the Agency officer responsible for boat operations on the lake, decided that he should accompany the troops on Lake Tanganyika, orders or no orders. He wanted to ensure that the newly arrived Swift boats would be handled properly and that the mercenaries would be put ashore at the proper place.

Everything went smoothly until the landing. The boats could not get close enough to shore, and the men had to jump into waist-deep or deeper water. Once in the water, a hidden heavy machine gun opened up on them. The operation was in jeopardy, but Mick saved the day by picking up a .75mm recoilless rifle in his boat and knocked out the machine gun with one well-placed round. The landing and the operation were successful but NBC and CBS television—invited by the leadership of 5 Commando, the mercenary unit involved in the operation—had captured Mick's action in living color. Mercenaries love publicity; the CIA abhors it.

When I heard of Mick's starring role, I tried to persuade the journalists to give me their film. I had met the CBS man socially and heard that the NBC man had been a U.S. Army ranger. I realized that halfway measures would not work with these men. They had some spectacular film on their hands. I had to take a chance and level with them and hope that their patriotism would overcome their journalistic instincts.

The CBS man listened attentively but said he could not give up his film because his NBC colleague—and rival—had similar film. Otherwise, he said, he would gladly give it to me. Taking him at his word, I rushed to see the NBC man who was staying in the same hotel. He had the same problem. He would give me the film but for the fact that CBS had it. I immediately called the CBS man to join us and, when I left, I had the film. I destroyed it that night.

The mercenaries chose one of their officers, Captain Cassidy, to command the fleet. He was an Irishman raised in England who had served in the British army and in Tshombe's mercenary forces in Katanga. He was reputed to be a fierce fighter and a competent leader. He appeared to be a good man for the maritime job but time was to prove otherwise.

Late one night, the senior air officer in Albertville called me on the single side-band radio to report that Cassidy had murdered one of his group's mechanics. Cassidy and the mechanic reportedly were friends, but they had quarreled while drinking earlier in the evening. The mechanic was reported to have told Cassidy that he was not tough when he was not armed, as was the case when they quarreled. (It was only after this incident that we were told that Cassidy had the reputation of enjoying killing and was thus considered unbalanced by some who knew him.)

Unfortunately, Peters was on leave in London, and Cassidy was the acting commander of 5 Commando. So, we had no one in Albertville to whom we could turn for help. The senior air officer asked if he should try to arrest Cassidy. I told him to keep his group in the hotel and remain there until I arrived the next morning.

The adjutant (administrative officer) of 5 Commando was in Leopoldville at the time. I called him and asked him to meet me at the airport at five in the morning. I did not tell him about Cassidy or what I was planning to do, fearing that if I did he would not turn up. Ken had a C–46 warmed up when I arrived at the airport. The adjutant was there, and we boarded the plane. It was only when we were in the air, heading towards Albertville, that I told him I expected him to place Cassidy under arrest and to take command of 5 Commando until Peters returned. To say that the man almost had a nervous breakdown would be an understatement, but he had nowhere to go.

I had radioed ahead requesting the senior air officer, along with a couple of mercenary officers, to meet me. As we were landing, I saw all of 5 Commando's officers, with the exception of Cassidy, lined up waiting for me. I was not sure what to expect but I disembarked and addressed them as though I were sure of myself. In response, they offered me condolences for the death of the mechanic. I thanked them and told them that their adjutant was taking over command pending the return of Peters. As for Cassidy, I pointed out that there had been a murder and that I had come to take him back to Leopoldville to be tried by a Congolese court.

The officers protested fiercely. They handled such matters themselves, they said. Their code protected them from being turned over to a Congolese court.

"Find Cassidy," I said, "and report to me at the command post. If you can take care of him to my satisfaction, then, fine. If not, I'm taking him to Leopoldville."

In short order, the mercenaries reported that Cassidy had disappeared. I pointed out that there were only two ways to leave Albertville without going through rebel-held territory—by boat, through Lake Tanganyika, which was 673 km long and 50 km wide, or by plane—and I knew no one had left by plane. I immediately ordered two T–28s into the air, one to fly north and one south over the lake. The mercenary leaders hurried away and returned quickly to report two P boats (the smaller boats that had been replaced with Swifts) were missing.

The pilot who had flown south reported two boats below him, one with one man and the other with two men, and requested authority to sink the boat with two men. He was hell bent on sinking it because the murdered mechanic had been a close friend. I refused his request for several reasons. Killing Cassidy would have caused major problems within 5 Commando, perhaps ending its usefulness as a fighting unit. Also, it would have meant that we would never have been able to work with the unit again. Finally, it would have entailed the loss of a boat, and I assumed that if the boat ended up on the Zambian end of the lake, where it seemed to be heading, we could count on the help of the Zambian government to get the boat and Cassidy back. I did not think of it at the time but, if I had said, "Go ahead," the mercenaries might have shot me.

I quickly sent a coded message to Jeff, my ex-deputy now in Lusaka, Zambia's capital, asking him to request the local police to arrest Cassidy when he arrived in Zambia. It turned out that Zambia and the Congo did not have an extradition treaty, but the Zambians arranged things à l'Africaine. Cassidy was duly arrested and escorted to the Zambian–Congo border. There, quite miraculously, he tripped and fell across the border at a point where some Congolese policemen happened to be waiting.

Cassidy was taken to Leopoldville, tried in a Congolese court, found guilty of murder, and condemned to death. The sentence, however, was commuted to life in prison because he had been awarded the Order of the Leopard, the country's highest decoration for valor. Before going to prison, Cassidy sent me a message:

"Some day, you son-of-a-bitch, I will get free and no matter where you are, I will find you and kill you."

Even in prison, the man remained a problem. Before returning from London, Colonel Peters sent me a message demanding that I have Cassidy set free. When I refused, his messages became threatening. One day, I was having breakfast with CIA's chief budget officer who was visiting several African posts. He was due to leave that morning on a SABENA flight and, as we were about to drive to the airport, a 5 Commando officer who was assigned to Leopoldville and kept me advised of developments within that unit, burst in to tell me that Peters was returning to the Congo on the incoming SABENA flight.

"Peters intends to have you killed if you don't get Cassidy off," he said. "The best thing for you to do now is shoot Peters as he gets off the plane before he can line up somebody to kill you."

The budget officer, whose CIA career had been limited to financial matters, was aghast. He looked at me in amazement. "This guy is suggesting that you murder someone before he murders you. This can't be true." I knew that I wasn't about to murder anybody, but I wasn't too sure about Peters. I excused myself and returned with a loose sports shirt that covered my revolver in its belt holster. As we departed for the airport, the budget officer asked if I were armed. When I said "yes," he looked away and shook his head. "I hope you've got Headquarters' approval."

At the airport, I arranged to have the budget officer's passport stamped and then we waited on the terrace for the arrival of the SABENA flight. As Peters got off, several large mercenaries greeted him. I wished the budget officer a safe journey and went into the terminal. I imagine the man had never been involved in such a situation, but he had the courage to offer to accompany me. I pointed out that he was not armed and might miss his flight.

I spotted Peters waiting for his luggage, but in order to avoid a high noon–like confrontation, I approached him from behind and spoke to him only when I was close to his group. His first reaction was to reach for the revolver he always carried. I told him not to be a damned fool. He asked if I was willing to arrange Cassidy's release. I shook my head. Peters picked up his bag and, without looking at me, said, "Either you do it or you die." With that, we separated, and I left for the long drive back to town.

Peters's large Mercedes soon caught up with my old Peugeot. I pulled out my pistol and waited, wondering what he was going to do, but he just pointed his index finger at me and with his thumb made the motions of the hammer falling. He smirked, and his car roared off. When I pulled up at the embassy, I noticed Peters's car parked down the street. I got out and Peters stepped out from behind some shrubs at the corner of the embassy. "I could have dropped you right there, Devlin," he said with a laugh.

From then on, it was a cat-and-mouse game with a series of telephone threats. But when that did not work, an unidentified caller warned me one night to be sure and think of Peters the next time I started my car. For the next few days, I avoided driving Colette and Maureen in my car. The next threat was the worst and sent me up the wall.

One Saturday afternoon a caller asked me if I knew where my daughter was. Then he hung up. I knew she was at the home of one of her friends at a party, but I immediately called the house and asked to speak to Maureen. She came on the line full of life, as only a young person can be when she is enjoying herself. She assured me that the mother of one of her friends would drive her home when the party finished, but I insisted on picking her up.

That night I went to the Memling Hotel where Peters was staying. I shoved my way past the mercenary guard at his door. Peters looked up as I came in.

"If you ever threaten my daughter again, or if one of your men ever puts a hand on her," I said, "I will kill you."

"I think you mean that," Peters said.

A few days later he called me to suggest a meeting. We lunched and he told me he was dropping the Cassidy matter and wished to confirm that 5 Commando would continue to receive air support in its campaign against the rebels. I told him he would get the support, and he never mentioned Cassidy again.

I later picked up a story about Cassidy that was pure hearsay but, if true, would have explained why some people were so keen to see him safely out of his African prison. He was alleged to have stolen a large amount of gold, worth several million dollars, when the mercenaries liberated the Watsa gold mines in the east of the country some months earlier. Cassidy buried the gold and the men who helped him suffered a series of fatal accidents within the next twelve hours, such as a bullet in the back of the head. It is clear, however, that Peters had some special reason for wanting Cassidy out of jail. One of Peters's men contacted Ken to ask him if he would be willing to use one of our planes to fly a shipment of gold out of the country in return for a large payment. Ken naturally refused. When Cassidy was released from prison seven years later, I could only assume that he bought his way to freedom.

THE LAST MAJOR FLAP during my second Congo tour came when a mercenary leader called Jean Schramme, often referred to as "Black Jack" by the press, tried to take control of Stanleyville. A Belgian planter who had run the family plantation in the Congo before independence, he had fought for Tshombe in Katanga but later, like Mike Hoare and Bob Denard, was recruited by Tshombe to work for the central government. Schramme commanded 10 Commando, a mixture of foreign mercenaries and Katangan soldiers.

Schramme failed to gain control of the city and Orientale province because Denard refused to join him. While not actively fighting against Schramme's forces, Denard took up defensive positions in the post office and the bank. Schramme, however, controlled most of the city, as well as the airfield where one of the air operations groups and a CIA operations officer were located. This meant that the planes were out of action and that the airmen and the operations officer were for all intents and purposes Schramme's prisoners.

I communicated with our operations officer by radio using a frequency that I suspected was monitored by Schramme. In that way, I used my conversations with the CIA officer to send messages to the mercenary leader.

Since the officer did not realize what I was doing, my statements to him concerning our supposed plans to bomb Schramme in Stanleyville must have convinced him that I had lost my mind. I mouthed all sorts of threats on the radio, even telling the officer that we might have to sacrifice him and the air group in order to prevent Schramme from succeeding. I have no idea whether Schramme believed the threats. We would never have bombed the city.

I also spoke with Denard, who immediately appeared to understand what I was doing. My first objective was to extricate the CIA officer and the personnel of the air group. Using the officer as an intermediary, I finally obtained Schramme's approval to send in a plane to evacuate our personnel. It was a difficult decision for both Schramme and me. Schramme gave up the hostages, and I had to risk the life of a pilot and the plane we eventually sent in to bring out our people. Ken flew the evacuation plane. In keeping with my earlier messages, I sent a message directly to Schramme threatening to level Stanleyville with bombs if he interfered with the departure of the air group. Ken succeeded in bringing out the men, and Schramme was soon forced to give up his hold on the city. Had Schramme succeeded, the Soviets and their African friends would have licked their chops as it would have resulted in yet more problems for the struggling Congo, which was just beginning to see a future without the bushfires of rebellion.

The last eight or nine months of my tour were uneventful when compared to the early days of my first tour or even the first year of my second tour. We were able to concentrate on normal intelligence operations, undisturbed by the likes of John Peters, gunmen in the garden, military coups, or mercenary revolts.

January 1, 1967, brought exciting news. A pouch from Headquarters reached us that day and, in it, was a personal letter from

Des Fitzgerald, announcing that I had been promoted to GS–16, the status of a super grade, a big step up the ladder and rather like a military man being promoted to flag rank. He also told me that he had personally selected me to be chief of station Laos for my next tour. He congratulated me on a job well done in the Congo, adding that there were other posts available if I did not wish to go to Laos. He indicated, however, that he would not advise me to refuse the assignment since it had been his own decision. He also knew full well that few officers were likely to turn down an assignment selected for them by the deputy director, operations. In any case, I had no intention of refusing Laos because it was one of the largest and most important posts in the service during the Vietnam War.

As the end of my tour approached, Mobutu expressed his personal thanks for the assistance I had rendered him and the country, and offered me truly extravagant gifts that I had to refuse. I explained that CIA regulations prevented me from accepting any but the most minor tokens of friendship. He was, however, not deterred.

I was busy packing on the Sunday I was scheduled to leave when the marine guard at the embassy called me to say that President Mobutu was there and wanted to see me immediately. It sounded like a bad joke, and I asked the guard if he was sure it was the president. He assured me he knew the president when he saw him. It was almost time to go to the airport, but I rushed to the embassy to find no one there except the marine guard. He said that when we had finished our call, Mobutu simply laughed and left the embassy. I was, to say the least, pissed off.

But when I got home, I found Mobutu's personal car—a white Chevrolet Impala convertible—in the driveway and the man himself standing on the front porch of my home with Colette and Maureen. As I got out of my car, he held up their arms to show a collection of ivory bracelets. He laughed and told me that the CIA could not accuse him of trying to buy me with a few bangles from the Kinshasa ivory market costing a few dollars. Before we parted, he gave me a large photograph of himself looking incredibly young and grave: *"A mon excellent et vieil ami L. Devlin pour tout ce que le Congo et son chef lui doivent."* ("To my old and excellent friend, L. Devlin, to whom the Congo and its chief owe so much.")

21

THE EVENTS DISCUSSED IN THIS BOOK occurred in what may seem to some the distant past, the 1960s at the height of the Cold War. It was a different era. Today, people may wonder why the two superpowers of that period, the Soviet Union and the United States, became so involved in the Congo. (Later, it was called Zaire and then the Democratic Republic of the Congo.) Until the late 1950s, the United States had generally avoided political involvement in Africa and had been content to deal with the continent through the European colonial powers that effectively blocked Soviet ambitions in Africa. The independence of Guinea in 1957, Ghana in 1958, and the prospect of a broad African decolonization changed the political climate. Those developments aroused the interest of the Soviet Union, and that interest aroused the United States.

Washington hoped the Congo would develop into a progressive parliamentary democracy under the guidance of Belgium. The mutiny by the Congolese army in July 1960, less than a week after independence, shattered that hope. Belgian civilians, who ran the economy and infrastructure, fled. Brussels sent in troops; and the mineral-rich Katanga and South Kasai seceded. Meanwhile, Lumumba, whose government and personal staff included known KGB agents and others believed to be under Soviet influence, threatened to turn to Moscow for military assistance. Washington's concern increased dramatically when it concluded that the Soviet

Union was actively seeking to gain a position of influence or control in the Congo.

Khrushchev regarded the Congo as a pawn in his effort to gain a power base in Africa. I believed then, and I still believe, that one of his objectives was to use the Congo as a stepping-stone to power and influence in Africa with the long-term objective of outflanking NATO on its southern flank.

The Eisenhower administration accepted many of the recommendations concerning the dangers posed by Lumumba that we offered from our perspective in the station and the embassy in Leopoldville. But unknown to me at that time, the administration was planning to go much further by ordering the Congolese leader's assassination.

The Kennedy administration began by making major changes in our Congo policy. Its liberal architects believed that the African non-aligned states would support the American position in international gatherings if we, in turn, supported their positions on African matters. They thus sought a compromise solution to the Congo problem. They were willing, if necessary, to work with Lumumba and, after he died, with his political allies. President Kennedy, however, was a realistic politician, and he soon realized that the United States would lose in the Congo if it continued to pursue this course and, in effect, returned to Eisenhower's policy of trying to exclude the Lumumbists from the political equation. He did not, however, go so far as to favor assassination.

The PROP operation has haunted me ever since "Joe from Paris" arrived in Leopoldville with instructions for me to assassinate Lumumba, instructions that he told me came from President Eisenhower himself. As for my role, I have pondered long and hard on whether I handled the matter correctly. I did not openly oppose the order despite the fact that I considered the assassination of Lumumba immoral, as well as unnecessary to achieve our goals in the Congo. Also, my refusal to obey would almost certainly have resulted in my immediate recall. My replacement would most probably have focused his energies on PROP to the detriment of our other clandestine operations. I thus explored the feasibility of mounting the operation while continuing to work on other less drastic means of removing Lumumba from power. The PROP operation posed far too many dangers for the United States. Also, I believed that the Congolese leaders would solve the problem in their own way. Thus, I neither refused to implement the operation nor did I devote an inordinate amount of time to exploring its feasibility.

When William Colby was named the CIA's executive officer, the number-three position in the organization, he sent a note to all hands requesting that he be told of any questionable or illegal operations in which the Agency might have been involved. I immediately thought of PROP. When I told Bill of the instructions I had received to assassinate Lumumba, he asked me to write a report on the matter and to send it to him, adding that, in his new job, he wanted to be aware of any problems that might come back to haunt the Agency. I agreed that it was wise to take such precautions. But I told him I would not put anything in writing because a written report might eventually fall into the wrong hands. I did, however, stress that neither the Agency nor any branch of the U.S. government had been involved in Lumumba's death.

Bill agreed that he did not need a written report, but I learned much later that he wrote a memorandum based on our conversation. He also received responses to his original memorandum from other officers and sent a comprehensive report to the White House, presumably for the president.

In 1975, President Gerald Ford let slip publicly information provided by Colby that the CIA had been involved in plots to kill several foreign chiefs of state. This news, especially in the immediate post-Vietnam and post-Watergate era, was grist for the congressional and media mills. That same year, the Senate created a special investigative committee, chaired by Senator Frank Church, to investigate the reports. Although I had retired from the CIA in 1974 and was working in Zaire (formerly the Congo), I received a letter from the committee asking me if I would be willing to return to Washington to testify.

Testifying before a congressional committee on a matter that had become a political football did not appeal to me. I had never discussed PROP, or any other CIA operation for that matter, with any unauthorized person. I regretted that the affair had become public, but I realized that there was nothing to do under the circumstances but to agree.

I testified under the name Victor S. Hedgeman, an alias given me by the committee, and was assured that my name would not be made public. The committee took this precaution at my request because I had been warned by old friends in the CIA that both the Black Panthers and Carlos the Jackal, a well-known international terrorist, reportedly had plans to assassinate me on the erroneous belief that I was responsible for the death of Lumumba. I did not want to make things easier for them by having the Senate announce my presence in Washington. Reports soon appeared, however, in the press that Lawrence R. Devlin, formerly chief of station, Leopoldville, had testified under the name of Victor S. Hedgeman. As a result of my involvement in the PROP operation, I have been depicted as being involved in the assassination of Lumumba in numerous books, articles, and even a ludicrous play.

In 1999, Ludo de Witte, a Belgian sociologist and writer, wrote *The Assassination of Lumumba*, a meticulously detailed book in which he demonstrated that Lumumba had been killed in Katanga by a Katangan firing squad on January 17, 1961. The book prompted the creation of a Belgian parliamentary committee that found that the execution was witnessed by Katangan ministers, a Belgian police commissioner, and three Belgian military officers. De Witte interviewed the Belgian who says he was ordered to cut up and dispose of the bodies after a firing squad executed Lumumba and two of his political associates. The parliamentary committee concluded that the Belgian government had a moral responsibility for Lumumba's death.

My name came up one more time during the investigation. Geert Versnick, chairman of the Belgian parliamentary Foreign Affairs Committee, visited Washington and contacted me, presumably to hear my side of the story. While the Church Committee leaks will always be with me, I can now point to the Belgian report that conclusively clears me of any responsibility for Lumumba's death.

CIA covert political action and military operations did, however, contribute to the removal of Lumumba from power and, subsequently, to the failure of Soviet efforts to control the Congo. But these operations, which had the full support of the various organizations working within our embassy in Leopoldville, as well as our government in Washington, would not have succeeded without the support of many individuals and groups in the Congo itself.

There has been a great deal of ink spilled in criticizing Mobutu, much of it by those who knew little about the Congo and even less about Mobutu himself. While not the ideal solution to the Congo problem, Mobutu provided the United States with what it wanted. He ousted Lumumba on September 14, 1960, and installed a government acceptable to the Western world as well as to the majority of Congolese in the areas controlled by Leopoldville. From September 1960 until November 1965 Mobutu remained chief of the army, but he also played a key political role. On the night of November 24, 1965, he led a bloodless army coup. Kasavubu resigned under pressure from the Congolese military, and Mobutu assumed the presidency.

A number of writers and journalists have alleged that I was in some way involved in the 1965 coup. I was not consulted nor was I in any way involved. The possibility that Mobutu might have political ambitions did not entirely escape me, but he always put me off with denials and statements that he was a military man, not a politician.

While far from democratic, Mobutu's style of governing was no worse than most African leaders and probably better than many. Mobutu inherited all the trappings of a parliamentary democracy, but he ruled as a tribal chief, the only form of government he really knew. He merely extended the role of the chief on a national basis. He was not alone in employing this form of government as it was, and is still, used by other African leaders.

I continued seeing Mobutu and other key political and military leaders until my second tour came to an end. It was my job to do so, and I submit that Mobutu was a popular and relatively successful leader in his early presidential years. With help from the United States and Belgium, he succeeded in putting down the Soviet-supported Stanleyville rebellion, and he brought some stability to the Congolese political system. Mobutu realized that tribalism was a deadly enemy of stability, and he managed to bring to his people a genuine sense of national identity. Most Westerners looked upon his mandated *abacos* (a French abbreviation of *à bas les costumes*, or "down with suits!," which resembled a vaguely Maoish suit for men) as a kind of gimmick. The *abacos*, however, was really no different from the coon-skin hat and Quaker suit that Benjamin Franklin wore while ambassador in Paris to emphasize his national identity as an American, not a transplanted Englishman. Dressed in their *abacos*, Zairians the world over recognized each other as Zairians and not primarily as a member of an African tribe.

I left Leopoldville to take up my Laos assignment in June 1967. I did not see Mobutu again until January 1971 when I returned in my new job, first as deputy chief and then chief of the Africa Division. We would meet when I visited the Congo or he came to Washington. Much had changed since my departure. The Binza Group no longer existed as a political force and the troika of Mobutu, Bomboko, and Nendaka, that had so influenced politics during the early years of independence, had been dissolved. Bomboko was shipped off to Washington as ambassador and Nendaka became Zaire's envoy to West Germany. Both men opposed Mobutu's plan to create a one-party state and were tried and convicted of treason, but later released.

In 1973, Mobutu nationalized nearly all foreign-owned businesses and plantations in the name of "Zairianization." The properties of *Union Minière*, the Belgian mining conglomerate that ran the copper and cobalt mines in Katanga, had been nationalized in 1966, but its technicians continued to manage and operate the mines for the government. The mines thus continued to play their cash-cow role for the government and foreign investors continued to be welcome.

The results of Zairianization were catastrophic. A large number of businesses and plantations were parceled out to Mobutu's friends and political supporters. Many of the new owners were not qualified to operate them while some merely sold off the stock, emptied the company bank account, and closed the door. Others tried, unsuccessfully, to manage their new acquisitions but went bankrupt. The result was a sharp increase in the number of unemployed and economic disarray. A year later, the bottom fell out of the copper market; a downward economic trend set in that has never been reversed.

Mobutu changed his mind and invited the property owners to return, but many, particularly small planters and businessmen, were not interested. In a paper on Mobutu that I prepared at that time, I described him as a political genius and an economic spastic. The United States and other Western countries continued to support him with aid programs and bank loans, but much of this assistance came to a halt with the end of the Cold War.

After three years as chief of the Africa Division, I retired from the CIA on June 28, 1974. Some people writing about the Congo have suggested that I continued working under non-official cover for the Agency, but that was not true. I returned to Leopoldville to manage Cainves Zaire—an American-owned company that managed mining interests in Zaire and developed projects in other African countries—and I saw Mobutu often during my time in that position. He would sometimes sound me out on his political plans, even though he understood that I was no longer in government.

Mobutu was alleged to have a personal fortune of five billion dollars. If true, I have often thought he must have received poor investment advice, because people writing about him used that unchanging figure for more than twenty years. Of course, I do not want to imply that Mobutu did not treat the public purse as his personal bank account. He certainly did. He became immensely wealthy. In complaining to me of allegations that his fortune amounted to five billion dollars, he once commented that he probably was not worth more than fifty million dollars. He may well have underestimated his worth, for he needed a great deal of money to maintain his political position and finance his extended family's luxurious lifestyle. For example, when he traveled in the interior, one of his aides usually carried a briefcase filled with bank notes for distribution to the village chiefs he encountered on his travels. The chiefs would expect their leader to do something for their village—a new roof for the local school, a new well, or some other good work—and, naturally, Mobutu expected the chief to insure that the village remained in lock-step with his government.

The world press greatly exaggerated the charge that Mobutu was responsible for the torture and execution of many Zairois. I spent some twenty-one years in the Congo, and, during that time, I dealt with people from all walks of life and from many tribes, clans, and political parties. I heard many complaints about Mobutu's regime, but I never heard him called a bloodthirsty man. Zaire never even came close to being a police state along the lines of the Soviet Union or Nazi Germany.

Realistically, Mobutu was the right man at the right time in September 1960. He had many faults but not as many as the media has attributed to him. He was a courageous man and a strong but realistic nationalist when I dealt with him in the 1960s.

Two major problems developed over the years. In an effort to eliminate serious competition and to insure his tenure as president, he removed many competent ministers and senior army officers, replacing them with "yes men." This inevitably resulted in a less caring, less effective, and more corrupt government.

The second problem was Mobutu himself. As the years passed, he appeared to become bored with the details of government, and, increasingly, problems just slipped through the cracks. He lost two sons to AIDS, one of whom Mobutu appeared to have been training to become his successor. In 1989, he was told that he had prostate cancer. Perhaps fearing the physical problems that sometimes follow prostate surgery, or perhaps believing he would lose his reputation as an iron man, he did not opt for surgery until it was too late. He died in September 1997. He should have groomed a successor, and he should have stepped down much earlier, but by the late 1970s he seemed under the illusion that he was the only person who could hold the Congo together. While perhaps true in the 1960s, he was unable to solve the problems of the 1990s, and he was defeated by Laurent Kabila, a brutal opportunist, in a long and bloody civil war in which both sides received aid and support from other African countries.

I thoroughly enjoyed my tours of duty in the Congo. It was a tough, tiring time, but accomplishing American objectives and contributing to the defeat of the Soviet Union made it worthwhile. Mobutu, Nendaka, and particularly Bomboko were my teachers, along with many other Congolese with whom I worked. Without their help, I might never have understood the Congo, its people, and its problems. Luckily, they were there when it mattered and were largely responsible for defeating the Soviets. I cannot help but wonder how the Congo would have turned out had my three "brothers," along with the rest of the Binza Group, continued to work together. But speculation achieves little. Khrushchev was defeated, the United States accomplished its Cold War objectives, and that, after all, was the *raison d'être* of my assignment as Chief of Station, Congo.

AUTHOR'S NOTE

I WAS ONCE ASKED WHY I wrote about my life and experiences in the Congo to the exclusion of other areas and assignments that were of importance and, certainly, of considerable interest. I served as Chief of Station, Laos, during the Vietnam War, yet I have not written about it to the same extent as I have the Congo. It was indeed a challenging position. One of my duties in Laos, in addition to my intelligence responsibilities, was to work with, manage, and operate an irregular army that varied in size from thirty to forty thousand Lao and tribal troops.

An irregular or guerrilla force, these troops reported on movements of men and material in the Ho Chi Min Trail area; destroyed trucks, supplies, and enemy troop formations whenever feasible; rushed to crash sites of American planes in an effort to rescue American crew members; and fought pitched battles with North Vietnamese army units and, in one case, captured an enormous North Vietnamese logistics base that covered the *Plain de Jars*. In the process, a North Vietnamese army division was so mauled that it took Hanoi more than a year to return the division to active service.

I met occasionally with the Joint Chiefs in Washington and regularly with General Abrams in Saigon to coordinate operations. I also worked closely with Department of State, White House, and CIA officials, as well as with members of Congress, and representatives of foreign governments.

But I was involved in a Hot War.

The Congo experience was unique in that it began in the relatively early days of the Cold War in Africa in the early 1960s. It was also unique and particularly challenging as it was an area little known or understood in Washington. The United States generally depended upon colonial powers, prior to 1960, to provide information on the area and to prevent the Soviets and Bloc nations from infiltrating Africa. All of this changed within a few days in the summer of 1960 when the Congo gained independence from Belgium.

The United States suddenly found itself in a face-to-face showdown with the Soviet Union. We were not prepared, but we had to block the Soviet Union's efforts to infiltrate, subvert, influence, and/or dominate key areas of Africa. This had to be accomplished rapidly, but, even more important, this had to be done with the weapons of the Cold War, such as political action, propaganda, subversion, and paramilitary operations.

McGeorge Bundy, who later became President Kennedy's *and* President Johnson's national security adviser, had stressed the importance of avoiding a Hot War when he recruited me for the CIA in 1948. This was a key reason why I joined the CIA. Allen Dulles, then director of the CIA, continually stressed the need to achieve our objectives without slipping across the thin line that separated the Cold War from a Hot Atomic War.

However, the CIA in the Congo was forced to use the intelligence techniques and operations that I recommended and employed there, but it did not use that ordered by Washington in the PROP operation, that is assassination.

CIA was staffed and managed to a great extent by men who had served in a Hot War (World War II), one that might have been avoided had the United States and its allies been organized and prepared to use Cold War tactics in the 1930s. We believed, almost to a man, that we must avoid another Hot War, but we also believed that the threat of Soviet domination must be stopped. Our experience convinced us that we did not want to find ourselves in a position similar to that reached by Great Britain under Prime Minister

Chamberlain and his predecessors, that is a position of weakness that forced Great Britain to enter a Hot War for which it was not prepared.

I realize full well that persons who have not borne such a responsibility may find it difficult to accept some of my methods. My generation had seen Hitler in action. We regarded Stalin and those who followed him to be just as dangerous as Hitler. We had to defeat the new threat of communism, and we made a considerable contribution to achieving this objective. In 1960, the Congo was on the front line of the struggle between the Soviet Union and the United States. We—Jeff, Frank, Dick, Dave, John, and many others—made a major contribution to preventing a Hot War, one that would have likely resulted in death and chaos never before experienced.

ACKNOWLEDGMENTS

My cousin John Gunn who, with his sophisticated knowledge of computers, provided invaluable assistance.

Michaela Wrong, an Africanist and author, who steered me in all the right directions.

Clive Priddle, my editor, whose advice and guidance greatly improved the original manuscript.

Jeff for his assistance in providing confirming memories and photos.

Frank for his assistance with photos.

My good friend Bill Mason for his comments and suggestions.

Ina Imbrey for locating phone numbers and arranging contacts.

Nicholas Godley for reading and commenting on the manuscript.

John de St. Jorre for his editorial assistance.

INDEX

LARRY DEVLIN was raised in California, enlisted in the army reaching the rank of captain in World War II, joined the CIA in 1949, and was appointed Chief of Station, Congo, in 1959. He subsequently served as Chief of Station, Laos, and Chief, Africa Division. He retired from the CIA in 1974. He resides in Virginia and Provence, France.

PublicAffairs is a publishing house founded in 1997. It is a tribute to the standards, values, and flair of three persons who have served as mentors to countless reporters, writers, editors, and book people of all kinds, including me.

I. F. STONE, proprietor of *I. F. Stone's Weekly*, combined a commitment to the First Amendment with entrepreneurial zeal and reporting skill and became one of the great independent journalists in American history. At the age of eighty, Izzy published *The Trial of Socrates*, which was a national bestseller. He wrote the book after he taught himself ancient Greek.

BENJAMIN C. BRADLEE was for nearly thirty years the charismatic editorial leader of *The Washington Post*. It was Ben who gave the *Post* the range and courage to pursue such historic issues as Watergate. He supported his reporters with a tenacity that made them fearless and it is no accident that so many became authors of influential, best-selling books.

ROBERT L. BERNSTEIN, the chief executive of Random House for more than a quarter century, guided one of the nation's premier publishing houses. Bob was personally responsible for many books of political dissent and argument that challenged tyranny around the globe. He is also the founder and longtime chair of Human Rights Watch, one of the most respected human rights organizations in the world.

•   •   •

For fifty years, the banner of Public Affairs Press was carried by its owner Morris B. Schnapper, who published Gandhi, Nasser, Toynbee, Truman, and about 1,500 other authors. In 1983, Schnapper was described by *The Washington Post* as "a redoubtable gadfly." His legacy will endure in the books to come.

Peter Osnos, *Founder and Editor-at-Large*

CPSIA information can be obtained
at www.ICGtesting.com
Printed in the USA
BVOW08s0137100917
494410BV00003B/4/P